POEMS
Please!

Poems Please.

Poems please,
delight, charm,
make me feel good,
make me laugh, cry, feel sad,
make me think of the olden days,
and pirates and highwaymen,
and fairies and elves in the deep, dark woods.

Poems please,
amuse, amaze,
gladden my heart,
bewitch me,
take me into other worlds,
tickle my fancy,
do my heart good,
warm the cockles of it, too.

Poems, please!
Give me lots of them,
short ones,
long ones,
old ones,
new ones, happy, sad, funny, glad,
rhyming and not,
cool and hot.

Poems, please!
show them to me,
read them,
sing them,
share them with me,
tell them,
invent them.

Every day,
in every way, Poems, please!

Poems please, oh yes, they do.

W.H.M.

POEMS
Please!

Sharing Poetry with Children

David Booth and Bill Moore

Pembroke Publishers Limited

© 1988 Pembroke Publishers Limited
538 Hood Road
Markham, Ontario
L3R 3K9

Canadian Cataloguing in Publication Data

Booth, David
  Poems please.

Bibliography: p.
Includes index.
ISBN 0-921217-22-6

1. Poetry and children. 2. Poetry — Study and
teaching. 3. Children's poetry. I. Moore, Bill.
II. Title.

PN1085.B66 1988   808.06'81   C88-093760-2

Research Consultant   Wendy Berner
Editor   Frank English
Jacket & Interior Design   Falcom Design & Communications Inc.
Typesetting   Jay Tee Graphics Ltd.

Printed and Bound in Canada by Webcom
0 9 8 7 6 5

For Bob Barton
the third side
of our poetry
triangle

Acknowledgements

Every effort has been made to acknowledge all sources of material used in this book. The publishers would be grateful if any errors or omissions were pointed out, so that they may be corrected.

Acknowledgement is gratefully made for the use of the following copyright material: Selection from *The Cow Jumped Over the Moon* by Earle Birney. Published by Holt, Rinehart and Winston of Canada, Limited (1972). "Wordhunter" by Judith Nicholls from *Magic Mirror* by Judith Nicholls. Published by Faber and Faber (1985). "Weather Is Full of the Nicest Sounds" by Aileen Fisher from *Out in the Dark and the Daylight* by Aileen Fisher. Published by Harper and Row, Publishers, Limited (1980)."Winter Cardinal" by Lilian Moore from *Think of Shadows* by Lilian Moore. Published by Atheneum Publishing (1980). "In My Mother's House" by Ann Nolan Clark from *In My Mother's House* by Ann Nolan Clark. Published by Viking Press, Inc. (1981). "What Are You Going to Do When You're Twenty-Two?" by Carolyn Graham from *Jazz Chants for Children* by Carolyn Graham. Published by Oxford University Press, Inc (1979). "Slow Reader" by Allan Ahlberg from *Please Mrs Butler* by Allan Ahlberg. Published by Penguin Books Canada Ltd. (1983). "Forgive Me for Walking Here" by Byrd Baylor from *We Walk in Sandy Places* by Byrd Baylor. Published by Atheneum Publishing. "Song 61" by Douglas Barbour from *The Poet's Craft* by Robert J. Ireland. By permission of the author. Published by Harcourt Brace Jovanovich, Inc. "Riddle" by Ruth Krauss from *Minestrone* by Ruth Krauss. Published by Greenwillow Books (1981). "I Wouldn't" by John Ciardi from *You Read to Me, I'll Read to You* by John Ciardi. Published by Harper and Row, Publishers, Limited (1962). "The Pocket" by Sean O'Huigan from *Scary Poems for Rotten Kids* by Sean O'Huigan. Published by Black Moss Press (1982). "Not Me But" by Arnold Adoff. Publisher, Lothrop, Lee & Shepard Books, Division of William Morrow & Co. Inc. "Every So Often" by Jean Little from *Hey World, Here I Am* by Jean Little. Published by Kids Can Press (1986). "Mum" by Michael Rosen from *When Did You Last Wash Your Feet?* by Michael Rosen. Published by André Deutsch (1986). "No Matter" by Lee Bennett Hopkins. Publisher, Curtis Brown. "Samuel" by Bobbi Katz. By permission of the author. "Spell of the Woods" by Leslie Norris from *Merlin & the Snake's Egg* by Leslie Norris. Published by Viking/Penguin (1978). "You're reading this too fast" by Ken Norris from *Canadian Poetry Now*. Published by House of Anansi. "Blessèd Lord, What It Is to Be Young" by David McCord from *One at a Time* by David McCord. Published by Little, Brown and Company (1986). "Bleezer's Ice Cream" by Jack Prelutsky from *New Kid on the Block* by Jack Prelutsky. Published by Greenwillow Books (1984). "Crackers and Crumbs" by Sonja Dunn from *Butterscotch Dreams* by Sonja Dunn. Published by Pembroke Publishers Limited (1987). "The Bird" by Patrick Lane. Published by permission of the author. "Tinkering" by Diane Dawber from *Oatmeal Mittens* by Diane Dawber. Published by Borealis Press (1987). Selection from "Evaluating the Poetry Children Write" by Jack Collom from *Teachers & Writers* Vol. 17, No. 2, (Nov.-Dec. 1985). Published by Teachers & Writers Collaborative. "Variations on the Culminating Event" by Harry Greenberg and Nancy Larson Shapiro from *Teachers & Writers* Vol. 19, No. 2, (Nov.-Dec. 1987). Published by Teachers & Writers Collaborative. "Johnnie's Poem" by Alden Nowlan from *Between Tears and Laughter* by Alden Nowlan. Published by Clarke Irwin and Company Limited (1971). "For Poets" by Al Young. Published by permission of the author.

TABLE OF CONTENTS

PREFACE

As teacher, you come to your classroom carrying a satchel of poems but, in truth, you are the words you read. Your children take in the teacher and the teaching as one — a single, complete event. Your life is your poem; your experiences illuminate your present classroom moments. The children discover your parents, your teachers, your personal poetry past, revealed in your choice of words, your manner of reading them, your attitude towards them, your eyes as you read them. You are the poem.

In this book, we hope to assist you in sharing poems with children, to help you examine your personal experiences with, and attitudes to poems, so that you can develop your strengths as a teacher who represents an honest, caring, and professional stance when working with poetry.

We have enjoyed our many years of sharing poems with children. To begin the book we took a few moments to reflect upon our own backgrounds — those people and events that led us to the poems and the children.

It is a journey we all must take — looking back at our roots and coming to know our origins as poetry users. When we confront our poetry past, rich or poor, full or empty, we can build our poetry future and develop programs and practices that will enable and empower the children with this special art form throughout all their lives.

David Booth . . .

At my mother's knee, I suppose. Those chestnuts of elocution: "The Boy Who Was Half-Past Three", "Little Orphan Annie", and we begged her to recite them again and again. At 18 she had had a small book of poems published privately by a patron, and that was the end of her career and the beginning of mine. I took all of the poetry books out of the Sarnia Public Library Children's

Section — I'm not sure why. I think it was the words — so many that I had never seen, special and from long ago, used so well and so strangely. Did "kind" rhyme with "wind", after all? In school, the occasional poem was read aloud, "How Horatius Kept the Bridge", "The Raven". I remember memorizing "Abou Ben Adhem" . . . "Daffodils" . . . some Kipling. But always I knew why it had to be commited to memory — some intangible homing device. Bits of poems in my school reader — ignored by the teachers, read by me. Bible classes, filled with verses read aloud and wondered over. Hymns and carols sung by me on religious radio programs. The realization, in French classes, that there were French poems, and French poets. "Paradise Lost" at university, when I wept that someone could know and use all those words.

Teaching my first classes of children, and meeting Bill Moore, my English consultant, who came into my classroom full of poems. He read them, modelling with his marvellous voice the quality of teaching. He returned, each time with more gifts, and I found the library again — the children's section — reliving and renewing my childhood, framing my teaching life. Teaching Speech and Drama on rotary to 600 inner-city Grade 7 and 8 children.

Assemblies to run every other Friday. Oh, the work! Choral speaking with 42 boys — and never having time to be afraid of their not liking the poems, or their not wanting to read them aloud in front of their peers. Thousands of lines dramatized, chanted, interpreted, sung.

Discovering all the anthologies — having left the children's section — discovering the power of the Brits, and the beauty of Stephen Vincent Benét poems. Working with and sharing Bob Barton's great talent; searching for the poems that worked with children. Being asked to teach a Language Arts Course for the Ministry of Education, handling poetry. And researching for six months to prepare. (I had never heard of those 10 kinds of rhyme!) Perrine pulled me through. And the poems that my students had written — my enrichment class, where I learned to teach. Poems every day, to the exclusion of Math, I fear. Discovering Sandburg and sharing him with 36 children, who became their own Sandburgs in room 24. Reading Hughes Mearns' *Creative Youth* (written in 1929 — is the world turning at all?). Discovering Myra Cohn Livingston's *A Tune Beyond Us* and realizing quality. Bringing back the classics along side Kenneth Koch. Sharing the treasures that Willa Pauli unearthed.

Using nursery rhymes for my first class in teacher training, as a professor, and realizing how much power was hidden inside them. Meeting Marion Seary at the Children's Book Store (where she still finds me those always new anthologies). Making up silly rhymes for my six year old, and basking in the joy of his proclamation "Dad is a poet". I am not, but perhaps a poeteur. Sharing poems with children through bringing them to teachers. Collecting what we poeteurs write — revelling in the poetic word, or line, or moment. Thirty years of poems. So many more I want to share. Find me a class. I'll just read one or two . . .

D.B.

Bill Moore . . .

I suppose the earliest influences were my parents.

My mother was a poet and a concert pianist. She sang songs to me from my very earliest years and loved the music of words. She had a lovely voice.

My father came from the north of England. He was a man in love with words. He delighted in showing me the difference between raise and raze, between wave and waive; when to use good old Anglo-Saxon words; and when to look for more sophisticated, Latin-rooted ones. Certain words he loved to roll off his tongue: fiduciary, meteorologically, iconoclastic, and adamantine. Every evening he would read to us children. *Alice in Wonderland,* I know, is a rather terrifying book for most children. For me it has never had terrors. I remember it with affection because of his voice doing all the characters.

I was lucky in elementary school. One of my teachers was a Longfellow nut and read us eight year olds long stretches of "Hiawatha". I still love Longfellow. Another specialized in rollicking pirate poetry. Then there was the Headmaster; imposing and Olympian, he would descend from his office and read stories and poems to us. Poetry he recited by the yard, on those wet winter afternoons, when the rain fell pitilessly on the lamplit slate roofs: "How Horatius Kept the Bridge", "The Pied Piper", "Look, Look the Spring Has Come", and ballads by the score.

In the higher grades, I was fortunate to fall under the spell of one of those unique eccentrics with which the British public schools are providentially filled. I can see him yet, standing in front of the class, hurling lines of poetry at us, like the skipper of a windjammer on his bridge in the roaring forties:

"The boy stood on the burning deck . . ."
(dreadful poetry, but great verse my lads!)

"My heart aches, and a drowsy numbness pains my sense . . ."
(Wonder what might have happened, had that poor beggar Keats survived a bit longer?)

"Now is the winter of our discontent . . ."
(Mark that feller Shakespeare, lads. He's a comer!)

On warm days we would sit out under a tree, as he read Swinburne and Morris, Tennyson and Browning, Clough, Hardy, Drinkwater, Southey and Masefield, along with "those young rebels, who may end up as classics": Eliot, Pound, Spender, Auden, and countless others. But that was 1939, and World War Two came along. I was suddenly snatched from the safety of school and into the arms of the Royal Air Force. There was not much poetry teaching there; but as everyone knows, war is 10 per cent sheer fear and excitement, and 90 per cent boredom. There was lots of reading time, and there were several books I carted around the various theatres of war with me: *New Paths on Helicon* and *The Albatross Book of Verse;* plus, of course, my battered but still serviceable *Palgrave's Golden Treasury.*

These were old-fahioned stuff, perhaps, but full of meat, and not a bad grounding. I read and re-read these, often in cold and windy spaces, under a bomber's moon.

There were a couple of other books I always had in my kitbag; one was *Through Literature to Life*. This was written long, long ago, and reissued in 1928. The subtitle explains the whole thing: "An enthusiasm, and an anthology". It was written by Ernest Raymond, and told of his introduction to the love of literature when he was a boy. I have never forgotten what he said about poetry:

There are three cries made by humans:

a moan — the cry of pain
a laugh — the cry of amusement
a cheer — the cry of approval.

The war was winding down in 1945, when, on the island of Malta, a fellow-officer gave me C. Day Lewis' wonderful book called *Poetry For You*. Lewis had written the book for his own children, in an attempt to help them share his love for poetry. I have read it over every year at least once. It is a simple book, in a way, yet there is always something new there.

These are books from the past. I make no apology for that: the books we read in our early years are usually the ones we cherish most. This does not mean that we ignore the new writers. We must read every new poet as he or she appears in print. We must maintain a voracious appetite, and clutch at every new idea that comes along to see how it improves our knowledge. I buy anthologies and complete works at used-book stores, garage sales, everywhere, and have a standing order with my local library: "Let me see the new ones as soon as you get them."

People and books, then, hooked me on poetry.

Some of the people include the thousands of children I have "done poems" with over the years, the hundreds of teachers who have thrashed out ideas with me, and two very special friends, David and Bob.

Most special of all: It was incredibly good fortune to marry a velvet-voiced actress, whose knowledge and understanding of poetry, along with her tolerance and compassion for all things, have combined to teach me more and more each day, over the past 45 years.

W.H.M.

1
Why Share Poems with Children?

Poetry

What is Poetry? Who knows?
Not the rose, but the scent of the rose;
Not the sky, but the light of the sky;
Not the fly, but the gleam of the fly;
Not the sea, but the sound of the sea;
Not myself, but what makes me
See, hear, and feel something that prose
Cannot: and what is it, who knows?

Eleanor Farjeon

What Is Poetry?

May Hill Arbuthnot said that "like music, poetry comes with healing in its wings; it carries its own therapy." Myra Cohn Livingston, in an article called "Not The Rose", wrote:

> *Poetry is not the rose with a name, a colour — a spot in the garden, an arrangement in a vase; not the food the rose has fed on, not the dust with which it is sprayed to keep the bugs away. It is the scent.*

Carl Sandburg said: "The first stuff for making poetry is words . . . of course, a feeling or a thought or both must come to a poet before he begins using the words that make a poem. But the right words, the special and particular words for this purpose in view, these must come. For out of them, the poem is made."

Poetry may prepare children for a new vision and this comes without their being told what they should be seeing in the poem. Teachers have to work hard to keep from imposing their own interpretations of a poem upon the children. If poetry is to work, we must help each child find for himself or herself the delight and truth in what he or she is reading or hearing. If we ourselves have lost the habit of reading poetry, then we must re-discover how this particular art form can matter to us, and therefore to them. In the end, the goal of our teaching is to help the children return to hear the voice of the poet on their own.

Poetry uses especially concentrated and connotative language. "The words mean more than the words mean," because the meaning and the form are wound together. A poet is able to deepen an everyday happening or an ordinary experience and make us see it through a magnifying glass, somehow broadening that experience. While poetry may illuminate and clarify life, it does more: it lets us see differently, develop new insights and new ways of understanding our world. It appeals to both thought and feeling, and has the power to call up rich sensory images in the reader and evoke deep emotional responses. It is not always an easy task. Somehow, the reader is inside the experience as well as reading about it. We have to work at poetry, go beyond the literal meaning, and discover the depths for ourselves.

Like film makers or photographers, poets manipulate our ears and eyes at the same time, using close-ups, long shots, slow motion, fast-forward, and soft focus. They juxtapose sound and image and make new meanings. They weave in subplots and overlap scenes; and they do it at lightning speed, in a few lines, in one word. They create or recreate experiences and then translate them into words. The poet gives form to feeling, thereby allowing us to recognize our own emotions as we begin to make sense of them, developing in us the intelligence of feeling. As reader or listener, we are educating our imaginations, using symbol, metaphor, allegory, without fear or pain, making meaning with our eyes, ears, and imaginations. That is a special kind of learning.

Some years ago a Dr. Mackenzie said this:

> We have all, for at least one period of our lives, loved the musical sound of rhyming words, and found delight in rhythmical measures. . . . Good poetry is intimately relevant to our lives. Poetry is that art that includes all others in its techniques. The poet paints pictures, makes music, utters prophecies, recounts history, produces philosophy, explains religion, all by the mysterious power of words. Poetry is the art that embraces all attitudes, for the poet expresses in his [or her] poetry emotional and intellectual

experiences that cannot be stated in prose, or by means of purely intellectual concepts. The aim of poetry is to give pleasure, and all other values accruing to it, political, theological, philosophical, sociological, or any other, are incidental — a bonus as it were.

The great poet, Robert Graves, said:

> Poetry is sense; good sense;
> penetrating, often heart-rending sense.

Anthologist Gerald D. McDonald has stated in his book *A Way of Knowing*:

> *Poetry can be wittier and funnier than any kind of writing; it can tell us about the world through words we can't forget; it can be tough or it can be tender; it can be fat or lean; it can preach a short sermon or give us a long thought (the shorter the poem, sometimes, the longer the thought). And it does all this through the music of words.*

The poet David McCord commented:

> *Poetry is so many things besides the shiver down the spine. It is a new day lying on an unknown doorstep. It is Peer Gynt and Moby Dick in a single line. It is the best translation of words that do not exist. It is hot coffee dripping from an icicle. It is the accident involving sudden life. It is the calculus of the imagination. It is the finishing touch to what one could not finish. It is a hundred things as unexplainable as all our foolish explanations.*

Writing in *Signal*, Griselba Greaves struggles to understand this art form:

> *It is possible that my personal history has made me particularly susceptible to poetry — the poetry found not only in poems with rhyme and metre, but also in the poetic moments that come in the best prose.*
>
> *For me, poetry is the crystallization of a concept, so that every facet of that concept may be seen. It can be grasped, if only partially, at one concentrated reading. Its true appreciation transcends mundane explanation: it is an emotional experience as much as it is an intellectual one, but both are there.*

It is pervasive, this thing called poetry:

*As well as being a particularly refined manifestation of
high culture in books which sell in small numbers, poetry
is an ancient, universal, and popular art form, and it is a
public phenomenon, found on gravestones and lavatory
walls, in advertisements and pop songs, in "In
Memoriam" columns, in the jokes of dirty young men (and
young women, for all I know), and in children's games. It
is also widely written in private, often in order to embody
or celebrate the most profound thoughts and feelings of
ordinary people and pupils: many of us have been struck by
that iceberg's tip when adolescents have shown us exercise
books filled with poems written in private about their personal loves and fears. For some, lines of poetry become
emblems of what they live by.*

Andrew Stibbs

It could be said that a poem is never really finished, because
every time you read it you add to its meaning. Poetry is dynamic:
it is not something you look at, but something you play with.

Poetry uses words; so does prose. What is the difference? It
has been said that prose meanders, verse marches, and poetry
soars. Poetry is an art and, like all arts, should be enjoyed. It can
be appreciated better if we know something of its underlying rules,
and write it as well as read it. Writing helps make us appreciate it.

Poetry is untranslatable. The words in their order are perfect.
Any change ruins the picture:

> There is sand at the bottom that bites at your feet,
> And there is a rock where the waterfall goes,
> You can poke your foot in the foamy part,
> And feel how the water runs over your toes.
>
> E. Madox Roberts

How much less delightful would it be this way:

> There is sludge at the bottom that sucks at your feet,
> And there is a fence where the waterfall goes,
> You can thrust your foot into the deeper part,
> And sense how the water goes over your feet.

*I was "doing poetry" with a group of young children
somewhere in the Canadian North. We had been talking*

about poetry and the way poets work. We read all sorts of poetry: funny poems, sad poems, nostalgic poems, and story poems. Then we tried to define poetry for ourselves. All kinds of definitions came up, but the one we all liked best came from a ten-year-old boy who said, "It's where the words mean more than the words mean." That seems to sum it all up very well.

> The words mean more
> The words mean
> The words
> Words
> More than
> More than words
> Words mean
> Mean words
> Mean more
> More than
> More than the words mean
> Words
> Mean.
>
> W.H.M.

Poetry for children is very difficult to define. Even poets have trouble. Much prose could be labelled poetry. The careful crafting of *Winnie the Pooh* stories demonstrates this poetical quality. We cannot use the description of "writing that is metrical and that rhymes", because much doggerel and simple verse is by no means poetic. Perhaps it is the quality of the writing which determines the truth of the poetry. Overly cute verse that helps us remember the days of the month or playful rhyming couplets may not be poetry. Some nursery rhymes are poems and others are not. We might say that it looks like prose, or that it may be written in verse form, but the distinguishing features are its qualities, its metaphors, its insights, its devices. It touches us aesthetically and contemplatively; we understand ideas better from the poet. All of us take pictures with cameras; some of us take photographs that are art. All can write verse; some can make a poem.

There is a natural relationship between childhood and poetry. It may be that, in spite of definitions, children instinctively understand what a poem is. As Emily Dickinson said:

If I read a book and it makes my whole body so cold no fire
can ever warm me, I know that is poetry. If I feel physi-
cally as if the top of my head is taken off, I know that is
poetry. These are the only ways I know it. Is there any
other way?

Children's poetry has a special appeal: the form and language of poetry speak directly to the child, to their senses, their imaginations, their emotions, their feelings, their experiences of childhood. Poems are metaphors for life: by looking through new eyes, at fresh images, children may reflect on their own lives. It is important that children's poems not be didactic or moralistic. Often, adults read a poem with a reflected light that children do not have. Nostalgia is rarely a quality of childhood. We must be careful of poems that are cute, that appeal to false emotions, or that are overly sentimental. Poems that are preachy and moralistic can actually interfere with literary appreciation. It is important that we find the best in poetry for children, because both adults and children respond positively to quality.

Andrew Stibbs says:

In choosing poems for pupils, I include the funny, the
crude, and the short — the poems most representative of
the vulgar traditions I have urged. An eventual taste for
the subtle and serious in poetry is more likely to be devel-
oped by enjoyment, experience, and knowledge of a mixture
of poems in school, including unsubtle and unserious ones,
than by an unrelieved diet of classics.

Poets feel something powerfully; they put their feelings into words and hope that we, hearing those words, will get some echo of their original feelings. Poets have always had the ability — under the influence of their own emotions — to produce sounds to vibrate in harmony with the reader's emotions. To exist as poetry, emotions have to be transmitted through language. Words, and the way they are grouped together to produce an emotional effect upon the listener, are the power of poetry.

" A Shared Adventure" — that's the key. What bedevils
poetry for the young is that so many adults insist on
reading verse and teaching it as though it were just
photographs-in-words; a representational medium for

telling us about what they would call reality — the "out there" externals of our lives. Sometimes verse is, of course, such a medium. But poetry is always more than that. It is Fiction. A world made by the writer in words.

Aiden Chambers

So many definitions. Here is one more:

"That's what a poem is," Leslie said, " a feeling about some special time or place or happening, pressed into as few lines as it will go."

Eleanor Cameron

Sharing Poetry With Children

Children come to poetry naturally, and then something happens to that linguistic emotional relationship. Is it the formality of teaching that takes away the appreciation? Is it the teacher's own attitudes that alter the child's enjoyment of this particular kind of print? For certain, something happens to many children, and the love of poetry as part of their life experience begins to wane. In adulthood very, very few people choose to read poems.

To begin with, we must accept the position that the poems we share with children have a value on their own, not only to make them future poem-lovers, but, as in play, an inherent developmental quality that helps children learn. Their poems, from the nursery, the street, the playground, the school, and the family, are linguistic and conceptual treasures that will enrich and support their growth. As teachers, we can tap into this storehouse and use poems as powerful learning situations. In order to do this, we must examine our own biases and attitudes to poems, and investigate how we can come back to poetry with insight and appreciation for its wonder and its potential. Poems must not be seen as icons or as intricate puzzles, but as part of childhood's rites of passage. If our students develop into adults who continue their relationship with poetry, then this is an added bonus. In this book, however, we will content ourselves with bringing poems to children, exploring both the process and the product as we engage chidren in reading, listening to, and writing poetry.

Teachers may have to work hard to overcome some concerns. We have had many people tell us their own fears about poetry. Why is poetry so difficult for so many teachers? Why did they develop this distaste for poetry? We will watch films, listen to music, admire paintings and prints, yet remain wary of poetry. It seems for many a bewildering subject. Often teachers will feel ill at ease when called upon to teach a poem. Perhaps we are products of schools where teachers felt this lack of motivation, preparation, or interest. It is a circle of sadness that must be broken. When poems are brought to children carefully, with joy and satisfaction, the children somehow find a deeper realization of life and fuller appreciation of the world. They seem to have a sensitive awareness of how to identify with the feelings of others, and realize that we all have those universal, emotional connections.

Do any of these statements apply to you?

- *I always used to hate poetry in school.*
- *I don't know what all those poets are talking about.*
- *I don't know why they didn't write in good, honest prose.*
- *I think my teachers felt the same way about the poems.*
- *All that memory work; learning stuff I didn't understand, and forgetting immediately. Poetry and memory work are synonymous in my mind.*
- *Nobody ever suggested to me that poetry should be fun. Nobody ever suggested to me that poetry was like music and art, something you enjoy more if you had some degree of choice, and weren't always tested on it.*
- *All the poetry lessons I remember were Simile Safaris. We tore them all apart, and laid the similes out like trophies.*
- *Teachers said, ''You don't understand or like it now, but years hence you will thank me for this.''*
- *Seems to me we always did poems about fairies and stuff like that.*
- *Nobody ever told me that writing my own was a wonderful way of learning to appreciate other poets' work.*
- *Nobody ever suggested to me that reading poetry aloud was a dramatic experience, filled with pleasure.*
- *Nobody ever suggested that the more I knew about how and why poets wrote the way they do would make poetry more enjoyable.*

Did no one ever suggest that poetry is the most compact, entertaining, brilliant, amusing, happy, sad, loving, angry way of using language, and that the resulting effect upon the user should be joy?

How can we re-educate ourselves poetically?

- By teaching the poems we enjoy ourselves;

- By searching out poets, old and new, that speak to us as teachers and as humans;
- By reading poems aloud to children with energy, passion, and delight;
- By risking the reading of poems: long poems, short poems, poems that touch us and release our feelings;
- By joining in with children, clapping along, tasting the words, sitting inside the circle;
- By encouraging children to write in a poetic fashion, using all of the tools that poets use, from models, shapes, and patterns to ideas and concepts;
- By sharing with other teachers poems that work, poems that draw children again and again;
- By using poems all of the time, in a quiet moment, as a lesson, as part of another subject's content;
- By scheduling times for poetry reading, by us, by groups of children, by individuals who are ready to share;
- By providing resources and dozens of poetry anthologies (by single poets, collections, picture book versions) for us as teachers to share, and for children to peruse on their own;
- By exploring poets as well as poems, letting the children come to know the writer of words, through meeting many poems by one poet, and perhaps by sharing information about the poet's life and work;
- By having records and tape recordings of poems for children at listening centres, so that they can experience the many interpretations of poetry;
- By inviting poets to share their poems with children in an artists-in-the-schools program;
- By reading poems to children that we personally enjoy, and for no other apparent teaching purpose;
- By making use of poems in big book formats, on overhead transparencies, on chart papers, on mobiles, incorporating them into visual arts, writing them large and small, in shapes of all kinds, with felt pens and chalk, and careful calligraphy;
- By not demanding a single response to a poem, but rather observing and listening to the responses of the children and building on them;
- By presenting as many poems, going inside the ones they enjoy, letting the learning happen;

- By not being afraid to teach about poems, thus giving children knowledge and information to strengthen their poem power, but never teaching the technique without context, without the child wanting or needing to know;
- By asking consultants, librarians, authors, book store clerks to keep us posted on new releases, so that our own poetry repertoire of children's poems constantly grows and changes;
- By singing and chanting poems and songs aloud and alongside the children, letting the joys of language reach them through the ear and the eye;
- By collecting poetic language to share with children from ads, stories, novels, songs, or magazines — letting the children learn from living language about the power of words;
- By letting children bring poetry to us, as they build their private anthologies, and write and share their own poems with the class.

Earle Birney summarizes our dreams of being teachers who honour poetry:

> The wistful purpose of this book then is to persuade anyone literate in the English language who thinks he does not like the poetry that he's missing a unique pleasure easily within his reach — and anyone who likes poetry a little, or only some kinds of poems, that he may extend his range and his pleasures.
>
> - it is a survival of primitive spells and exorcisms, and cannot be entered into by anyone who has excluded wonder and mystery from his life
> - it is the use of words to combine the pleasures of music and dancing, and so cannot be adequately enjoyed without being heard in the inner ear at least, and felt in the body's rhythms
> - virtually all human beings are born with the abilities needed to delight in and to make poetry, but unimaginative concepts of education can muffle and even destroy these abilities
> - the essential "education" for both a poet (and his reader) is exploring indefinitely his medium, understanding words as they are spoken and written, and especially as they have been shaped into the poetry of his generation
> - this education begins naturally with the lullaby and the

*nursery rhyme, and it can continue into the school only
if the teachers offer so-called adult poetry in the same
childish spirit of sharing the magic of rhythm and fancy,
and of expecting no more from it than pleasure, comfort,
and perhaps reconciliation with the darker moments of
being alive*

- *the best "teachers" of poetry are therefore those who
attempt not to teach but to be fellow students and practi-
tioners in the making and enjoying of an imaginative
craft*
- *"courses" in poetry are of no use without provision of
the real things: books of poetry, disks, tapes, and films
incorporating it (without censorship on the score of content or language); programs involving readings of poetry
by the poets themselves or by imaginative readers; and
discussion (not "classes") with poets and other artists in
relaxed situations and settings.*

The Usefulness of Poetry

Poems have a worth of their own, not just as motivating strategies, curriculum content, or reader activities, but just as the art form
called poetry. As in the arts of painting, dramatic play, movement,
and games, children grow through poetry. Poems work as all artistic
experiences do — cognitively and emotionally at one time. The children think and feel about what they hear or read; and this special
aesthetic experience causes them to develop in all aspects of their
learning within a context of both pleasure and language use. The
poem can be a concentrated teaching package, its effect long-
reaching and long-lasting. Teachers must trust the arts and trust
the educational power that lies in their use. Poems on their own
are fulfilling, satisfying, and educational experiences for children.
They can provide a powerful stimulus for all kinds of learning,
because they are powerful learning tools:

- on their own they provide artistic and aesthetic experiences for
children;
- they demonstrate language in unique patterns and forms, trig-
gering new linguistic meanings;
- they offer ideas and concepts as seen through artists' eyes, giving children new and original perceptions of life;
- they give teachers opportunities for reading aloud to children,

forming an inexhaustible supply of stimulating and satisfying experiences with oral language;

- they present children with opportunities for joining in, participating in meaningful language experiences, even as non-readers;
- they impart to children language patterns that, first learned through the ear, can then be understood later in print;
- they demonstrate the musicality and lyricism of language;
- they are memorable and stay in the children's minds to be brought forth when needed;
- they can tell stories in a unique, compressed fashion, entwining the plot and the emotion at once;
- they can be read aloud chorally, involving everyone — the rhythm and rhyme patterns drawing the children in, letting readers of different abilities become part of the reading experience;
- they let us work our tongues, lips, and vocal cords in unusual and intricate fashion, as we twist and turn around language patterns unfamiliar yet intriguing;
- they give our reading eye strength, as we interpret language that causes us to look closely, think carefully, and make different meanings each time we meet the poem;
- they let children see and hear print that is comprehensible yet complex;
- they encourage response as children grope towards meanings — both public and private, both individual and collective;
- they open up backgrounds and cultures new and different from our own, and let us see with different eyes and feel with different sensitivities
- they touch our spirits and draw us into unique perceptions that transcend day-to-day life;
- they encourage us to manipulate both words and ideas as writers, letting us explore patterns of language and rework our thoughts;
- they give us private strength to be called upon in lonely or difficult times;
- they join us with the past, integrate us with the present, and lift us into the possibility of the future.

Poetry may be technically useful in teaching, but it also may be emotionally essential to living.
- Is understanding important? Then so is poetry.
- Is tolerance of others important? Then so is poetry.
- Is the ability to dream important? Then so is poetry.

It is not always easy to read, but then hopscotch is not easy to play. Some of the delight comes from meeting the challenge. On the other hand, most little children tend to be rhythmic and poetic unless it is crushed out of them in school.

We teach poems for so many reasons:

- The pleasure of rhyme and rhythm — all children have rhythm: the rhythms of life as they breathe, their heart beats, their feet marching on the stairs, their wooden spoons beating on their tables
- the pleasure of sharing the experience of the poet's universality — recalling personal experiences: "what oft was thought yet ne'er so well expressed"
- a simulated imagination — "Where there is no imagination there tends to be cruelty and prejudice."
- increased powers of observation — "I never thought of it that way before!"
- the chief reason for poetry is PLEASURE — There may be spin-offs, such as a deeper appreciation of language, an ability to see into some one else's life, the beginning of tolerance and under-standing; but the chief reason for the existence of poetry is pleasure.
- poetry may be better than prose for a good story — although not all poems tell a story. The language of poetry is tighter, more compact, more emotionally suggestive; poems can be spookier, funnier, more exciting, more loving, briefer, and more fun than almost anything else. The poem might be as short as:

> Jack be nimble
> Jack be quick
> Jack jump over the candlestick

or it might be a long, cumulative story, which we can say along with the reader:

> This is the house that Jack built.
> This is the malt
> That lay in the house that Jack built, etc.

It is rather like a special puzzle.

- We tend to like interesting comparisons. Poetry is full of these.
- The joys of recollection are great: "Oh, yes. I remember those lines: "The wind was a torrent of darkness. . . ." Recollection can be of lines, or of feelings: "Yes, that is exactly the way I felt

when that happened."
- Poetry is an art, it is music, and is a rigorous work-out for the mind and the imagination.
- Poetry is the essence of language distilled.
- Poetry is an experience crystallized in language.

A poet uses words the way an artist uses shapes and colors. Both want to produce an effect upon the emotions.

We must attempt to preserve the natural affinity that children have for poems — the love of rhythm and rhyme, the joy of jingles and skipping games, and singing the lyrics of the songs they share.

By its very nature, poetry encourages subjective, personal response. With poetry, there is hope for children to have responses that come from their worlds and correspond in some way to how others are thinking and feeling. If, however, a poetry program is based on criticism, structure, and obligatory response, there will be no room for pleasure and, therefore, no learning. Because poetry creates a personal response, there is no road map clearly defined as to how to understand a poem, and this can create anxiety in the reader or listener, or in the teacher. If different interpretations are allowed and indeed encouraged, if the poet's vision can be perceived in more ways than one, then poetry can be our avenue towards wider and higher-level thought processing.

Imagine using a poem as a punishment lesson for failed printing! Or using poetry to teach road safety with ill-thought-out rhymes! Or writing haiku eight years in a row! If poetry in teaching is useful, if poems are worth reading for whatever reason, then how we teach them is of prime importance.

A Way of Thinking

For children, one of the most important aspects of poetry is that it demands meaning-making processing at the highest level. We depend on our past for meaning-making. We struggle to make sense of print because of what has gone on in our lives before. It is a trail of associations that allows us to understand and negotiate between the print and our lives. Poetry may be the best medium, the most holistic element, that pulls together all of the aspects of language and shows us how to build and make meaning. Therefore, the poem must become part of our experience. It is full of potential, possibility, and opportunity. We read poems tentatively, with the poetry experience giving us the licence and discipline to explore, to recognize, and to respond. Poets make poetry by translating experiences into words, patterning and ordering their thoughts through language. Poetry requires that we translate what the poet says in terms of what our life experience says and who we are. The children are an important part of that negotiating process, contributing their unique backgrounds of language and feeling, and coming to grips with those of the poet. Using imagery, metaphor, and analogy, the reader or listener incorporates the experience into personal meaning frames. Because poems use a particular kind of language, as the poet creates with carefully chosen images, precise words, and effective patterns, the children begin to develop a sensitivity to words, rhythms, and images as they experience them, need them, and use them.

If we read several poems and share our responses, then different ideas and viewpoints of the same idea or image will broaden the children's understanding. A poet uses words to conjure up feelings, images, sounds, and ideas. Poetry encourages thought of a special kind — poetic thought.

> There is the inner life, which is the world of final reality,
> the world of memory, emotion, imagination, intelligence,
> and natural common sense, and which goes on all the
> time, consciously or unconsciously, like the heart beat.
> There is also the thinking process by which we break into
> that inner life and capture answers and evidence to support
> the answers out of it. That process of raid, or persuasion,
> or ambush, or dogged hunting, or surrender, is the kind of
> thinking we have to learn and if we do not somehow learn
> it, then our minds lie in us like the fish in the pond of a
> man who cannot fish. . . . I am talking about whatever
> kind of trick or skill it is that enables us to catch those
> elusive or shadowy thoughts, and collect them together,
> and hold them still so we can get a really good look at
> them.
>
> *Ted Hughes*

It helps children know something in a new way. As teachers, we can help rouse awareness in children, help them to see things that they did not notice, and help them to see other things anew. We wake up children with new impressions of life. They begin to think with a metaphoric mind. Because poetry deals in relationships, metaphor, and analogy, it invents and challenges traditional ways of thinking. It makes a new whole out of pieces by synthesizing them into poems. Poets bring pattern and order to the universe and, if we have opened our minds to metaphor, we can join them in making meaning. The associations of poetry touch us to our very core. They open up springs of memory and of emotion. Teachers can encourage poetry, celebrate it, value it, model it, and make it available. Perhaps poetry is the most thought-provoking language form we have.

Poetry is an intellectually and demanding art form. Poems work on multiple levels with all kinds of subtext and complex stages working one on the other. The language is disciplined, meticulously chosen, intense, compressed, and powerful. The meanings grow after every reading. With guidance, children can comprehend the most seemingly difficult poems as they talk, focus, explain, and rephrase ideas with the help of a skilful teacher. The poet observes a singular event and then gives it universal significance with interpretation and form, tying the reader's response to a broader human experience. This lets the child listen to and read poems written throughout the centuries, contrasting past and present views, recognizing historical and literary significance, learning that the perspective of the interpreter and the poet together determines historical significance. Letting our children hear poems and read poems from the past gives them strength, background, and a balanced view from which to make decisions and come to understandings.

Language Growth Through Poetry

Word play is a large part of language education. Chukovsky said that, in their early years, youngsters exhibit a kind of linguistic genius as they master intricate aspects of language form and function. This task is generally accomplished without the help of adult instruction. Word play is a large part of the process as children reconstruct language learning, using rules of the systems they discover. They examine the make-up of the system called English. Word play has within it a systematic explanation of language function. As they play linguistically, children are learning valuable information about how language works. Poetry, with all its intricate word-play systems, is part of that exploration. The activities that grow from it are valuable resource materials for language programs.

It is the poets who continually remind us that how something is said is as important as what is said. In order to communicate, children need a command of the forms and function of language. Through poetry, they isolate, scrutinize, magnify, and elaborate their store of words. Poetry is a perfect test for what language can do. It is full of word play.

Poets have always used language in special ways. In poetry, we have a vehicle for looking at the use of words, the choosing of the one special word that fits perfectly. Reading poetry, then, is a wonderful way of tuning children in to the power of language. One way to do this is to read and explore SHORT, SHARP BITS. We read short pieces, two or three lines. We look at them, and talk about the special words, their aptness, the way the lines flow, and so on. In this way the children learn the power of language in a pleasant fashion, using material that is brief enough to be encompassed in a very short time. These lessons, which could occur two or three times a day, should never take longer than three or four minutes. The technique is as follows:

1) The lines are displayed on primary paper, written in felt pen.
2) The teacher reads them, and the class listens.
3) General discussion takes place, with special words being pointed out, comments are made on interesting turns of phrase, etc.

Often these lines can be used as a base for the children's writing. (A certain amount of borrowing is quite permissible.) Writing the lines on paper is better than writing them on the board, because once the day is over, the papers can be stored for future reference. Here is a short, sharp bit from F.R. Scott:

> Hidden in wonder and snow, or sudden with summer,
> This land stares at the sun in huge silence.

There is a copy before the class. We read it, and talk about the words used . . . "Sudden with summer", how true that is. In this country — one minute it is spring, and then suddenly, it is summer. Unlike the seasons in Europe, we do not have a long and gentle spring. "Sudden with summer", the alliteration is pleasing to the ear. Then, again, so much of the year the land is "hidden in . . . snow . . . ." Why did he put that "wonder" in there? Possibly, because the amazing beauty of snow. And this is an empty land, as well, which does "stare at the sun in a huge silence". If you have ever been out on the rocky shores of a northern lake, you are aware of that "huge silence". The rhythm of the lines helps them to be read with a swing, which helps to impart the message. "Hidden" — maybe the wonder is that much of the land is still hidden from us, so much of it is unexplored. The alliteration has been mentioned. The assonance, where the vowels agree, in "wonder . . . sudden summer. . ." adds to the music.

Wordhunter

My brother chases frogs —
well, eggs to be precise,
that jelly-baby spawn
which lurks near murky weed
after the winter's ice.
Takes them from the very doors
of hairy water-boatmen's jaws.
But me,
I'm a wordhunter.

Now my uncle,
he hunts butterflies,
Searches nettles, heaps of dung
for Purple Emperors, cabbage white,
Swallowtails with painted wing —
I'm sure you know the kind of thing.
Not me,
I'm a wordhunter.

See my sister Sue.
She chases — daydreams.
Laugh or tease, she just replies
"What do I care?"
Closes eyes and quickly flies
back to her castles in the air.
Not me,
I'd rather be

A WORDHUNTER.
Judith Nicholls

Perhaps nowhere else in print do words have such impact as in poetry. Each one matters. Where it is placed on the page matters. How it sounds, alone and in relationship to the next word, matters. Each meaning conjured up in your head and heart matters. Words are the veins of the poem. They carry the blood of its ideas and feelings. Children may not become poets, but they can be word-hunters.

Poems Across the Curriculum

Children can observe the natural world through their own eyes and through the talent of the poet. For example, many poets are fascinated by the changes in nature and communicate those feelings in their poems. Teachers can use poetry in science by gathering together a collection of poems and broaden and deepen the child's aesthetic appreciation of the world of science. For example, Aileen Fisher understands both children and nature. She writes of the woods and the meadows, of creatures feathered and furry, of weather and night, and helps the child in the simplest and freshest of language and image to see the world, through artful poetry.

Weather Is Full of the Nicest Sounds

Weather is full
of the nicest sounds:
it sings
and rustles
and pings
and pounds
and hums
and tinkles
and strums
and twangs
and whishes
and sprinkles
and splishes
and bangs
and mumbles
and grumbles
and rumbles
and flashes
and crashes.

Aileen Fisher

Lilian Moore, another poet who writes about nature, uses her close and acute observations of her surroundings to heighten the children's senses of the world around them:

Winter Cardinal

Fat
and elegantly
crested,
clinging to the branch
of the stripped tree
like
one bright leaf that
bested
every wind and lived
to show
its red
against
the astonished snow

Ann Nolan Clark's "In My Mother's House", a lyrical poem of quiet beauty, creates an image of a place and time that brings a gentle magic to a lesson on mountains or memories:

Mountains are the high places;
They reach up and up
To the blue-blue above.
They stand around us,
Looking down at the people
In the pueblo.
In the plaza,
In the fields.
I like to know
That mountains are there,
Around me,
So quiet
So big,
And so high.

I have heard
That the Thunder sleeps
In the mountains,
With his great bow
And lightning arrows
By his side.

I have heard
That clouds gather
In the mountains,
And that rainbows
Make bridges
Over them.

I have heard
That mountains
Are the home
Of the winds
And the night.

Perhaps
These things are true;
I have heard them.

Poems can give us entry points into every field of learning. They form complete educational packages of their own, and touch on all areas of curriculum. They point us in new directions; they help us reflect on what we have seen; they bring us new perceptions and viewpoints of all life, all subjects, all interests. We need no special hour for poetry; we need poetry for every hour.

In the writings of aboriginal peoples we find the roots of all poetry — the perception, the form, and the feeling. For children, these writings hold promise of the belief and values of poetry, and can lead to sensitive understanding and modelling.

> I arise from rest with movements swift
> as the beat of the raven's wings.
> I arise
> To meet the day.
> My face is turned from the dark of night
> To gaze at the dawn of day,
> Now whitening in the sky.
>
> *Inuit* (Arctic)

> What is this I promise you?
> The skies shall be bright and clear for you
> This is what I promise you.
>
> *Chippewa* (North America)

> I the singer stand on high on the yellow rushes;
> Let me go forth with noble songs and laden with flowers.
>
> *Aztec* (Central America)

Poems For All Children

All children can benefit from poetry — the pre-school child who claps along, the gifted reader who seeks out the most sophisticated poets, the reluctant reader who finds that short, sharp poems taste delicious, the child new to English, who finds the rhythms and the rhymes memorable, the young adult who finds his or her feelings reflected in the words.

Small children in every culture tune in to the rhythm of language. No matter our background, experience, or age, we sing along with tunes throughout our lives. There are poems in every language. The Inca created poems and songs for loved ones 500 years ago. Poems know no language barriers. Children learning to speak English bring with them a sound basis of language structures in their native language. Poetry can tap into linguistic knowledge through the ear, and the child can participate almost immediately. Carolyn Graham uses the structure of poetry in her excellent patterns for children learning English as a second language.

What Are You Going To Do When You're Twenty-Two?

What are you going to do when you're twenty-two?
                    I haven't decided.
                    What about you?

                    I might climb a mountain.
                    I might go to France.
                    I might write a story.
                    I might learn to dance.

Where are you going to be when you're twenty-three?
                    I might be in Paris.
                    I might be in Rome.
                    I might be in Turkey.
                    I might be home.

What are you going to be when you're ninety-three?
                    I'm going to be old
                    when I'm ninety-three.

What are you going to do when you're one hundred and two?
                    I haven't decided.
                    What about you?
                                        Carolyn Graham

The gifted child can use experiences with poems to mine the subtle levels of meaning, to explore the nuances of language, and to build new patterns for his or her own writings.

Children in Special Education classes traditionally have been deprived of poetry in the quest for skill development, robbing them of the very language processes they need the most. Effective teachers of Special Education realize that:

• poetry is an exceptional asset to children with special needs;
• we need to build it into every aspect of their programs;
• we can read poems aloud, choosing ones with refrains and repetitions so the children can join in;
• we can incorporate big-book formats of poems so children can see the words as they hear them;

- we can use overhead transparencies of poems for easy access by limited readers;
- we can build upon the structure of the poem — patterning, substituting, predicting, and inventing.

We can let all children express themselves in their own poetic writings, and they will feel the success of putting their ideas and feelings into print. We can read aloud the poems the children cannot read but can understand with the help of an adult who brings meaning to the ear and offers them concepts for thought and feeling: We can enrich the lives of the children we teach through bringing poems to all of them regardless of label.

Slow Reader

I-am-in-the-slow
read-ers-group-my-broth
er-is-in-the-foot
ball-team-my-sis-ter
is a ser-ver-my
lit-tle-broth-er-was
a-wise-man-in-the
in-fants-christ-mas-play
I-am-in-the-slow
read-ers-group-that-is
all-I-am-in-I
hate-it.

Allan Ahlberg

Poems in Our Schools and in Our Lives

There are a few basic guidelines adults should remember when sharing poetry with young people:
- choose poems that children will find interesting, and ones that you enjoy as well;
- stress the pleasure of poetry, the satisfaction of the poetic experience;
- select poems in which the meaning and the language are appropriate for the background and experience of the children, and help them come to the poem;
- consult children on the choice of poems;
- prepare the poetry you are going to read aloud before sharing

it: know it, care about it, share it well;
- let children rehearse poems before they read them so that both reader and listener enjoy the experience;
- don't let children memorize poetry until they re-read it for meaning voluntarily;
- don't dissect poetry: explore it and explain when necessary; do take it seriously;
- read poetry frequently, grouping poems together: spend 5 minutes sometimes, 50 minutes other times;
- allow informal controversial talk about the poems and don't make children afraid that they might say the wrong thing.
- use tape recordings and records to assist you when reading poetry to children;
- interact personally, voicing opinons and joining in; but don't lecture or dominate;
- have many anthologies available for children, books of all types by all kinds of poets;
- seek out the ideas and views of the children: listen to them and respect them;
- find poems that children can read with you, poems they can read easily and recall with minimal effort;
- relate the writing of poetry to the reading of poetry;
- allow for an emotional response by the children, and respect their feelings;
- read poems for your own enjoyment: buy a new anthology, and lend it to a friend.

A student spoke to me after a class on using poems with children about her father who wrote poems all the time, but did not publish them. Instead, he bound them into booklets and shared them with his family. His daughter, naturally, was very proud of her dad's efforts, and when she was given as assignment by her Grade 11 English teacher to choose any Canadian poet, research his or her life, and read a collection of his or her poems in order to build a poet profile, the student chose her father. Upon submitting the work, she received a failing grade and, when she questioned the mark, was told that a poet is not a poet unless he is published. After explaining the situation to the teacher, the student received a note saying that both she and her father should be ashamed of trivializing

poetry, and that her father had no right to call himself a
poet. She was then assigned Earle Birney as punishment.

   Later that year, the teacher's mother died, and in
remembrance, she read aloud a poem to the class as
memorial to a lost loved one. Breaking down in the middle
of the reading, she wept, then explained that poetry was
the highest of art forms and could touch us most deeply.
No student was moved by the teacher, her loss, her emo-
tion, or the poem she had chosen to share. The students
had long ago recognized the elitism of this teacher as she
presented pearls of poetry outside their grasp. Hurrah for
fathers that feel they are poets! Hurrah for daughters that
read their fathers' poems!

D.B.

The Poem

It is only a little twig
With a green bud at the end;
But if you plant it,
And water it,
And set it where the sun will be above it,
It will grow into a tall bush
With many flowers,
And leaves which thrust hither and thither
Sparkling.
From its roots will come freshness,
And beneath it the glass blades
Will bend and recover themselves,
And clash one upon another
In the blowing wind.

But if you take my twig
And throw it into a closet
With mousetraps and blunted tools,
It will shrivel and waste.
And, some day,
When you open the door,
You will think it an old twisted nail,
And sweep it into the dust bin
With other rubbish.

Amy Lowell

2

THE WORLD OF CHILDREN'S POETRY

Shallow Poem

I've thought of a poem.
I carry it carefully,
nervously, in my head,
like a saucer of milk;
in case I should spill some lines
before I can put it down.

Gerda Mayer

What is Poetry for Children?

The question arises: *What is a poem for a child and what is a poem for an adult?* Can both enjoy the same poem? Is poetry itself like a universal folklore enjoyed by both children and adults? Should poets who write poetry for children be restricted to particular words and ideas and shapes? Why do children seek out poems written for themselves as well as poems written for adults, and seem to find in them reasons for including them in their reading? Is it because poetry itself offers delights that go far beyond a child's conscious understanding? Of course there are experiences shared by the adult world that children cannot comprehend. Perhaps, as in every story ever read or told, children choose those aspects they can possess and put into order and ignore what they cannot understand. As in all tribal universal sharings, the members absorb what they can. Because poetry has such appeal to the ear, an undertow pulling the listener in, the child may join the adults in experiencing the ear tune that the heart also somehow understands. All good poems operate on many levels for readers of differing ages. When we give children poetry only because of its verse qualities, its labored rhyme or awkward rhythm, then we limit the child's capac-

ity for responding to the poetry. If we romanticize or sentimental-
ize childhood, use doggerel for teaching simplistic morality, or
accept into the definition of poetry anything that has an apparent
poetic look, we cheapen our own values. Then we run the great
risk of making poetry not worth reading in the eyes of the child.
This is not to say we do not want light-hearted verse, humor, even
jingles and skipping rhymes, but we do want something that has
its own value, where the poem itself is a worthwhile experience,
not a technique for teaching some hidden skills.

Until recently, many anthologies for children selected poems
from the work of adult poets in order to introduce children to adult
poetry. They gathered the poems under themes, genres, issues,
holidays, or by nations, and selected from adult writings the poetry
that would appeal to children, including folk and aboriginal poetry.
Where the anthologies worked, the poems appealed to the children's vision, often from the viewpoint of the child or reflective
of childhood.

*Poetry that children like and poetry intentionally written
for them may be two different things. What is children's
poetry? Is it a modified version of poetry for adults,
expressing a simpler view of life? Is it nonsense verse or
playful rhymes that a child can "understand"? Is it concerned only with happy events, other children, friendly
animals, and fanciful tales? Or can it be said that poetry is
simply poetry and that all of it belongs to children except,
as Herbert Read has pointed out, for poems that incorporate those "particular and many experiences which children do not share with grown-up people"? This is probably
true, with the caveat expressed by Lillian Smith in* The
Unreluctant Years: *"In giving poetry to children it is
well to remember that they understand far more than they
can express. Children apprehend by intuition and imagination that which is far beyond their limited experience." It
might further be said that there are no boundaries to children's sense of wonderment.*

Sheila Egoff

What to include in poetry for children is not an easy task. In his anthology, *Children's Verse in America*, Donald Hall states:

> It is difficult, editing such a collection, to remain truly consistent. On the one hand I refuse to consider Longfellow's intentions when he wrote about village blacksmiths or skeletons in armor; on the other hand, I omit some sections from Whitman's "Song of Myself," anthologized for children in recent anthologies, on the grounds that they are not "for children" either by intention or structure or history. If I one day edit a collection of poems in which I select what children might like, and not what children have liked, perhaps I will print other examples of Whitman — and verses by Wallace Stevens about Chieftain Iffucan of Azcan in caftan, or by Robert Bly about horses in snowy fields. In this book I mean to be historical. Yet on another hand (anthologists require three or four hands) I include Robert Frost's "Stopping by Woods on a Snowy Evening" because anthologists of children's verse have used it for several decades; it has even been illustrated and published as a children's book by itself. Does it belong in The Oxford Book of Children's Verse in America? If we know anything about Robert Frost, we know he did not write it for children. I reprint the poem because it has become a poem for children — but I do not include it without doubt. It is a poem passed on to children for their own good, not because of an intrinsic or structural intention, like a pipe for crawling through.

The antecedents of today's childhood poetry and verse lie in the distant past — fragments of poems, sea shanties, ballads, scraps of doggerel, superstitions, admonitions, slogans, charms. They come from the period when the language was changing from Old to Middle English. Context helps us deduce the meaning of archaic forms and phrases, and there are wide variations in the length, the style, and the tone of the pieces. The modern descendants of popular folk songs can find their roots there.

This folk poetry provides rhythm and music for the play that children engage in. It includes riddles, tongue twisters, rhymes, games, word play, lullabyes, folk songs. Finger plays traditionally taught rhythm, muscle control, and word play. The children use their fingers, hands, and arms to help tell the verse, and include body movements, such as bending, jumping, and skipping.

This subculture of game, verse, song, and rhyme has been collected in Great Britain by Peter and Iona Opie, and in Canada by Edith Fowke. These compilations are the oral poetry from the playground and introduce children to the world of poetry as an organic and living force. (They can also provide entry points for introducing children to the poetry of print.) This oral lore was sung and recited by adults to children, and can help children in the transition from their play verse to the cadences and humor and more subtle qualities of poetry. Raffi, Fred Penner, and Sharon, Lois, and Bram have sung and recorded songs drawn from the verse of children. Sometimes they are printed in books illustrated by artists. These give us valuable source material for joining with children in the universal collaboration called children's folk verse.

Mother Goose

Nursery rhymes are used before children can talk. The rhymes often provide the children's first introduction to poetry. The musical quality of the rhymes spoken aloud is part of the happy relationship between parent, child, and poem. There are alphabet rhymes, counting rhymes, finger plays, chants, rhythm, humor, and strange people and situations. The word play, the imagination, the sounds, the rollicking rhythms, the merriment, and the excitement all introduce us to poetry and makes us friends of poetry. Contemporary poets have taken the well-known rhymes, the slapstick humor, the wit, the comic spirit, and used similar techniques for their own writings. The short verses, repetition, sound work, action, rhythm, and rhyming create a physical involvement as they are read.

> Nothing seems to stop the nursery rhymes, neither attacks on their violence and amorality by overzealous concerned adults, nor the archaic language and unfamiliar images and unexplicable behavior. We do not know if nursery rhymes are hidden pockets of political satire, refer to historical personages, or reveal social history, but we do know they survive. Many children still know rhymes that one would think had passed on, and many parents can still quote from memory the tunes of "Little Bo Peep" or "Pussy In The

Well''. Perhaps it is their appeal to both adults and children that has caused their longevity. Children rarely demand explanations for the incongruities of nursery rhymes. They still amuse and delight, and are much more than historical curiosities. They work for the parent or adult who wants to amuse or comfort the child. They work for the child who is vulnerable and subordinate to the adult.

Joanne L. Lynn

The rhythms in nursery rhymes intrigue and satisfy. In nursery rhymes, sense and nonsense co-exist. It is a magic world:

. . . a fantastic world beyond the prose of knowledge. A child can build for himself, at a moment's notice, a world as perfect, useless and beautiful as a soap bubble.

Robert Lynd

There is drama here:

> Little Miss Muffet
> Sat on a tuffet,
> Eating her curds and whey;
> Along came a spider
> And sat down beside her,
> And frightened Miss Muffet away.

Who was Miss Muffet? Why was she sitting there? Why did the spider come? How would I feel if a horrible spider sat down right there beside me?

Children love the rhythms and the rhymes. Why is rhyme so dear to most of us? Maybe it is the repetition of the sound: we hear it the first time, and then again, and that pleases us. We anticipate that it is coming up once more. That ability to project and anticipate: perhaps that is one of the chief pleasures of language.

We learn that life can be sad:

> Little Bo Peep has lost her sheep,
> And doesn't know where to find them.

but it will turn out all right:

> Leave them alone, and they'll come home
> Wagging their tails behind them.

We learn that some disasters can be faintly comic:

> Jack and Jill went up the hill
> To fetch a pail of water;
> Jack fell down and broke his crown,
> And Jill came tumbling after.

In nursery rhymes we learn about merry people:

> Old King Cole was a merry old soul,
> And a merry old soul was he . . .

There is humor and laughter, nonsense and, above all, appeal to the imagination.

> There was an old woman who lived in a shoe,
> She had so many children she didn't know what to do.

And you remember old Mother Hubbard, who:

> . . . went to the cupboard,
> To fetch the poor dog a bone;
> But when she got there,
> The cupboard was bare
> And so the poor doggie had none.

There are many slightly different versions of nursery rhymes, just as there are differing versions of ballads. They tell us about love and hate, and the inevitability of fate. They liberate us, through imagination, into a fantastic and unreal garden of delights.

> Mary, Mary, quite contrary,
> How does your garden grow?
> With silver bells, and cockle shells,
> And pretty maids all in a row.

Lines like these are fun and easily roll off the tongue, and quickly commit to memory.

Nursery rhymes offer us total and complete romance:

> Ride a cock horse to Banbury Cross
> To see a fine lady upon a white horse.
> Rings on her fingers, and bells on her toes,
> And she shall have music wherever she goes.

They show us sadness and death as in "Who killed Cock Robin?"

They exist in a child's world, where time and space are totally flexible:

> How many miles to Babylon?
> Three score and ten.
> Can I get there by candlelight?
> Yes, and back again.

They take us into the realms of the imagination:

> I had a little nut tree;
> And nothing would it bear,
> But a silver nutmeg,
> And a golden pear.
> The King of Spain's daughter
> Came to visit me,
> And all because
> Of my little nut tree.

The words themselves are perfect — honed through time.

> A diller, a dollar,
> A ten o'clock scholar,
> What makes you come so soon?
> You used to come at ten o'clock,
> But now you come at noon.

As in all good poetry, nursery rhymes have sound, sense, and imagination, repetition which we love, and form windows into a world of wonder.

The Evolution of Poetry for Children

Children's fiction has evolved into real literature, and poetry is following along at a quick rate. At the turn of the century much of the poetry written for children was sentimental, patronizing, and didactic. Much contemporary poetry for children is light-hearted and vigorous. The best of it, such as that of Dennis Lee, Eve Merriam, Jack Prelutsky, and Shel Silverstein, is simple and yet well-crafted. It incorporates the oral traditions of playground verse and the cadences of Mother Goose. These poets use sound patterns that have the satisfying rhyme of the memory gems of childhood and the compelling beat that enables them to be remembered. Like playground content, much of contemporary light verse for children just skirts the forbidden and the taboo. Anarchy, titillation, and the risqué counterpoint feeling and sentiment. Word play is a big part of this poetry — puns, tongue twisters, scrambled words, and near rhyme. The children perceive both the themes and the linguistic exploration as part of their meaning-making approach to life. Colloquial rhymes, the rhythms of the speaking voice, the storytelling quality, along with the subjects of a child's life, make the poems accessible to children and introduce poetry as a natural phenomenon, without pain.

We can introduce children to poems both old and new, poems written especially for them, and poems that can be shared by adults and the young — the whole human tribe.

The subtlety of Walter de la Mare, the lyricism of Ted Hughes, the metrical cadences of Robert Louis Stevenson, the memories awakened by A.A. Milne, the word play of Ogden Nash and David McCord, and the haiku of Harry Behn are all representative of children's poetry.

> . . . you're back again where you began. You're back with the mystery of having been moved by words. The best craftsmanship always leaves holes and gaps in the works of the poem so that something that is not in the poem can creep, crawl, flash, or thunder in.
>
> *Dylan Thomas*

Poems written by poets ages and ages ago are interesting to children today because the feelings people have, their emotions and delights, are just the same now as they were hundreds of years ago. William Blake, in the 18th century wrote:

> When the green woods laugh with the voice of joy,
> And the dimpling stream runs laughing by . . . .

and at the end of the 18th century, William Wordsworth said:

> The cock is crowing,
> The stream is flowing,
> The small birds twitter,
> The lake doth glitter,
> The green field sleeps in the sun . . . .

From roughly the same time came Kate Greenaway's lines:

> Little wind, blow on the hilltop;
> Little wind, blow down the plain;
> Little wind, blow up the sunshine;
> Little wind, blow off the rain.

Alfred, Lord Tennyson, the great Victorian poet, wrote:

> I chatter over stony ways,
> In little sharps and trebles,
> I bubble into eddying bays,
> I babble on the pebbles.
>
> I chatter, chatter as I flow
> To join the brimming river,
> For men may come, and men may go,
> But I go on for ever.
>
> from *"The Song of the Brook"*

One of the first poets to write especially for children was Robert Louis Stevenson. This is from his poem "Autumn Fires":

> In the other gardens
> And all up the vale,
> From the autumn bonfires
> See the smoke trail.

There are many illustrated editions of *A Child's Garden of Verses* by Robert Lewis Stevenson in print today, which suggests his popularity is everlasting. Poems from the turn of the century and from our grandparents' childhood, as well as our own, are still accessible to children.

Elizabeth Coatsworth continued the tradition of poems just for children:

> I heard a mouse
> Bitterly complaining
> In a crack of moonlight
> Aslant on the floor —

Christina Rossetti wrote:

> The city mouse lives in a house; —
> The garden mouse lives in a bower,
> He's friendly with the frogs and toads,
> And sees the pretty plants in flower.

A.A. Milne built a poetic world around nursery life and the solitary existence of one child. With the beginning of the 20th century, Walter de la Mare created an incomparable body of work, including fantasy and reality, ranging from nonsense to mood pieces of the deep unknown, folklore, fantasy, and mysteries of the dark woods, conjuring up images and imaginings for children. The content of poetry during these years was full of fairies, folklore, nature, and the images of the ideal childhood. It was a poetic world of pleasant childhood, full of the cadences and miracles of the lives of children.

Although today's children enjoy modern contemporary poets, with careful selection and interpretative oral reading, they can begin to visit poems from the past with as much delight as the children who first read them.

There are so many wonderful poets to choose from. The "older" poets we enjoy sharing with children include:

Dorothy Aldis
Herbert Asquith
Rhoda Bacmeister
Dorothy Baruch
Harry Behn
S.V. Benét
Rowena Bennett
William Blake
Lewis Carroll
Guy W. Carryl
Chas E. Carryl
Elizabeth
   Coatsworth
Hilda Conkling
Chas. S. Calverley
W.H. Davies
Walter de la Mare
John Drinkwater
Ivy O. Eastwick
Eugene Field
Robert Forst
Rose Fyleman
Rachel Field
Eleanor Farjeon
Kate Greenaway
Arthur Guiterman
W.S. Gilbert
Harry Graham
Kenneth Grahame

Robert Herrick
S. Hoffenstein
Pauline Johnson
John Keats
Charles Kingsley
Rudyard Kipling
Edward Lear
Vachel Lindsay
H.W. Longfellow
John Marquis
John Masefield
Hughes Mearns
Mildred Plew Meigs
E. Vincent Millay
A.A. Milne
Christopher Morley
Ogden Nash
Henry Newbolt
Moira O'Neill
Dorothy Parker
Matthew Prior
Edgar Allan Poe
Beatrice Potter
Sir Arthur
   Quiller-Couch
William Brightly
   Rands
Lizette W. Reese
Laura E. Richards
James W. Riley

Elizabeth M.
   Roberts
Edwin Arlington
   Robinson
Christina Rossetti
Carl Sandburg
Duncan Campbell
   Scott
Robert Service
William
   Shakespeare
Robert Louis
   Stevenson
Edna St. Vincent
   Millay
Jonathan Swift
Sara Teasdale
James Tippett
Nancy Byrd Turner
W.M. Thackeray
Walt Whitman
Frida Wolfe
Humbert Wolfe
W. Wordsworth
Eleanor Wylie
Annette Wynne
E.B. White
John Greenleaf
   Whittier
W. Butler Yeats

In the sixties and seventies, many poets rejected much of what they claimed were stereotypical views of childhood and began to explore the social concerns and situations in which today's children find themselves. Now we also find poems full of urban angst, family problems, personal pain, and moral dilemmas. Some poets explored variations on rhythms and word play along with the new content and they produced a sophisticated type of verse for children: Eve Merriam, Dennis Lee, Lilian Moore, Jack Prelutsky. Lucille Clifton, Nicki Giovanni, and Arnold Adoff began writing of the black experience. Ted Hughes observed the world for children and reported on its darker side, presenting a philosophical stance inside his carefully controlled cadences. Shel Silverstein was the king of the contemporary poets during the seventies, and with savage wit, described the foibles of childhood. He included slang, wry commentary, and patterns from the street. Spike Milligan's British comic poetry and Charles Causley's allegories bring us into the contemporary world of children's poems. Now, we have for our use all styles, from hard-edged comedy to subtle philosophy. David McCord, Myra Cohn Livingston, and Karla Kuskin are exploring the syntax and movement of language, working tricks with visual and verbal puns, finding empathetic touchstones for children. Perhaps poetry has come of age — complex, child-oriented, and philosophically attuned to both developmental stages of the child and of the society in which the child lives. We have teachers and parents bringing the poems back to the oral tradition, reading them aloud, memorizing them, singing them to and with the children.

Today's anthologies are full of new rhyme patterns and new content. There are poems of the pain of childhood, unfairness, even death. Now an individual finds life pictured in all of its aspects, and poetry for children takes on a broader, more honest, and more far-ranging nature. We still find the beautiful moments, the child-like laughter, and the sentiment of honest feelings, but these are counterpointed with the complexities of family and friends, school life and dreams, eulogies and cheers.

There are many poems published today for the children's market. The poems are often less formal and more spontaneous than in the past, and the language patterns are representative of children's own talk and writing. The subject matter has changed in children's poems, and adults must be open to the great variety of content now pictured in poems for today's children. They must help the children become as aware as possible of the full range of poetry.

Today, there is a new generation of poets writing for children. Their work is often humorous, witty, and perceptive. Family experiences, situations, children's precarious positions in society are all material for these poets. For example, Michael Rosen's narrative poems, often about family relations, in unusual poetic style and using all kinds of talk patterns, create intricate and well-crafted stories to touch today's readers. Often they are illustrated by Quentin Blake with his characteristically cartoon-type drawings. Children may respond readily to the contemporary poets and then work backward in time visiting poets who wrote in a different manner about various topics. Arnold Adoff uses the patterns of language to slow the reader and to emphasize each word in his poems. Cynthia Rylant, in her book *Waiting to Waltz*, chronicles growing up in a small town in Appalachia.

How many of the "Newer Poets" have you explored with your children?

Arnold Adoff
Allan Ahlberg
Frank Asch

Harry Behn
Jill Bennett
Rowena Bennett
Earle Birney
N.M. Bodecker
Phillip Booth
Elizabeth Brewster
Gwendolyn Brooks
Margaret Wise
  Brown

Ian Campbell
Charles Causley
Remy Charlip
John Ciardi
William Cole
Countee Cullen

e.e. cummings

Roald Dahl
Diane Dawber
Beatrice Schenk
  de Regniers
Fitzhugh Dodson
Michael Dugan
Sonja Dunn

T.S. Eliot
Willard J. Espy

Max Fatcher
Paul Fleischman
Robert Francis
Robert Frost

Theodore
  (Dr. Seuss) Geisel
Chief Dan George

Nikki Giovanni
M.B. Goffstein
Eloise Greenfield

Donald Hall
Phyllis Halloran
Seamus Heaney
John Hegley
Robert Heidbreder
Florence Parry
  Heide
David Helwig
Russell Hoban
Mary Ann
  Hoberman
Felice Holman
Langston Hughes
Ted Hughes
sean o huigan
Lucie and James
  L. Hymes

David Ignatow

Paul B. Janeczko
Randall Jarrell

Bobbi Katz
X.J. Kennedy
James Kirkup
A.M. Klein
Ruth Krauss
Karla Kuskin

Philip Larkin
Irving Layton
Dennis Lee
Jean Little
Myra Cohn
  Livingston
Arnold Lobel

Gwendolyn
  MacEwan
Wes Magee
Margart Mahy
David McCord
David McFadden
Phyllis McGinley
Roger McGough
Eve Merriam
Spike Milligan
Cynthia Mitchell
Lilian Moore
Edwin Morgan

Christian
  Morgenstern
Lillian Morrison
Susan Musgrave

Judith Nicholls
Leslie Norris
Alden Nowlan

Mary O'Neill
Gareth Owen

Brian Patten
Mervyn Peake
Redmond Phillips
Nancy Prasad
Jack Prelutsky
Al Purdy

James Reaney
Duke Redbird
James Reeves
Laura E. Richards
Marci Ridlon
Theodore Roethke
Michael Rosen
W.W.E. Ross
Joanne Ryder
Cynthia Rylant

Clive Sansom
Vernon Scannell
F.R. Scott

Maurice Sendak
Ian Serraillier
Shel Silverstein
Lois Simmie
Stevie Smith
William Jay Smith
Raymond Souster
William Stafford
James Stephens
May Swenson

Sara Teasdale
J.R.R. Tolkien
Henry Treece

John Updike

Judith Viorst

Miriam Waddington
William Wallace
Clyde Watson
Carolyn Wells
Colin West
Siv Widerberg
Nancy Willard
William Carlos
  Williams
Valerie Worth
Kit Wright
Tim Wynne-Jones

Jane Yolen

Charlotte Zolotow

*. . . many poets have claimed that the thrust of their work
is to recall something left behind in childhood — a sense of
direct living, of unity, of the joy in constant discovery that
goes far beyond mere nostalgia. — The poet who keeps
alive the intense memories of childhood will create poetry
suffused with respect for children's intelligence, imagina-*

tion, and perceptions. This will be a poetry that is not a nostalgic reminiscence about childhood for adults, but rather a celebration of childhood, as gritty and stimulating as it is, for all children.

Janet Saltman

The Difference Between Poetry and Prose

Tolstoy once wrote in his diary, "Where the boundary between prose and poetry lies, I shall never be able to understand. The question is raised in manuals of style, but the answer to it lies beyond me." We do know that poetry is an economical, intense, and efficient form of literature. Every word matters. Nothing can be skipped. The reader has to concentrate on each deliberate word and sentence. Eve Merriam says a poem is like a can of frozen juice: when you add three cans of water, you get the prose version. Some poems can be written in a paragraph form and some authors write prose that is highly poetic. On the whole, poetry is poetry when the language becomes so condensed that every single word is part of the heart and soul of the text. Many children would define poetry as rhyming lines, but the rhymes of poetry are complex and difficult to create. Norma Farber says, "Let our children learn to speak two languages from birth — the two languages of their mother tongue — poetry and prose." The language of poetry is close to the language of children. Sound exploration, rhythm, and rhyme are created spontaneously by children. Teachers can intervene and reclaim the lost language of poetry, finding the poetic language within different print forms.

> The night wind has a dismal trick of wandering round
>   and round a building of that sort,
> And moaning as it goes,
> And of trying with its unseen hand, the windows and
>   the doors;
> And seeking out some crevices by which to enter.
> And not content with stalking through the aisles,
> And gliding round and round the pillars,
> And tempting the deep organ,
> Soars up to the roof, and strives to rend the rafters;
> Then flings itself despairingly upon the stones below,
> And passes, muttering, into the vaults.
> Anon it comes up stealthily,

And creeps along the walls,
Seeming to read, in whispers, the Inscriptions sacred
   to the Dead,
But high up in the steeple!
There the foul blast roars and whistles.
High up in the steeple,
Where it is free to come and go through many an airy
   arch and loophole,
And to twist and twine itself about the giddy stair,
And twirl the groaning weathercock,
And make the very tower shake and shiver!
High up in the steeple;
Where the belfry is,
And iron rails are ragged with rust,
And sheets of lead and copper, shrivelled by the
   changing weather,
Crackle and heave beneath the unaccustomed tread!
And birds stuff shabby nests into corners of old oaken
   joists and beams.

This is taken from *The Chimes* by Charles Dickens, and surely it meets all the desired criteria for poetry: it has rhythm, comparisons, word pictures, and repetition. The choice of words is poetic and the emotional response demanded is clear. We re-arranged the lines.

Look into some of your favorite books and find some "poetic prose" that you could reshape into a free-verse poem. *Charlotte's Web* and *Tom Sawyer* would be good starting places.

Byrd Baylor has written many fine books for children. Her style is poetic, and great care is taken in the arrangement of words in chunks of meaning, like the perfect veins still seen in a fossil. The shape dictates how we read the words; and our reading builds unique meaning. Children can quickly realize how the words, chosen and placed on the page, determine what we will think and feel:

> Forgive me for walking here,
> Brother Lizard.
>
> Forgive me,
> Sister Quail.
>
> I know this is *your* sand,
> not mine,
> You've left your tracks
> to make it yours.
> You've left a hundred
> tiny roads.

Spiders
and snakes
and beetles and mice
don't worry.

You can see that
I walk
lightly
here.

I never ruin
the paths
you've made.
I only follow them
because
they are good paths
to follow.

They're maps
that show
where
small feet
crossed the desert
all last night
and where those feet
circled
and stopped
and where they turned
and chose a hill
or met a friend
or went alone . . .

Some people read tracks
like they'd read a story.
(The story is true.
It's written
in sand.)

Poetical prose is a window into poetry, and can give children
the special sight required for understanding the reading and the
writing of this art form.

> Poets are fishermen crying
> "Fresh catch from sleep,
> Fresh as the mackerel sky
> Or a salmon's leap
> Is the catch we offer.
> Come buy, come buy!"
> *Anne Wilkinson*

3

How Do Poems Work?

Song 61

　　What does poetry do
then? he asked me
not having liked my poems
not thinking them ''poems'' at all he said.

& what could i say to him i had
nothing to offer beyond
　　(the poems)/

　　　& i have
no answer for you
no answer that would do
　　what you want it to, what
you want me to
　　　　do, writing poems
　for you/for
what? that you might say
　　you like them/&who
　　　else.

All else failing　this answer:

　　If possible, poetry sings.
　　Sings poetry, if possible.

no answer/no response
　in his eyes/i
could not be seen could not be
　　　heard?
i must still
　　however
　　　　sing.

Douglas Barbour

Painting Pictures with Words

Poets paint pictures with words, as painters do with color and shape. They often compare things we would not usually think of as being alike.

Writing about a dandelion, Hilda Conklin said:

> O little soldier with the golden helmet,
> What are you guarding on my lawn?

Now, who would have thought of comparing a dandelion with a soldier? Yet, it works: the kind of helmet, like the ones Roman soldiers used to wear, with plumes on top — often golden. This is all-important. Part of the pleasure we get from poetry comes from these interesting, and often arresting comparisons.

> The ghosts of dandelions haunt the land
> And the sky folds grey and close around
> The place that hummed and chuckled in the sun.
> > V. Francis

You have seen dandelions, after the flower dies, and only the "clocks" are left. They are the color of ghosts, and they are ghosts because they are what is left after the flower dies. They are ghosts because of the way they drift, silently. All that is suggested in that one word "Ghosts". "Hummed" and "chuckled". . . . make the place alive through personification.

There are many more word pictures. Here is one:

> The children have gone indoors
> to gobble and chatter their way
> spilling the day's adventures through the evening meal.
> > H. Ball

> *The grey sea and the long, black land;*
> *And the yellow half moon large and low;*
> > Robert Browning

> . . . *long, black land*

Ryan, aged 13, wrote this poem:

Trux

Chest-high tires crush the asphalt.
Endless flames belch from long stacks.
Windshield dirty with dust particles.
Headlights stare like enormous eyes.

Chrome glistens atop the cab.
The trailer simulates huge shoulders.
Sunlight flashes from the hood ornaments.
Thunder rumbles from the mighty chassis.
The horn roars out its fury.
The cast-iron grille smiles murderously.
All cars are dwarfed by this huge steel monster
Boy, do I love my truck?

Here is a picture from a poem about icicles, by John Ferns:

Monster's teeth,
nails of the silver witch,
sun words splinter
as we fight, unicorns flashing brilliant
beyond sight.

(Have you ever thought that icicles look like the teeth of a Tyrannosaurus Rex?) And where does the unicorn come in?

Pictures are painted by poets using all the senses: sight, hearing, smell, sound, and touch.

This is a picture of a spooky house:

All day within the dreamy house,
The doors upon their hinges creaked;
The blue fly sung in the pane: the mouse
Behind the mouldering wainscot shrieked.

Alfred Tennyson

We skated on stream and pond; we cut
The crinching snow.

Robert Bridges

Perhaps he made up the word "crinching". It paints the right picture — when it is so cold the snow makes a creaking, crinching sound, as you walk over it.

Here is an olden-days description of a pretty girl at a wedding:

Her feet beneath her petticoat
Like little mice stole in and out.

Sir John Suckling

It is a miracle that the pictures created in words by poets seem so vivid and real. It is as if a slow-motion camera has captured for an instant a sight or a sound, and magnified it so that we can see it and feel it. Poets use very few words, and yet a flood of images fills our minds as we read them. Poems can be a photo album of our country, created without camera and film. Picture poems. (Worth a thousand words)

How many images does Ruth Krauss' word-play poem conjure up?

Riddle

hot-maker / snow-melter / river-sweller /
bud-buster / watermelon-ripener / pattern-maker-through-forest-trees-one /
rooster-waker / people-browner / shadow-of-migrating-bird-maker /
in-the-east-one / in-the-west-one / straight-up-one /
neck-breaker / Moslem-bender / noodle-dryer /
hypnotizer-of-morning-glories / bell-ringer / spitfire /
made-small-shining-in-my-eye-one / parade-encourager / picnic-monger /
democratic-one / undemocratic-one / silhouetter-of-tall-pines-in-the-air /
candle-lighter / dragon-lighter / red-sky-at-evening-lighter /
thunder-maker / groundhog-fooler / pot-boiler
who-threw-the-first-stone-one / Old-Sol / New-Sol /
duck-sitting-on-own-self-in-lake-maker / Soleil / Eye-of-Mexico /
uns / snu / nussy / shine-in-the-coal / moon-hider /
sky-cleaner / and-makest-thou-the-wind-to-blow / makest-thou-the-balloon-to-bust /
the-streams-that-are-hot-in-the-cold-sea-maker / leaf-turner / century-turner /
sky-ticker / what-would-happen-if-you-skipped-a-day-one /
blood-light / vein-light / bone-light /
phoenix-imitator / daisy-symbol / Indian-giver /
apple-on-the-head-of-Sir-Isaac-hitter / on-the-topmost-tip-of-the-mast-gleam /
old-dogtail-wagger / shady-side-of-the-street-maker / shine-on-shoe-maker /
in-the-puddles-one / in-the-tide / lighting-the-mountain /
right-at-my-own-doorstep-you-are-one / stoop-sitter / moth-maker /
lunchtime-bringer / bogeyman-assistant / old-x-behind-the-x-ray /
to-stud-nightfall-with-sparks-one / old-sunnyside-up-in-the-sky / pretty-day /
bringer-of-bluebells / buttercup-yellower / strawberry-reddener /
dark-horse-of-another-color / who-saw-the-Golden-age-one /
second-fiddle-to-Nero / glacier-giver / engine-driver

Poets enlist sensory memories in creating images in their work. Children are able to identify with these sense feelings in the poems they hear and read, and they sharpen their sensory perception. Young children see the whole world through those senses, and poetry lets children recapture and re-investigate their worlds of memory.

The Sounds of Poems

Poets are wordsmiths. They spend their lives choosing words, bending them, shaping them, teasing them, playing with them. The sounds of language fascinate them so. They create poems that make our ears sing. (Read a poem slowly; notice the sounds that make the poem come alive.) Those special sounds in poetry happen when poets select a particular rhythm or beat, when they choose words that imitate the sounds they represent, when they create rhymes with words that go well together. Out-loud language makes meaning in our minds. Poems are full of the sounds of poetry. We can read them, chant them, sing them.

The natural rhythm of childhood holds the beginning of the understanding of a poem. From the chants of tribespeople to the working song rhythms, from the lullabies to the pat-a-cake rhythms, the built-in metre has a music of its own, and draws the child to it. The rocking-horse rhythms of Mother Goose, the galloping horses of Stevenson's "Windy Nights", Mrs. Peck Pidgeon bobbing for bread, David McCord's "Pickety Fence", jump-rope rhymes, street games, all are part of rhythm in verse and poem. The poet manipulates the rhythm for various effects — to show contrast, to allow a new element to appear, to highlight a particular moment, to surprise, to frighten, to hold in awe.

Rhyme brings out the musical quality of poetry and lets the words sing. Young children enjoy making up rhyming verse. Mother Goose poems let rhyme come before meaning in making those wonderful poems of childhood. Games in the street and playground verses are the beginning of poetry for many children. Along with rhyme, there are other aspects of sound that poets make use of — alliteration, assonance, repetition of letters, and coined words, all adding to the music, the melody, and the sound of the poetry.

There is comfort in the traditional rhyme patterns of familiar poems, and there is excitement and surprise in the new sounds that we discover as we meet a wide range of poetry.

The poet John Ciardi twists and turns his way through all types of rhyme patterns in this poem:

I Wouldn't

There's a mouse house
In the hall wall
With a small door
By the hall floor
Where the fat cat
Sits all day,
Sits that way
All day
Every day
Just to say
"Come out and play."

To the nice mice
In the mouse house
In the hall wall
With the small door
By the hall floor.

And do they
Come out and play
When the fat cat
Asks them to?

Well, would you?

Don't forget that the rhythm of language is one of the greatest helps to extending understanding, and the sounds of language are intimately bound up with meaning. I have a passionate conviction that this is the stage when poetry becomes a special way of saying things, a kind of enchantment for which there is no substitute. A Child's Garden of Verses and Come Hither are so surely part of my childhood that I want every child to know what words make, as well as to understand what they say. When school reading takes over from the pleasures of early discovery of books and stories, reading aloud will be all the easier if the child's fluency in spoken language is also grounded in a poetic tradition older than writing.

Margaret Meek

The Shape of Poetry

Poets shape their poems by the way they arrange the words on the paper. They group them into verses, place them in unusual places on the page, twist them into pretzel ideas, arrange them to look like what they are talking about, write all the letters in capitals (or use none at all), fool around with punctuation, write the lines as dialogue. By placing letters, words, sentences, carefully on the page, poets can focus our attention on patterns that give power and strength to what they are trying to say. As we read poems, their shapes help us to hear what the poet is trying to say.

Contemporary poets enjoy using experimental verse forms, often abandoning the conventions of punctuation, capitalization, or versing for original and inventive new concepts, using shape, sound, and effective concrete structures. The poet sean o huigan uses seemingly formless shape to poke fun at those things that fascinate children; and through contrasting grotesque violence with humor and wit, he presents images that delight them:

The Pocket

i reached
into my
pocket
and much
to my surprise
something in
there
grabbed me
and pulled
me right
inside
i felt
its clammy
fingers
all bony
cold and
thin

i tried to
keep my
head out
no use
it all went in
and that
was not
the end
of it
the pocket
seemed
so deep
and dark
and strange
and scary
i felt i
had to

"shut up
you silly
creature"
a voice
yelled
in my
ear
and then
my feet
were
pulled inside
and i had
disappeared

sean o huigan

The look of a poem is an important aspect of its total effect, building a unity of meaning, sound, and intent. The typography and placement of words, phrases, and lines, the use of stanza, rhyme, and metre, all determine the poetic response.

Arnold Adoff has developed a unique shape style that children will come to recognize as only his, even when the poem may be left unsigned.

Not Me But

cows walk up and beg to
            be
        burgers

chicken legs
  will tap dance
            to
                my
      teeth
and
oatmeal cookies
        have
        been
            known
to fly
    out of their jars
    as i pass by
                Arnold Adoff

Details Large and Small

Poets make good reporters: they see and hear with special eyes
and ears. As they observe different people in special places doing
all kinds of things, they seem to be able to recreate in their poems
not just what went on but how people felt about what was happening, and how people felt about what they had seen (even if
they had only imagined what they thought they saw.) Reporters
in newspapers may only give the facts; poets have the power to
somehow put you right in the middle of the event, so that you
become an invisible participant, seeing and feeling as those in the
poem do. Poems can actually take you inside what is happening.
(You can record your thoughts in the notebook of your mind.)

Michael Rosen calls upon a sad memory to generate his report:

Mum

When mum was dying
some people came
some stayed away.

some people came and saw
her grey face

some people came and saw
the hole in the side of her head
but some stayed away

some sat and talked
some brought her old books
some saw her fingers drumming
but some brought nothing
because they didn't come

sometimes I met them
in the street
in other people's rooms
getting into cars

always the same
"How's Connie?"

What held them away
from our door?
Was it the dark rooms?
The rows of bottles of tablets?
The heavy scent of her perfumed cushion?
Or the sight of her shiny skin
stretched over the bones of her skull?

They kept their distance
they kept her in her place
they left her for dead
months too soon.

Jean Little takes a moment in her family's past to chronicle a particular and significant experience:

Every So Often

Every so often, my father tries making bread.
He's too impatient though. He puts it on top of
    the radiator to make it rise faster
And I doubt if he kneads it as long as the books
    say he should.
He likes to see results.
When it's baking, the whole house smells like heaven.
But you do have to hurry and eat it while it's fresh.
The next day, it's almost too heavy to lift.

The mood only strikes him once every couple of years.
Mother shakes her head and gets out of his way
But I sit around and cheer and get as excited
   as he does.

I've no idea what starts him off on breadmaking
But I'm glad he does it.
It makes him ridiculous, mysterious, and my
   own particular father
Like nobody else in the whole entire world.

Jogging the Memory

You may meet yourself in a poem. Some poems will remind you
of our own experiences. Something in the poet's words may trig-
ger vivid recollections from your past — people you have met,
places you've been, events that involved you, smells, sights, tastes,
and sounds mentioned in the poem, that were conjured up by the
poet's memories. You may meet your own life's experiences in the
poems you read. Or you may just reflect upon the happenings
painted in your imagination by the poet. What happens to people
in life can be the inspiration for a poem, and you may come to
understand yourself through reading about moments in the lives
(real or imagined) created by poets. (black and white memories.)

   When we read this poem, we all rejoice in the memory of coolness that the poet conjures:

No Matter

No matter   or
how hot-burning
it is   cut deep into
outside   a fresh, ripe watermelon

when   you can
                             feel
you peel a   coolness
long, fat cucumber   come into your hands.

Lee Bennett Hopkins

   Perhaps this poem of loss will help children recall or reflect
upon the death of a family pet, or help them understand the fragile
quality of life that the simplest creatures show us:

Details noticed by the poet, missed by our busy eyes, bring images and memories sharply into focus.

Tonight
After supper
When it was dark
My Dad and I went to post letters.
And we walked through the back alley,
Between the leaning-over houses;
We saw a fat dog,
And a new moon hung up
In the branches of a tree.

W.H.M.

Samuel

I found this salamander
Near the pond in the wood.
Samuel, I called him—
Samuel, Samuel.

Right away I loved him.
He loved me too, I think.
Samuel, I called him—
Samuel, Samuel.

I took him home in a coffee can,
And at night
He slept in my bed.
In the morning
I took him to school.

He died very quietly during spelling.

Sometimes I think
I should have left him
Near the pond in the woods.
Samuel, I called him—
Samuel, Samuel.

Bobbi Katz

The Voice of the Poem

In some poems, the poet creates a voice that is speaking aloud, talking to someone, to you as you read the words, to a special person, an animal or an object, It may be to the spirits who listen to the poet's voice crying out in pain or wonder (or maybe the poet is just talking to himself). The voice can warn us, or direct us, apologize to us, thank us. Poets can choose any voice to speak through, and they can imagine any audience as listener. Poems are full of voices whispering, chanting, arguing, praying. The children can add their own voices and read them aloud.

Don't Tell Me That I Talk Too Much

Don't tell me that I talk too much!
Don't say it!
Don't you dare!
I only say important things
Like why it's raining where.
Or when or how or why or what
Might happen here or there.
And why a thing is this or that
And who is bound to care.
So don't tell me I talk too much!
Don't say it!
DON'T YOU DARE!

Arnold Spilka

When children find the voice of the poem, by exploring the words and their sounds, deciding when to pause, when to slow down or speed up, they come to understand the heart of the poem (and they gain much practice in language and thought).

Spell of the Woods

Listen, the trees are singing
And the wood is full of voices.
From the lake's edge
Trembles the willow's song
And poplars
Fly high, silver whispers
On the carrying air.
All the trees are singing.

Sing then, alder and ash!
Sing, mellow-sounding beech!
And you small animals,
Keep still among the roots;
Birds, do not shout your notes
From any thicket!
Keep silent now while the wood

Makes its ancient music
And the trees sing, all the trees sing.

Oh, the wood is a great choir.
From a green dark
The deep oaks chant
In their mossy voices
And the wind
Sounds its sobbing cellos
In the elm trees.
The trees toss aloft their branches
As they sing, as loudly the trees sing.

Leslie Norris

Story Poems

Long before most people could read or write, stories and tales were remembered through ballads and songs. As the minstrels wandered through countries, they reported on the news they came across — heroic deeds, great battles, tragic incidents. Poets have continued to tell stories. Some poems spin tales and report on people, places, and events, all done with the ear and the eye of the artist. Everyone has a story to tell.

Not all poems tell stories, but many of them do. Some of the nursery rhymes are narrative explorations:

Pussy cat, pussy cat
Where have you been?
I've been to London
To look at the queen.
Pussy cat, pussy cat,
What did you there?
I frightened a little mouse
Under her chair.

Lucy Locket lost her pocket,
Kitty Fisher found it;
Not a penny was there in it,
Only ribbon round it.

(How you could lose your pocket. Ours are firmly stitched into our trousers and skirts. Then we found out that pocket, in those days, meant a kind of purse. In some areas, they still call a purse a pocketbook.)

As we get older we like the stories that ballads tell:

> The king sits in Dunfermline town,
> Drinking the blood-red wine:
> "O where will I get a skeely skipper
> To sail this new ship of mine?"

Don't you like "blood-red wine"? Sir Patrick Spens is the man chosen, and off he goes, despite warnings from all and sundry that there is going to be a terrific storm. And it came:

> They had not sailed a league, a league,
> A league but barely three,
> When the luft grew dark, and the wind blew loud,
> And gurly grew the sea.

The dialect is a bit difficult, but the ballad was made up long ago. In the end, everybody drowns:

> Half owre, half owre to Aberdour,
> 'Tis fifty fathoms deep,
> And there lies good Sir Patrick Spens,
> With the Scots Lords at his feet.

Like all good ballads, this one tells a straight, unvarnished tale. Like many ballads, it is tragic, and ends with death.

Some ballads are adventure tales, like the ones of Robin Hood.

> When Robin Hood was about twenty years old,
> With a hey down down and a down,
> He happened to meet Little John,
> A jolly brisk blade, right fit for the trade,
> For he was a lusty young man.

There are hundreds of ballads about Robin Hood, and about killings, murders, revenge, and thwarted love. Most ballads were written without children in mind, thus not all are suitable for them.

There are poems written in a ballad style, but not true ballads, because they were written first, not made up and sung or recited by wandering troubadours. "Paul Revere's Ride" is such a modern one, and "Young Lochinvar" by Sir Walter Scott, along with many others he wrote. Tennyson's "The Charge of the Light Brigade" is also a narrative poem.

> Half a league, half a league,
> Half a league onward,
> All in the valley of death
> Rode the six hundred.

There were also the "Pied Piper of Hamelin" by Robert Browning, and "The Highwayman" by Alfred Noyes.

Longer story poems used to be more popular than they seem to be today. Possibly it was because people had no radios, television, or VCRs, and quite often most people could not read very well, if at all; so they liked listening to a tale well-told. The rhyme and the rhythm of the poetic form helped to shape the story better in their minds; and offered them help in remembering it.

For these reasons, story poems are effective for choral speaking and dramatizing.

Some stories are short; some are long. Some are built around plot; others have stories hidden beneath the lines. Sometimes the story lies only in the reader's or listener's mind.

I Met An Old Woman

I met an old woman
Climbing a hill
She sat down beside me
Silent and still.
I gave her some water
From my little jug;
She wiped her lips gently,
And gave me a hug.

D.B.

A Little Old Man

Can you believe it?
A little old man
Walks down the lane
As fast as he can.
He lives all alone
In a tiny old house,
(Well, not quite alone
There is a small mouse.)
They seem to agree
On things large and small,
And they never argue
At all, at all.

D.B.

The Rescue

The wind is loud,
The wind is blowing,
The waves are big,
The waves are growing.
What's that? What's that?
A dog is crying,
It's in the sea,
A dog is crying.
His or hers
Or yours or mine?
A dog is crying,
A dog is crying.

Is no one there?
A boat is going,
The waves are big,
A man is rowing
The waves are big,
The waves are growing.
Where's the dog?
It isn't crying.
His or hers and still it cries.
Or yours or mine?
Is it dying?
Is it dying?

The wind is loud,
The wind is blowing,
The waves are big,
The waves are growing.
Where's the boat?
It's upside and down.
And where's the dog,
And must it drown?
His or hers
Or yours or mine?
O, must it drown?
O, must it drown?

Where's the man?
He's on the sand,
So tired and wet
He cannot stand.
And where's the dog?
It's in his hand,
He lays it down
Upon the sand.
His or hers
Or yours or mine?
The dog is mine,
The dog is mine!

So tired and wet
I stroke its head,
It opens its eyes,
It wags its tail,
So tired and wet.
I call its name,
For it's my pet,
Not his or hers
Or yours, but mine—
And up it gets,
And up it gets!

Ian Serraillier

Tricks of the Trade

Metaphor, simile, alliteration, personification, and analogy are everyday language strategies that children use. They begin creating them long before they know what they are doing. As children make connections between things, they use these high-level thought processes that we call the poet's tools. No child needs to define these terms at first: they need to use them. As children require information about them to promote talk and understanding of the poem, teachers and reference books can help them to acquire the technology of poetic writing.

Children are part of the world of poetry from the beginning. As they make sense of their world, they use shapes, colors, sounds, sensory words, smells, and tastes to describe it.

*In these respects I suspect the mature artist is not different
from the creative scientist, the mathematician, the explorer,
the philosopher. All are energized by an obsession to make
real and clear and formally memorable what began as only
a cloudy guess. It moves eventually into the discovery of
final form, into a sense of completing, of saying something
as well as one can. There is a movement from mind-
stretching to mind-controlling, from a mere swimming
about in chaos to a search for land.*

Earle Birney

*Unless you pay some attention to the technical side of
poetry, you are unlikely to know the full range of poetry's
domains. In such instances, appreciation stops short of feeling the power of the poet's language, and you are likely to
miss opportunities for bringing a poem to life.*

*We know that taking a position is swimming upstream
against a current of modern thinking that attributes all dislike of poetry to forced poetic analysis.*

Sam Sebesta

Certainly there is a strong feeling that "forced analysis" of a poem has done more than almost any other thing to make many people dislike poetry. On the other hand, the "emotional bath" approach can lead to sloppy thinking and lessen the true enjoyment.

The more you know about clothes or automobiles, the greater your ability to discriminate and to enjoy clothes and cars. If you know something of the technical tricks poets use, the greater your enjoyment of the poetic experience. For instance, if you recognize alliteration, you may get more pleasure out of alliterated lines. You no longer are vaguely aware that something rather pleasing has occurred. You know what the writer did, what he or she was aiming at, and get a quiet satisfaction out of recognizing his or her ability.

It is not suggested that teachers teach technical terms to the class. How unfortunate an approach it would be to say, "This morning, class, we are going to learn all about hyperbole." At this point practically everyone stops appreciating anything. On the other hand, the teacher must know the technical tricks of the trade — for that is what they are. Poets do not necessarily say, "I think

I'll use a couple of synonyms, and then in the third line I'll throw in a touch of zeugma and, just to top it off, maybe a little sniff of oxymoron.'' But poets are aware of these techniques, and thus attempt to use them effectively. We as poetry readers and writers should be equally aware of the techniques. Then, when the magic moment arises, and a child or a group wants to know how the poet accomplished an effect, and what it is called, we are ready to assist.

Word Choice

The very first skill the poet must employ, before all others, is the choice of the right words.

All words have meaning. Many words in our language have two kind of meanings: *denotation*, the meaning you might find in the dictionary; and *connotation*, the emotional extra weight attached throughout the years.

Poets know this, and use the emotional connotation of words to make us react in the way they desire. Words have emotional weight. Some words are what have been called PURR words: *mother, baby, love, darling,* and so on. Other words are called GROWL words, and have unpleasant connotations: *death, shadow, fear, spectre, etc.*

One problem with that is that no two persons have exactly the same response to any one word. Three people might read or listen to a line about pirates and their base in the town, by the harbor. One person finds *tavern* the perfect word, with all its romantic associations of Jamaica Inn, Captain Henry Morgan, or swashbuckling pirate movies. For another reader or listener, *inn* is the *mot juste*; while yet another prefers *hostelry*, because she or he was in Devon once, and stayed at a place by the sea: fifteenth century, oak beams, secret passageways, where the pirates used to smuggle in the rum. It was always called the Smugglers' Hostelry.

Words are tools, learned late and laboriously, and easily forgotten, with which we try to give some part of our experience a more or less permanent shape outside ourselves. They are unnatural, in a way, and far from being ideal for their job. A word is its own little solar system of meanings, yet we are wanting it to carry some part of our meaning, of the meaning of our experience. But the meaning of our experience is finally unfathomable: it reaches into our toes and back to before we were born and into the atom, with vague shadows and changing features, and elements that no expression of any kind can hold.

The struggle truly to possess one's own experience, in other words to regain one's genuine self, has been the human's principal occupation, wherever one could find leisure time for it, ever since humans developed this enormous surplus of brain. Humans have invented art — music, painting, dancing, sculpture, theatre, and the activity that includes all these, poetry.

It is occasionally possible, just for brief moments, to find the words that will unlock the doors of all those many mansions inside the head and express something of the crush of information that presses in on us, from the way a crow flies to the way a person walks, from the look of a street to what we did one day a dozen years ago. Words that will express something of the deep complexity that makes us precisely the way we are, form the force that created humans distinct from trees. Words say something of the inaudible music that moves along in our bodies from moment to moment like water in a river. They tell something of the spirit of the snowflake in the water, something of the duplicity and the relativity and the merely fleeting quality of all life, something of the almighty importance of it and something of its utter meaninglessness. And when words can manage some part of this, and manage it in a moment of time, and in that same moment make out of it all the vital signature of a human being — not of an atom, or of a geometrical diagram, or of a heap of lenses — but a human being, we call it poetry.

We all have differing approaches to words.

"The moon was ghostly galleon . . ." is perfect for almost everyone, because *galleon* has all the romantic associations of pirates, the Spanish Main, hidden treasure, palm-fringed sandy beaches, deep blue seas, Caribbean islands, Drake and the Spanish treasure ships . . . and so forth. A ghostly *boat* would never do, nor a *ship*.

Words are the tools with which the poem is built, and we must be aware of their power. The poet writes and wants to manipulate the reader's mind. The emotional connotation of words is one of the chief weapons.

One interesting way to pursue this idea is to give a line, and have the children fill in the missing word, which *they as individuals feel* might be best.

The knight galloped up on his . . .

(*plug, nag, horse, steed, stallion, charger*?)

If the class is sufficiently at ease to tell the truth, there will always be disagreement. No group of students will *all* pick the same word. The intriguing part comes when they are sufficiently at ease to say *why* they picked that particular word. Try these:

The pirates scrambled up the . . . castle wall.

(*old, ancient, decrepit, antique, etc.*)

You can often get useful words out of a thesaurus. Here is one example: we told the class that this was to be used in a poem describing an extremely ugly, terrifying villian.

The cook was the most . . . person I had ever seen.

(*ugly, disfigured, forbidding, unsightly, unseemly, shapeless, monstrous, graceless, inelegant, uncouth, awkward, frightful, hideous, odious . . . etc.*) The list goes on, and every word comes from one page in an ordinary *Roget's Thesaurus* (children love to play this game).

The next step is to give a line or so already written by a poet. Some words are left out, and the students try filling in the *best word for that particular line*. You give them clues, and they have to justify their choice.

> Stone walls do not a prison make
> Nor iron bars a . . . (cell, cage, prison, dungeon)

Cage was Richard Lovelace's choice. Why? Is it still the right word, or have we changed since the 17th century?

> And what is so rare as a day in June?
> Then if ever come . . . days. (lovely, gorgeous,
> perfect, nice)

Perfect was James Russell Lowell's choice. Again, we can discuss our reasons for the choice. Things change, and maybe that word will not suit 20th-century children.

> My room's a square and candle-lighted . . .
> In the surrounding depths of night afloat.
> (ship, galleon, boat, skiff, yacht)

Frances Cornford chose *boat*. The rhyme, of course, demanded it.

> The fog comes
> On little . . . feet. (quiet, slow, grey, cat, ostrich, jolly.)

Carl Sandburg chose *cat*. Why? The possibilities are endless and can lead to effective discussions and realizations about words.

One of the techniques, **alliteration** ("Big, brawny, beer-bellied Bart!") is a fast way into wordcare. Alliteration can make use of beginning vowels as well as consonants:

> An Austrian Army Awfully Arrayed
> Boldly By Battery Besiged Belgrade . . . etc.
>
> *Anon*

> A dream, and more than a dream, and dimmer
> At once and brighter than dreams that flee,
> The moment's joy of the sward swimmer
> Abides, remembered as truth may be . . .
>
> *C.A. Swinburne*

Alliteration was used in early English poetry. Rhythm and rhymes came much later.

Rhyme is defined as "a correspondence of sound in the final accented syllables or group of syllables of a line of verse . . . etc." We all KNOW what rhyme is. We will go into the matter of rhyme in some depth. (Some people prefer to spell it *rime* by the way.)

Rhythm is defined as "sounds characterized by regular alternation of stressed and unstressed impulses." We all know what rhythm is. We will go into it too later. (Nobody seems to want to spell rhythm any other way.)

Rhyme

Rhyme (or rime) is as old as Chaucer, and much older. Rhyme, in the days before universal literacy, meant that lines could be memorized. People often did memorize useful little bits, such as:

> Thirty days hath September,
> April, June and November . . .

Rhyme has an attractive feel to it. The repetition of sounds is pleasing to the ear. There are several varieties:
a) single rhyme:

> Jack be nimble,
> Jack be quick,
> Jack jump over
> The candlestick.

b) double rhyme:

> Faster than fairies, faster than witches,
> Bridges and houses, hedges and ditches.
> > *Robert Louis Stevenson*

> Here's a church, and there's a steeple,
> And there, inside, sit all the people.

c) triple rhyme!

> The waters glistening,
> And us here listening.

or

> I am the very model of a modern Major-General,
> I've information vegetable, animal, and mineral;. . .
> > *W.S. Gilbert*

d) internal rhymes, where the rhyme occurs in the middle of the line:

> Then up with your cup,
> And match me this catch . . .
> > *Sir Walter Scott*

e) printer's rhyme, where the words look as though they rhyme, although we pronounce them differently:

> It might be said
> He wore a plaid.

My favorite dislike is a rhyme like *kind* and *wind* (breeze).

The most popular ways to rhyme ends of lines are: AA, ABAB, ABBA, ABAC, ABABCC, and so on. The poet chooses the rhyme scheme that seems to fit and do the job.

Sometimes poets will rhyme one sound over and over, just for fun:

> Or if I drop upon my toe
> A very heavy weight,
> I weep—for it reminds me so
> Of that old man I used to know-
> Whose look was mild, whose speech was slow,
> Whose hair was whiter than the snow,
> Whose face was very like a crow,
> With eyes, like cinders, all aglow,

Who seemed distracted with this woe,
Who rocked his body to and fro,
And muttered, mumblingly and low,
As if his mouth were full of dough,
Who snorted like a buffalo—
That summer evening long ago,
A-sitting on a gate.

(That was Lewis Carroll's White Knight speaking.)
Nursery rhymes are full of almost-rhymes, as in:

Nineteen, twenty,
My plate's empty.

or

Little Tommy Tucker
Sang for his supper.
What shall we give him?
Brown bread and butter.

We like the sound of vowels that are nearly alike, and that is one of the reasons for **assonance**. In assonance, the vowels sound almost the same, even though there is no rhyme in the perfect sense, that is, with the consonants agreeing:

The bat is black.

There is a sense of rhyme, although it is not true rhyme, but it pleases.

Along the same lines, we have **consonance**. Here the vowels are different, but the consonants are the same:

Among the leaves he lives.

I lean alone, against this wall.

These are interesting technical tricks, and we should never fall into the trap of thinking that poets are people who know all about them, and nothing else. Conversely, if we know what they are, we can understand the poem and the poet in a deeper sense.

Rhythm

Let us look at **rhythm.** This is "the beat" everyone loves in music, especially in Rock and Roll. From our earliest years, we love that beat. A little child in a high chair beats a spoon to the rhythm of the radio, or dances to the rhythm of a commercial on T.V.

To market, to market,
To buy a fat pig;
Home again, home again,
Jiggetty jig.

Star light, star bright,
First star I see tonight.

Ring-around-a-rosy,
A pocket full of posies.

Or it might be a more complicated beat:

No longer for me when I am dead
Than you shall hear the surly sullen bell.

Wm. Shakespeare

The main thing to remember about rhythm is that it must be used to make the poem more meaningful. Fast, skipping rhythms go with jolly, happy poems; slower and more stately rhythms fit more sombre and serious themes.

The ostrich is a silly bird,
With scarcely any mind.
He often runs so very fast
He leaves himself behind.

M.E. Wilkins Freeman

or

At the equinox when the earth was veiled in a late rain,
    wreathed with wet poppies, waiting spring,
The ocean swelled for a far storm and beat its boundary,
    the groundswell shook the beds of granite.

Robinson Jeffers

It is interesting to know about rhythms, but we must never let ourselves fall in to the trap of thinking that rhythm is more important than the feeling, the emotions, the use of words in a poem.

It maybe useful to know the names of the patterns of rhythm: **Iambic** is the commonest English metre. It consists of a light beat followed by a heavy beat:

alone

before

remote . . . many English words fall naturally that way.

If you have only one of these things — we call them *feet* — in a line, it is called *monometer:*

> I fear
> She's here!

with two, it is called *dimeter;*

> I see my boat
> Is still afloat.

with three, it is called *trimeter;*
with four, it is called *tetrameter;*
with five, it is called *pentameter.*

Five in a line, and all **iambs,** gives us the metre in which Shakespeare wrote much of his poetry: **iambic pentameter.**

> A horse! A horse! My kingdom for a horse!

There are other kinds of feet, although they are not used very often: **trochaic** has a heavy beat followed by a light beat:

> By the shores of Gitchee Goomee,
> By the shining great sea-water.
> > *H.W. Longfellow*

> *Carrots, apples, lobsters too,*
> *All were thrown into the stew.*

Anapaestic has two light beats, then one heavy:

> Tis the voice of the lobster, I heard him declare,
> "You have baked me too brown, I must sugar my hair."
> > *Lewis Carroll*

> The Assyrian came down like a wolf on the fold.
> > *Lord Byron*

Dactylic has one heavy beat, followed by two light beats:

> Fell like a cannon-shot,
> Burst like a thunderbolt,
> Crashed like a hurricane.
> > *Alfred Tennyson*

Spondaic has two heavy beats together:
Pyrrhic has two light beats together.
Choriambic has heavy beat, light beat, light beat, heavy beat.

Other Technical Tools

Onomatopoeia, a lovely Greek word, means that the sound of the word is like the sound of the thing it is describing: pop, bubble, slurp, crash, boom. Poets have been using this technique for a long time:

> Pop, pop, pop!
> Says the popcorn in the pan;
> Pop, pop, pop!
> You may catch me if you can!
>
> *Louise Abney*

> Double, double, toil and trouble.
>
> *Wm. Shakespeare*

> Boomlay, boomlay, boomlay boom!
>
> *Vachel Lindsay*

> Dry clashed his harness in the icy caves.

> Susie's galoshes
> Make splishes and sploshes
> And slooshes and sloshes.
>
> *R. Bacmeister*

Allegory is a story where persons and events are meant to represent something other than themselves alone:

> Because I could not stop for Death
> He kindly stopped for me;
> The carriage held but just ourselves
> And Immortality.
>
> *Emily Dickinson*

In modern poetry the writer often refers to commonly known stories, characters, etc. This is called **allusion,** for example:

> He was a very Hercules, and I a famous coward.

> He out Herod's Herod.

Allusion is tricky. Your brilliant word play devolves into nothing if your readers do not understand your allusion. For example, you might refer to Noah in a piece about floods, but, if your readers are not familiar with the Bible story of the Ark, they will fail to understand your reference. However, allusion can be an effective way to put ideas across in brief and intriguing form.

Metonymy is the technique whereby we suggest many in one. For instance, consider "All hands on deck." It is not just the hands we mean, but the sailors (who incidentally will be using their hands). Other examples would be:

The *White House* stated . . .

The *press* made known . . .

The *school* believes . . .

Paradox is a statement which apparently contradicts itself:

> Thence
> Shall life succeed in that it seems to fail
>
> *Robert Browning*

Oxymoron (a squashed or compressed *paradox*)

Where two apparently opposite ideas are put together. The shock value is enormous:

> an open secret
>
> jumbo shrimp
>
> Freezing fire, burning ice
>
> *John Milton*

Hyperbole is exaggeration:

> The streets are paved with gold.
>
> The gutters ran with blood.
>
> He swallowed oceans of tea daily.

Repetition is one technique that has always been popular. This may take the form of a chorus:

> A frog he would a-wooing go.
> Hey, ho! says Roley!
>
> The old wife sat at her ivied door,
> (Butter and eggs and a pound of cheese)

Or there could be the repetition of words, groups of words, or whole lines:

> Blow, bugle, blow, set the wild echoes flying.
> Blow, bugle; answer, echoes, dying, dying, dying.
>
> *Alfred Tennyson*

This little piggy went to market,
This little piggy stayed home;
This little piggy had roast beef,
This little piggy had none;
But this little piggy went
Wee-wee-wee-wee-wee-all the way home!

Finally, there is the whole matter of **comparison.** Poets are always comparing one thing with another:

Shall I compare thee to a summer's day?

Wm. Shakespeare

Her face was like the rising sun.

He looked as though he had swallowed a porcupine.

His voice was cold as ice.

There are three ways of comparing: simile, metaphor, and personification. They are slightly different from each other, but the main thing to remember is that they are all ways of *comparing one thing with another, so as to illuminate the first thing.*

In poetry, these comparisons are often unusual, and jolt us into awareness:

Although the night is damp,
The little firefly ventures out,
And slowly lights his lamp.

I have seen old ships sail like swans asleep.

J. Elroy Flecker

Night's candles are burnt out.

W.M. Shakespeare

Sometimes the comparison is not directly stated. Here the leaves are compared with a person:

When the leaves in autumn wither,
With a tawny, tanned face,
Warped and wrinkled up together . . .

J. Silvester

The white mares of the moon rush along the sky
Beating their golden hoofs upon the glass heavens.

Amy Lowell

Teach technical matters as the need arises. One still hears of teachers who present students with four, five, or more page, single-spaced lists of poetic terms to be studied or memorized (or both). Possibly, some rare students may come to have a positive feeling for poetry by studying definitions of simile, onomatopoeia, mood, alliteration, etc., but it is doubtful. Certainly, knowledge of the English metric system enhances the (advanced) poetry lover's enjoyment of Yeats' "Sailing to Byzantium" or Eliot's "Macavity, the Mystery Cat". The danger is that the intellectualizing, coming too soon, may stunt the growth of love and desire for poetry.

The issue of how much theory and how much terminology the student needs to know is a difficult one but one which must be faced by each teacher. "If I force too much technical information on the class," the teacher must ask himself or herself, "do I stifle all interest in the poem?" "If I neglect all attention to form, to metrics, to nomenclature, do I deprive students of the chance to enjoy and appreciate poetry at higher levels?" One way of treating the problem is to focus on meaning, ask what the poet seems to be saying, and then, after arriving at some agreement, the class can go on to consider the words, figures of speech, form, rhyme, and so on.

A poem is not simply something printed on the page. A poem is an event, and it happens when a poet and a reader meet inside the form in such a way that the reader makes personally real those connections between things that the poet saw as real in the construct of his or her own world and as possible to be communicated. The reader makes this confirmation in much the same way that the poet made the suggestion: by using intellect, imagination, and memory. Reading a poem is an act of participation, where the reader not only makes the performance whole, but makes it, in one essential sense, uniquely his or hers.

The human insight of the poem and the technicalities of the poetic devices are inseparable. Each feeds the other. This interplay is the poem's meaning, a matter not of what it means (nobody can say entirely what a good poem means) but *how* it means — a process one can come much closer to discussing.

Ars Poetica

A poem should be palbable and mute
As a globed fruit,

Dumb
As old medallions to the thumb,

Silent as the sleeve-worn stone
Of casement ledges where the moss has grown -

A poem should be wordless
As the flight of birds.

A poem should be motionless in time
As the moon climbs

Leaving, as the moon releases
Twig by twig the night-entangled trees,

Leaving, as the moon behind the winter leaves,
Memory by memory the mind —

A poem should be motionless in time
As the moon climbs.

A poem should be equal to:
Not true.

For all the history of grief
an empty doorway and a maple leaf.

For love
The meaning grasses and two lights above the sea —

A poem should not mean
But be.

Archibald MacLeish

4

When Children Read and Listen to Poems

You Are Reading This Too Fast

You are reading this too fast.
Slow down, for this is poetry
and poetry works slowly.
Unless you live with it a while
the spirit will never descend.
It's so easy to quickly cut across the surface
and then claim there was nothing to find.
Touch the poem gently with your eyes
just as you would touch a lover's flesh.
Poetry is an exercise in patience.
You must wait for it to come to you.
The spirit manifests in many guises;
some quiver with beauty,
some vibrate with song.
What is happening?
Slow down, slow down,
take a few deep breaths,
read the poem slowly,
read the lines one at a time,
read the words one by one,
read the spaces between the words,
get sleepy, this is poetry,
relax until your heart
is vulnerable, wide open.

Ken Norris

Teaching Poetry

The matter is not so much the teaching of poetry but how the teacher takes to the surprises that happen when children talk about, and write poetry. William Stafford suggests that we not use the word "poetry" if possible, that we not codify, classify, and label in approach to "this shimmering and unexpected field of goodies." He says that poetry will always be a wild animal. "Something about it won't yield to ordinary learning. When a poem catches you, it overwhelms, it surprises, it shakes you up. And often you can't provide any usual explanation for its power. They seep into the world all the time, and lodge in odd corners almost anywhere — in your talk, in the conversation around you. They can be terribly irresponsible." As teachers we must seek our children's views, listen to their interpretations, treat them with respect and seriousness, interact with them in consultation and conferences, allow conversation and informal discussion, and encourage the explorations of their own experiences in relation to the poems. We must not make them afraid to say the wrong thing, but enable them to voice their own ideas. We can provoke the children into the surprise of coming to know, rather than checking them for comprehension of content or poetic techniques. Open-ended, divergent thinking helps children formulate their own questions about poetry. Aesthetic learning comes from experiences provided by teachers where the poem is understood in the deepest way possible, with the mind and the heart, in what is called the cognitive/affective learning mode.

Much of the reading of poetry depends upon the expectations of the children, how they see poems as a useful vehicle for learning. Have they had a wide variety and a steady diet of poems they have enjoyed, laughed at, and wondered over? Does the teacher demonstrate an interest in, and a fondness for all types of poetry? Have they met various poets — in print, in person, on tape — from their own area, their own country, and from other countries?

It is important that the teacher set the atmosphere for the poem or the poems they are going to share. The content or shape of the poem may determine that some prior experience occur before the poem is met. On the other hand, as the children meet poem after poem by one author or on one theme, they themselves may begin to build their own knowledge and their own expectations of what they want to find in those poems.

In school, children meet poems in their reading anthologies, on tapes, in books chosen from the library, and as teachers read and recite them. What do children think about poetry at the conclusion of the school years? Theorists claim that the effect of a school system on children's perception of poetry may be damaging and negative. The Plowden Report suggested "it is doubtful poetry has ever been well treated in schools."

Many teachers feel uncertain about how to proceed in the teaching of poetry. Michael Benton refers to it as "a double misfortune: neglect where it needs attention, and concern where it is best left alone". In too many cases, a poem is seen as a stimulus for other important and product-centred learning, such as writing, painting, or discussion. In this type of teaching, the poetic experience is seen as a stimulator for the child's follow-up activity, rather than an interactive process by which the child's thought and feeling change. Traditionally, we see poetry as that which is taught in the classroom to all by the teacher rather than what the children read by themselves. In this system, the teacher chooses all the poems because it is felt that the children will not make the necessary connections with their reading done outside traditional classroom work. The truth of the matter is that poetry is not prose and probably cannot be taught in the same way. The child is at once a reader and a writer and a listener. What happens in school must complement what happens outside school. What we teach children in school must give them strength and courage to read and write outside school. Poetry must be taught and seen as an art form on its own. The insights will come because of the truth of poetry, not because of the tricks and techniques that will promote literacy. A belief in poetry will give the child a cosmology of poetry, a universe outside other types of print, a way of perceiving and understanding both the form of language and the message embedded in it.

> Let us intervene. Let us pretend, if we must, that we ourselves, prosaic adults, feel a greater need, a wilder enthusiasm for that fugitive other language than we may rightly claim. Let us claim that birthright vital in the mind and memory and in the mouth and ear of our children — even though, for whatever reason, we have let it die in ourselves. Let us take up armsful of poems signalling the years from the Queen of Hearts to King Lear — anthologies furnish us abundantly. Let us speak poems

aloud at home, in the school, in the library, in the open,
wherever they may resound. Let us ourselves memorize
them, or at least their memorable lines, so that readily and
ear-to-ear we may share them with young listeners,
swiftly, urgently, on any pretext, at the drop of a
reminder.

For the light of common speech is not enough. There
are further glories to be witnessed in all our noisy years.
They must be sought out, claimed, hailed in their rich
complexity. Sense and the senses must become prepared,
line by line and poem by poem, for the great master sounds
and master images yet to be heard. Let the children grow
sensitive and strong to receive the poems that still await
them. Let them become fluent of imagination to fathom
metres and meanings. Let them grow agile of tongue to
taste the most sonorous cadences. Let them listen.

"And hear the mighty waters rolling evermore."

Norma Farber

Eve Merriam says that some children feel that poetry is a
speciality served up only on red letter days like Thanksgiving turkey or Christmas plum pudding. She feels that children have to
be taught to dislike poetry.

As adults, we may read poetry framed by its history, the poet,
the style, the form, the philosophical approach, or any other attributes. For the child, the relevant question must be what this poem
is saying to him or her now, at this time and in this situation. Then,
as they become familiar with poetry and with the features of poetry,
they can relate the art form to the content and the response can
come from both form and content. Surely the picture we are painting is the important aspect of art, not the type of paint we are using.
We find scissors so we can cut shapes; we don't cut shapes so we
can use scissors. In looking at the poem, we look at the poem first
and the print second. We must not be afraid of form and art, nor
let children think we are afraid of it, nor be nervous about bringing relevant information to meet the words on the page. We first
enter the poet's life through what he or she says to us, through
his or her sharing of experiences.

For children, the poem does not exist until they have responded
to it. It is this negotiation between poet and child, between print
and reader, that creates meaning. Collectively, we can find many

universals; privately, we make our own worlds, our own meanings. By letting children respond personally and by sharing those responses, we enlarge our frames of reference and we increase our spheres of meaning. Poetry, being an art form, encourages all types of response. The teacher must see this activity as a building of frames for learning, rather than a collection or dissection of accepted ideas. We use the poems we have read to enrich our background and as building blocks for making more meaning in life. We look at not only the content, but the poet's perceptions and the ways in which ideas and feelings are expressed. We look at the poem as a whole and we respond to it holistically.

How Will a Poem Affect a Child?

It is best summed up in David McCord's poem:

> Blessèd Lord, what it is to be young:
> To be of, to be for, be among —
> Be enchanted, enthralled,
> Be the caller, the called,
> The singer, the song, and the sung.

There are times when the child becomes one with the poem — the singer, the song, and the sung.

Because poetry is a special way of knowing and a special way of seeing, it takes everyday thoughts, feelings, and experiences and turns them into art. Poetry is a very powerful form of print; it is a "living through" experience. We must be concerned with how the child is responding to the poem, what he or she is feeling, seeing, thinking, and living through. We must be concerned with what happens as the child reads the poem, not only with what is left or taken away.

We have the experience first, and sometimes we share that experience. However, it may remain a secret to be drawn upon later. We must not judge the success of our poetry time with children by deft analysis but rather by holistic meaning-making. As teachers we ask open-ended, subtle, meaningful questions that help the children negotiate between their own lives and the representation of life created by the poet. We must tune our ears and eyes to the poem and then make sense of our perceptions.

The way we teach poetry will determine how children respond to it. Those people in life who dislike poetry, who are afraid of it, nervous of it, and distrustful of it, are often people who have had negative school experiences with poetry.

As teachers, we must be able to find the strength of a poem ourselves. Even if we have been scarred by our past poetry experiences, we must make sure that the poetry we now explore and use with our children touches us personally. Children can sense when we are pretending; they can sense when we are preaching; they can sense when we are teaching something because we have to.

- You can read poems in preparation by selecting favorites from different, new anthologies.
- You can write poems with the children, say them aloud, join in with them, and bring songs you enjoy into the classrooms.
- You can build an enthusiasm for poetry from a past that was poetry-poor. Many teachers have done it. The new anthologies will give you hope. (See the bibliography at the end of this book.)

You can learn to treat poetry as a normal aspect of the school day. It can be read aloud together and it can be written. It can be used in various subject areas, to begin a lesson and/or to summarize one. It can be used to create a mood or atmosphere, or to accompany the reading of a particular story or novel. It can be part of a general theme or general unit of study. It should not be treated as a fragile vase, but as the clay that was used to make that vase. The beauty and strength of the poem will come from the experience of the listener or reader, because a poem needs an audience to complete it. Bringing that experience to children in positive, energetic, emotional, and enthusiastic ways is the art of teaching.

In sharing poems with children, we must explore them first, find the spots that present difficulties, such as changes in rhythm, internal rhyme, etc, and master the poems so that the experience with the children can be simple and joyful. Don't be afraid to read the poem aloud while you prepare to teach it. It is not necessary to memorize, but memorizing a poem can be a treat and a delight for a class and can show that the teacher models what she or he believes in.

Teach the craft of the poem when the children need that information in order to write their poems. Let the technology of poetry be taught organically. Once the children are inside the poem, they themselves will note the elements that created it. Do not worry about covering all the qualities of poetry or the elements of poetry. If enough poems are shared, those qualities and elements will emerge clearly and effectively. The children will draw attention to the components of poetry writing that are necessary for full meaning. Dissecting and analyzing are only valid when the children have to do that because their own needs demand it.

Choose poetry for the children who are ready for it, poetry that they can accept. Do not be afraid of long words or unusual topics. The power of the poem that is chosen carefully will reach the child. Kenneth Koch, in *Rose, Where Did You Get That Red?* demonstrates that the classical poem can touch the Grade 5 child very deeply when presented by a compassionate and interesting teacher. It is not necessary that poetry be taught for a specific part of the day, as in a half-hour writing or reading lesson. Three poems will take less than five minutes to share with children. The response for the poems may take the rest of the time. Read different types of poems to children, and have them explore different genres and styles themselves. Don't demand that children read particularly difficult modes of poetry before they have experienced all types themselves.

Re-read poems that the class has enjoyed, or have the children read them aloud to you. In the case of poetry, quantity often breeds quality. Sharing three or four poems means that children can compare each one with the others. Thereby, they can develop standards and taste. We must allow a response to poetry that is natural and child-centred. Have no hidden responses or answers up your sleeve. In small groups, children can discuss poems they have heard or read. Then they can share with the class having explored their ideas in the smaller group setting. Allow children to respond through art and movement and drama. The arts connect with each other, so that every time an experience is represented through one art, other arts can touch that representation. Choose poetry that demonstrates all types of feeling and thought, sensory poetry, emotionally laden poetry, humorous poetry, narrative poetry that pulls us into the lives described on the page, and poetry that paints pictures so clearly that all children can image them in their minds.

Children need the opportunity to be alone with a poem, to read and re-read it, making meanings by themselves, to read at their own rate, choosing what to linger over and what to skip, when to wonder, and when to wander. If we accept poetry as legitimate art for the classroom, then we must provide opportunities for a child to read poems alone, from classroom anthologies, from their own library books, from the works of a single poet. Sometimes the responses can be shared and sometimes the experience can remain private.

Poems in a reading anthology must not be seen as filler, but as vital and significant reading. When children read these selections, the experience should be considered as important as the reading of the preceding story or other form of writing. Often these poems are treated lightly or ignored so that the children's perception of the value of poetry is lessened.

What Happens When We Read Poems?

The teacher must encourage the public pleasures of sharing poems, and the private pleasure the children gain from reading them on their own.

By beginning with earprint, with poems and songs and rhymes that they can remember, children can meet words on printed pages and read them immediately and easily. They have a whole print-success on the first contact. Bill Martin, Jr. says the child "can zoom through with joyous familiarity, reading on his own for personal pleasure what he has heard from loving adults who share with him the wondrous world of poems." As children are part of the print, they learn how the author has crafted the poem and they begin to work to find out how all this takes place. They begin to verbalize their intuitive insights and organize them into skills that enable reading to occur. Cumulative rhymes, interlocking sequences, choruses, patterns, cultural sequences, and chronological sequences help engage the child in the structural insights of what they are reading. Poems and songs are perfect vehicles for helping children to exercise these problem-solving skills.

Poems work differently from stories. All the words on the page take on special significance and the ways in which a poet places the words are endless. The reader makes meaning from the poem by seeing them as a three-dimensional object, looking under, around, on top of, beside, and behind. There is no linear action for the eye to follow, no time frame. Our viewpoint, or vantage point, will determine the meaning we take from the poem. This can change as we look around the words for the meanings. Every word can matter: the words are used to stop the eye, to move the eye along, back, and forth. The rhythm alters our perception of the language.

Poetry converts feeling into form — the intelligence of feeling. Form dictates what the eyes see and how the eyes read. The structure of a poem determines our perception of the ideas, using a special sense of energy, concentration, image, and meaning. An effective poem allows the reader to be both participant and observer at once. Beginning with the role of the onlooker, the reader thinks and questions and observes, then becomes drawn in, and finally reflects on the effect of the poem on his or her emotional self. Because poems allow the reader to think and feel at the same time, poetry has the power to affect a child's awareness of what language is and what language can do, in a more significant fashion than almost any other kind of print.

As children explore a poem from a whole perspective, changing through each reading and exploration, they begin to respond to what interests them, and the meaning begins to emerge from the poem. The more the poem is looked at with feeling and thought, the deeper the understanding becomes. In poetry, the images symbolize the meaning, and as those images become clearer and alter and change, the meanings do as well. It is as if the reader is looking at a photograph or an object as the light is changing: the object also appears to change constantly. What we see looks different. T.S. Eliot called the sound and rhythm of poetry "the auditory imagination", penetrating far below the conscious levels of thought and feeling, invigorating every word. The patterns of words, the rhymes, and the rhythms bring meaning to what we hear and read.

Rather than having a particular learning goal in mind for the children, the teacher has to see poetry for what it is, an exploration that is unique in print. When children hear a poet they enjoy, they then want to seek out other poems by that poet or by poets who write in a similar vein. They can read them alone or together and then share them. They can write poems in the patterns of the poems they have read. They can collect poems by a poet and prepare them for sharing. They can research information about the time in which the poet wrote, the poet's life, and the poet's attitudes. They can order and relate the poem to other poems in a particular sequence and create a critical overview that connects the poems. They can rehearse them, tape record them, and share them with others in the class and outside the school. They can see poems as living entities full of life and emotion to be shared with others. If the children leave school disliking poetry, not wanting to read more, not wanting to listen or locate or learn about other poems, we have failed in our mission of either using poetry for appreciation or using poetry as a means of learning.

Talking Our Way into Poetry

Allowing children to respond to poetry, to immerse themselves in it, to be responsible for choosing it and reading it, and using it in the content area — makes poetry part of the core of the curriculum. While some teachers have used discussion after poetry to the point of reducing the poem to questions and answers, talking with and about poetry can be a most important feature. Through discussion about a poem or a group of poems, children can come to understand shared universal meanings; they can hear each other and modify, clarify, and extend ideas and feelings; they can compare and contrast the poems they have read; they can re-read a poem for emphasis to prove a point; they can talk about the ideas of the poem, its feelings and form; they can recall experiences as suggested by the poem; they can describe incidents or people that the poem conjures. There should be no fear of having children discuss poems they have heard or read: it should be a natural response to the aesthetic and artistic experience.

Children should feel free to speak their questions, concerns, and feelings after hearing poems or reading poems. This may be handled better in small groups, especially with older children where they can share opinions and ideas, intimate settings, and then report in a more general fashion to the whole class.

Discussion . . . . shorter pieces

While the exposure to large numbers of poems and lines is most beneficial, there does come a time when one poem might be discussed thoroughly. This would come after the children have been given hundreds, possibly thousands of lines, many of them in short, sharp bits.

Looking at more than one poem on the same topic, or by the same author, or with some kind of connection, is a good step towards a deeper examination.

Remember, always, that the object is not dissection. The analogy one might draw is between the poem and the rose: you might take your rose and dissect it so that you have the petals, the sepals, the stamens, the pistil, the thorns, and the stem spread out upon the bench before you. But, where's the rose? And more importantly, where's the perfume?

This does not mean that we never take poems apart to answer some of these questions:

- What do you think made the poet write this one?
- What is the emotional tone?
- What was the poet thinking about when he or she wrote it?
- Is there one word, or series of words, which shows you how the poet felt, and how you are supposed to feel?
- What about the imagery? Is it all visual, or are the other senses employed? Is it new and striking?
- What particular bit hit you hardest?
- How about the rhythm? Is it obtrusive? enough? suitable?
- Are there any parts which seem not quite right?
- Does the rhythm suit the mood?
- How about honesty? Simplicity?
- Is there rhyme? Does it help? (Does lack of it hinder?)
- Does the pattern help?
- How about an irregular pattern? Why did the poet choose that?
- Is there any repetition? Does it help? Do you like it?
- How about comparisons?
- Is the figurative language helpful in giving you the immediate picture, or is it too obscure? ("Dick the shepherd blows his nail . . ." — means it is cold. Is that too difficult?)
- How many senses are appealed to?
- Could you pick out some music to accompany the poem?
- Is this supposed to be funny? What kind of humor is the poet using—straight/satirical/cruel/etc.?
- Does the sound meet with the sense?
- How do you feel about the characters (if any)?
- Is the setting useful? How does the poet do it?
- Is imagination used and called for in the reader?
- Is this a universal thing? (Does it apply to all people, at all ages, and in all places?)
- Is the message understood?
- Is it worth reading?

The practice of asking questions about poetry has negative connotations for many educators. Perhaps this is due to the fear that too much discussion and analysis of a poem destroys its artistic unity. But, does questioning necessarily make it so? Questioning is, after all, a natural element of the teaching art.

Patrick Groff suggests that questioning need not be destructive, as long as we observe at least three critical precautions:

- "First, *the poetry about which we ask children questions must not be overly difficult in content and form.*
- A second *precaution is that no questions about poetry should be asked children until they have heard many different kinds of poems, have been immersed in the varieties of poetry, as it were.*
- A third *forewarning about asking questions is the consideration of what responses these questions are intended to elicit from children. I take the stand that questions about poems should be seen by the child as just another encounter or personal exploration of the poem.*"

Groff suggests these 30 questions to give us pointers for poetry talk:

1. Why is this a poem? Is it different from a story? Is this poem at all like a story? Did it make you feel any different than you feel when you read a story?
2. Why do people write poems? Why don't they write stories instead?
3. Why did this poet write this poem? (if not people, then animals, mineral, material, or vegetable life) Are they like people you know? Do they talk in the same way as people you know?
4. Are there people in this poem? (if not people, then animals, mineral, material, or vegetable life) Are they like people you know? Do they talk in the same way as people you know.
5. Where does this poem take place? Is it like any place you know? Would you like to be in this place?
6. Is this poem funny, fast, light, frightening, exciting, happy? What other word does this poem make you think of?
7. Is this a beautiful poem? Should all poems be beautiful?
8. Did the events in this poem actually happen? Have they ever happened to you?
9. What things are there in this poem to see? Are these things you have seen before? How often have you seen them? Where?
10. What things are described in this poem? Are there any descriptions different from ones you have read before? Are they done in the way you describe things?
11. Is this poem honest or true? Do you believe what it says? Does

it tell you something you should know or believe?

12. What things happened in this poem that you would like to have happen to you? Did anything happen that you would not like to do? Could not? Should not? Would be afraid to do?
13. Did this poem try to teach you something? Is this something that boys and girls need to learn?
14. What might make this a better poem? What part, if any, would you change?
15. Are there any words or ideas in this poem you do not understand?
16. Find a word in the poem you think is interesting. Is this word used in the way the dictionary describes it?
17. What words rhyme in this poem? Are there any words that rhyme in a single line? Does each line rhyme with the next line? Are there any words that almost make a rhyme?
18. What happens to this poem if you change words in it? What happens if you change a rhyming word with another word?
19. How many different kinds of words are used in this poem? What kinds of words are used most?
20. Are there some words in one line of this poem that begin with the same sound? Can you imagine why a poet would do this?
21. Are there words in this poem that sound like what they mean? (whizz, pop)
22. Are there things or animals in this poem that act or speak as if they were people? What makes them sound or look like people?
23. Are the lines in this poem short or long? Can you guess why?
24. Are there any sentences in this poem that look as though they were twisted around? Why would a poet twist sentences around?
25. Could you sing this poem? Does it sound as if it might be the words to a song?
26. Do you feel that someone in the poem is telling what is going on? How much does he or she know about the people and things that are happening? Does he or she like what is going on?
27. Is something said in this poem that is intended to mean something other than what it says? Does something mean the opposite from what it says?
28. What poetry language (figures of speech) is in this poem? (This would require the teacher to have had children previously find some of these in poems; for example, metaphor, simile, irony,

personification. Some of the previous questions are aimed in this direction.)

29. Can you say in one sentence what this poem is all about? Why, or why not?
30. What two things or actions in the poem are contrasted or set against each other? Which one wins out? And finally, would you like to write a poem like this one? How many of the things about poems we have talked about do you think you can put into a poem? What would be interesting things to write poems about?

Comparisons

Model I

The Cow

Poem 1

The friendly cow all red and white,
I love with all my heart;
She gives me cream with all her might,
To eat with apple tart.

Robert Louis Stevenson

(You might have to explain the British love of cream on pies . . . known as tarts.)

She wanders lowing here and there,
And yet she cannot stray,
All in the pleasant open air,
The pleasant light of day.

(Is it permitted to use the same word twice?)

And blown by all the winds that pass
And wet with all the showers,
She walks among the meadow grass
And eats the meadow flowers.

(Another repeated word: meadow!!)

"What is the mood? Peaceful. How does he or she do it? Are cows peaceful? What lines did you like best? Read them to me — two will be enough. Is there any one verse you prefer? What word pictures do you get? . . . and like?"

"This is a brief one. Is there a line you like best? What word pictures? Is this a true picture . . .etc.?"

Poem 2
This crinkly brown bag,
On four skinny legs
Stares and munches placidly.

Poem 3
There they stand, knee deep in mud
These cows, chewing their lazy cud.
Switching their tails to drive off flies.

Poem 4
Gazing at me from liquid eyes.

Poem 5
Watch those cows
Browse!

"Now! — Which poem did you prefer? Can you tell me why?"
(This will work only after some expertise has been gained by the
children in this technique.)

Two more brief poems:

Poem 1
Daffadowndilly
Has come into town,
In a yellow petticoat
And a green gown.

Mother Goose

Poem 2
In spite of cold and chills
That usher in the early spring,
We have the daffoldils.

Anon

After you have discussed these two, and found out who liked
what, try adding this one:

Poem 3
I wandered, lonely as a cloud
That floats on high o'er vales and hills,
When all at once I saw a crowd,
A host, of golden daffodils;
Beside the lake, beneath the trees,
Fluttering and dancing in the breeze.

Wm. Wordsworth

"Now, which of the three did you like best? Which lines, etc.? Is there one word in any poem which struck you as being perfect? Poets, you know, spend their lives looking for the perfect word."

—"I like 'fluttering and dancing'."
—"I liked 'ayellow petticoat and a green gown'."

Model 2

Try comparing the following epitaphs, all by unknown wordsmiths:

Poem 1
Stranger! approach this spot with gravity!
John Brown is filling his last cavity.

Poem 2
Here lies Will Smith, — and what's something rarish,
He was born, bred, and hanged, all in the same parish.

Compare:

Poem 1
The splendor falls on castle walls,
And snowy summits old in story;
The long light shakes across the lakes,
And the wild cataract leaps in glory.

with

Poem 2
A bitter day that early sank
Behind a purple, frosty bank
Of vapor, leaving night forlorn.

Both are by Tennyson, but one upbeat, and the other down.

Walter de la Mare did not write his poem this way:

Now the moon, in her silver shoon, slowly, silently,
walks the night; she peers this way and that, and, upon
silver trees she sees silver fruit. The casements, one by one,
   catch her
beams beneath the silvery thatch.

His words are so wonderfully chosen that, even in prose form there is beauty. However, this is the way he did it:

Slowly, silently, now the moon
Walks the night in her silver shoon;

This way, and that, she peers, and sees
Silver fruit upon silver trees;
One by one the casements catch
Her beams beneath the silvery thatch.

This is a wonderful way of showing children that the shape, the form is important, as well as the choice of words.

Cloze Method

Another technique we can use with children is to leave out certain words which they then try to fill in. We have all done this with little children many times:

Wee Willie Winkie went through the . . .

and the child fills in the word *town*. Very tiny children can do this. The technique works wonderfully with young and old. For example:

We have a secret, just we three,
The robin, and I, and the sweet cherry . . . (tree)
The bird told the tree, and the . . . told . . . (tree/me)
And nobody knows it but just us . . . (three)

Anon

Everything is black and gold,
Black and gold, tonight!
Yellow. . .yellow moon, (pumpkins)
Yellow candle. . . (light)

Sometimes the poem is presented with a written copy on the board or on an overhead transparency. Other times, it is done orally. The more complex poems, naturally, must be written down, for the children to be able to figure out the missing words.

The flowers of the summer have faded away,
And Autumn is here with her mantle of. . .(grey)

A. McLachlan

Sometimes I give them a selection of words to fill in. They pick the words they feel fit best.

For weeks and weeks the autumn world stood . . .
Clothed in the . . . of a . . . haze;
The fields were dead, the . . . had lost its will,
And all the lands were . . . by wood and hill,
In those grey . . . .

Here are some words. Pick the ones you feel fit best:

Line one: quietly, dead, still
Line two: ghost, spook, shadow, fiery, scarey, smoky
Line three: people, animals, wind, snow
Line four: quiet, silent, empty, hushed
Line five: wretched, horrible, cold, withered, awful, lonely, nights, days, times, lands

Again, this helps the children to see the importance of *le mot juste*.

More Comparisons

You might begin with some short, sharp bits for comparison. Here is the first:

> No spring nor summer beauty hath such grace
> As I have seen in one autumnal face.
>
> *John Donne*

You talk about the apparent paradox: "How can old, autumnal faces be beautiful?" Talk about grandparents, dear old characters from literature, like the Hobbits, etc. Then discuss the form and the rhyme. There is the possibility of being held up momentarily on the old-fashioned word *hath*, etc.

And the second:

> One smile from her lips will never be forgot.
> It refreshes like a flower from a watering pot.
>
> *Unknown Victorian Gardener*

Is it intentionally funny? Is it funny? Does he mean it? Is it meaningful? The comparison is a bit odd, but then, it was written by a gardener. Maybe it is just as honest as Donne's couplet.

Model 1

Moonlit Apples

At the top of the house the apples are laid in rows,
And the skylight lets the moonlight in, and those
Apples are deep-sea apples of green. There goes
A cloud on the moon in the autumn night.

A mouse in the wainscot scratches, and scratches, and then
There is no sound at the top of the house of men
Or mice; and the cloud is blown, and the moon again
Dapples the apples with deep-sea light.

They are lying in rows there, under the gloomy beams;
On the sagging floor; they gather the silver streams
Out of the moon, those moonlit apples of dreams,
And quiet is the deep stair under.

In the corridors under there is nothing but sleep,
And stiller than ever on orchard boughs they keep
Tryst with the moon, and deep is the silence, deep
On moon-washed apples of wonder.

John Drinkwater

Here are some questions you might ask:
- Why do you think he wrote this poem?
- Have you ever been somewhere like that?
- What is the emotional tone?
- Can you find words that suggest it?
- Pick out two lines you particularly liked. Why did you like them?
- The poet used long vowel sounds to help the feeling. Find some.
- Does it rhyme? Are you aware of the rhyme? Does it help?
- Why are the lines this length?
- Does the length of each line help?
- Should you read it slowly or quickly?
- What do you suppose he meant by:
    deep-sea apples of green
    dapples the apples (note the assonance, the vowels)
    gloomy beams (why "gloomy"?)
    silver streams out of the moon
    moon-washed apples of wonder
- He uses some lovely words: wainscot (you might have to look it up) and "keep *tryst* with the moon" — another hard one.
- Is there any repetition here?
- Did you notice that the fourth line of each verse is shorter than the others? Why did the poet do that?
- Read Walter de la Mare's "Silver" and compare the two.

Model 2

Discord in Childhood

Outside the house an ash tree hung its terrible whips,

And at night, when the wind rose, the lash of the tree
Shrieked and slashed the wind, as a ship's
Weird rigging in storm shrieks hideously.

Within the house two voices arose, a slender lash
Whistling she-delirious rage, and the dreadful sound
Of a male thing booming and bruising, until it had
   drowned
The other voice in a silence of blood, 'neath the noise
   of the ash.

D.H. Lawrence

Some discussion and questions we might have about Lawrence's
poem. . .possibly after a reading by the teacher.
• This is not a happy poem. Give me some words that tell
  you this.
• Give me some groups of words, or even whole lines.
• What mood would the poet have to be in to call the
  branches of the ash tree "terrible whips"?
• Is there any special significance in the word "whips"?
• Here are some words, in column A the words are from the
  poem. In column B there are synonyms. Try linking them
  up:

A	B
lash	cane/rod/scourge
shrieked	peculiar/odd/unusual
weird	shouted/called/cried
delirious	howling/shouting/noisy
booming	insane/mad/crazy

• Would any of the synonyms have fitted in the poem better than
  the words he used? Why are the words he used so perfect?
• Do you feel that it is overdone, at all?
• Why does he say "she-delirious"?
• Why does he say "male thing"? Why *thing* rather than *person*?
• Can you find any places where he has used alliteration? Is this
  effective?
• Are these things suggested or actually stated in the poem:

Everyone was unhappy.
It was night, in the winter.
The child was listening in horror.
The people fighting inside were his parents.

- Sometimes things suggested are more powerful than when you actually describe them.
- The poet speaks in what kind of voice? shocked/resigned/surprised/etc.
- Can you think of any scene in a film or story that parallels this? (This one might be too dreadful for direct personal experience.)
- Could you give it another title?
- You might explore the whole idea of the "pathetic fallacy" here — the chaos in the weather echoing the chaos in the home.

Discussing Longer Poems

When we read a longer poem, usually a narrative one, such as "How They Brought the Good News" or "The Pied Piper", we can approach it in three ways:

1. The teacher reads the whole poem. (Sometimes it is on tape, read either by the teacher or by someone else.)
2. The teacher reads part, and the children read other parts *silently* to themselves. (Read the next 10 lines, and when you have finished, let me know.)
3. The children read the entire poem by themselves.

In Style 1, the poem is introduced, some setting is given, and the teacher reads it, stopping from time to time to throw in an explanation, or to ask a brief question. The question must be brief, so as to *not* interrupt the flow of the poem. Sometimes you can go for many lines without a question. If it is obvious that certain things are lost, that the children do not understand, then a quick word from the reader tells them and obviates frustration.

In Style 2, again, there is an introduction, and the teacher starts reading. (Again, it could be a tape).

At an appropriate point the reader stops and says: "Read the next six lines and tell me what happened." Or: "Read the next seven lines and tell me how you feel about so and so." Or: "Read the next seven lines, and tell me where they are going." Usually the questions asked about this silent reading are pretty factual, and help speed the reading along. Never have the really exciting bits read silently. Never have bits where there is conversation read silently.

Then the teacher reads on, until coming to another part which the children can read silently: "Read the next 10 lines to yourselves and tell me so and so."

Rarely, very rarely, the children themselves can read aloud on the initial reading. This Oral-Silent or Half-and-Half technique works beautifully with longer, narrative poems.

In Style 3, the technique, where the children read it all to themselves, calls for these steps to be followed:

Step One: Introduce the poem and say, "Read through the poem. Then, pick up the Quiz Sheet I have made for you, read the poem over again, and answer the questions on the Quiz Sheet.

Step Two: When all have completed Step One, you have a discussion of the poem, the children using their Quiz Sheets to help them talk about it.

The questions on the Quiz Sheet fall into several categories:
a) about the character/setting/plot;
b) the style;
c) the reader's feelings;
d) the words used.

How they Brought the Good News

I sprang to the stirrup, and Joris, and he;
I galloped, Dirck galloped, we galloped all three;
"God speed!" cried the watch, as the gate-bolts undrew;
"Speed" echoed the wall to us galloping through;
Behind shut the postern, the lights sank to rest,
And into the midnight we galloped abreast.

Not a word to each other; we kept the great pace
Neck by neck, stride by stride, never changing our place;
I turned in my saddle and made its girths tight,
Then shortened each stirrup and set the pique right,
Rebuckled the cheek-strap, chained slacker the bit,
Nor galloped less steadily Roland a whit.

'Twas moonset at starting; but while we drew near
Lokeren, the cocks crew and twilight dawned clear;
At Boom, a great yellow star came out to see;
At Düffeld, 'twas morning as plain as could be;
And from Mecheln church steeple we heard the
    half-chime,
So Joris broke silence with, "Yet there is time!"

At Aerschot, unleaped of a sudden the sun,
And against him the cattle stood black every one,
To stare through the mist at us galloping past,

And I saw my stout galloper Roland at last
With resolute shoulders, each butting away
The haze, as some bluff river headland its spray;

And his low head and crest, just one sharp ear bent back
For my voice, and the other pricked out on his track;
And one eye's black intelligence—ever that glance
O'er its white edge at me, his own master, askance!
And the thick, heavy spume-flakes which aye and anon
His fierce lips shook upwards in galloping on.

By Hasselt, Dirck groaned; and cried Joris, "Stay spur!
Your Roos galloped bravely, the fault's not in her,
We'll remember at Aix" — for one heard the thick wheeze
Of her chest, saw the stretched neck and staggering
  knees,
And sunk tail, and horrible heave of the flank,
As down on her haunches she shuddered and sank.

So we were left galloping, Joris and I,
Past Loos and past Tongres, no cloud in the sky;
The broad sun above laughed a pitiless laugh,
'Neath our feet broke the brittle bright stubble like chaff;
Till over by Dahlem a dome-spire sprang white,
And "Gallop," gasped Joris, "for Aix is in sight!"

"How they'll greet us!" — and all in a moment his roan
Rolled neck and croup over, lay dead as a stone;
And there was my Roland to bear the whole weight
Of the news which alone could save Aix from her fate,
With his nostrils like pits full of blood to the brim,
And with circles of red for his eye-sockets' rim.

Then I cast loose my buffcoat, each holster let fall,
Shook off both my jackboots, let go belt and all,
Stood up in the stirrup, leaned, patted his ear,
Called Roland his pet-name, my horse without peer;
Clapped my hands, laughed and sang, any noise,
  bad or good,
Till at length into Aix Roland galloped and stood.

And all I remember is — friends flocking round
As I sat with his head 'twixt my knees on the ground;
And no voice but was praising this Roland of mine,
As I poured down his throat our last measure of wine,
Which (the burgesses voted by common consent)

Was no more than his due who brought good news
from Ghent.

Robert Browning

Here is how a Quiz Sheet looks. Remember, the children answer in as brief a form a possible. They are simply jotting down notes, to help them recall their reactions when they are discussing the poem at a later point.

Title: "How they brought the good news from Ghent to Aix", by Robert Browning

QUESTION	LINES	COMMENT
Who are the heroes?	(actual bits of	Approve?
What are they doing?	lines are written—	Good?
Who drops out first?	to be quoted in	Believable?
Who drops out next?	later discussion	etc.
How did the hero manage to get to Aix?		
How does the poet get the feeling of excitement?	Quotes written for use in the	What you think about the
Does the rhythm help? Why?	discussion	words? — Too hard?
How about all those hard words for horse's harness, etc.?		Off-putting?
Do they bother you, or are they right?		
How does the poet deal with each horse's collapsing?		
Is there any repetition? Does it help?		
How do you feel about the story?	Quotes to support	Mostly comment here
How did you feel when Dirck could not go on?	comments	
Did you think the hero would get there? Why?		
How did you feel when he got there?		

QUESTION	LINES	COMMENT

Who was the real hero—the
man or the horse?

Find three words used to
suggest speed.
Find three words which
suggest excitement.
Find three words you did
not know but could *guess*
from the sense of the line.
Find two words you could
not guess and had to look
up.
Find a line or two you
especially liked.

Once the children have completed the quiz sheet, the general
discussion begins.

You ask one of the class the first question, and everyone is
invited to join in, backing up their remarks with quotes from the
poem.

It is only *after* all this, which could take some time, that the
poem is read aloud by the teacher, as the wrap-up to the lesson.

This technique works well with longer pieces. After you have
done several this way, the children themselves can make up Quiz
Sheets for the rest of the class.

Some Teaching Points

- Choose poems with interesting rhythms.
- Choose poems, at first, which are either funny or spooky.
- Choose poems which play with words in ways the children can
  grasp.
- Choose poems which have sharp and intriguing images.
- Choose poems, to begin with, where there is a pretty straight-
  forward story.
- Don't ever choose poems written down to what somebody
  thought might be the children's level.
- Choose poems which cause children to say, "Yes, that is just
  how I felt."

- Choose poem which make them remember something from their lives.
- Choose poems which have universal appeal.
- Choose poems which can be read over and over and over with ever-increasing pleasure.

Here are a few thoughts to bear in mind as you teach a poem:
- Poetry should be experienced before it is analyzed. Analysis is fine, as long as it aids in the enjoyment. This applies to discussion of the poet's technical abilities; there is nothing more likely to cause greater enjoyment than some knowledge of how the poet did what he did, and why.
- Poems should never be approached as artifacts, as something venerable or sacred. Any good poem can be questioned and argued over.
- Children must be exposed to a great number of good poems, and allowed to mull them over, to re-read them, to pick out ones they particularly like.
- Especially with younger children, the response should be physical as often as possible. Clapping, stomping, jiggling, and giggling are all fine. Joining the chorus is as old as the hills, and pre-dates printing.
- The best response might be for the child to find a poem which reminds him or her of one you have just done. ''I found this in a book at home, and it made me think about the poem on a dog we just read.''

Some ways in:
- Begin with ones they love — nursery rhymes, bits of poems, etc.
- Read them aloud to the children.
- Teach them to read the poems aloud/chorally and/or individually.
- Let them memorize (three rules)
- Let them select and bring poems or bits to read to the class.
- Have personal anthologies and a class anthology — done with good penmanship/calligraphy.
- Encourage them to illustrate.
- Have a bulletin board constantly updated.

Some things to think about when leading children into the enjoyment of a poem:
- Choose one you like that you feel is worth teaching.

- Prepare yourself for that initial reading. Do not insult your listeners with a poorly rendered first reading.
- Help the listeners/readers to see what it's all about.
- Help them to realize the mood.
- Encourage each child to react personally.
- Explain to them that they do not have to like every poem.

And at the same time:
- Don't use long introductions, with complete biographies of the poets.
- Don't drill vocabulary.
- Don't do all the interpreting — though at first you might have to do quite a lot, to help them gain security.
- Don't forget that the main thrust is supposed to be pleasure.
- Don't forget that sometimes the best "way out" is silence.
- Do try writing.
- Do try dramatizing
- Do try choral speaking.
- Do try memorizing for future pleasure in recollecting.

> *It soon became clear, in our discussions of any poem, that there were as many interpretations of a poem as there were readers of that poem. The poem is the catalyst in the transmission of an experience from the mind of the poet to the mind of the reader. I saw that, as a teacher, I had a personal responsibility for every poem that spoke to me; never to be didactic, but always to give room for each child to have his individual experience of that poem.*

Griselba Greaves

Northrop Frye says that ideally, our literary education should begin with things like "This Little Piggy Went to Market" or "Bye Baby Bunting" (and this is very important) *where the rhythm is accompanied by physical action,* like bouncing up and down. The child who has these experiences responds much better to poetry than the child who does not. That is a very important way in.

What To Do With a Poem

1. The children may want to sketch quickly the poem's images. They may then later, after discussion or exploration, decide to work on one particular drawing that somehow represents the poem.

2. The children may jot down their first impressions of the poem as they read it, or as they read the group of poems, and then join a group to share what they had written. This gives them the protection of reading what they want to read aloud, and opportunities of elaborating and clarifying their own reponses.

3. The children may jot down their thoughts and feelings as they are reading the poems, almost in a stream of consciousness with associations, connotations, and reflections. This may help the children to understand their own processes of reading poetry and contribute to the discussion after the poem has been read.

4. Children may want to write up their own questions about the poem that can become the focus of their group work or the discussion.

5. The poem can be shared without a title; the children can then decide on an appropriate or possible title after re-reading the poem. These titles can be suggested, discussed, and voted upon.

6. As children contribute ideas and feelings, the perception of those taking part alters. It is important that children have shapes and constructs in which to share their feelings and thoughts, so that they feel safe, and so that the work becomes focussed. They can use cue sheets, questions, guide points from the teacher, or contrast the ideas of another group.

7. Children can classify poems by the opinions represented. They can arrange poems by viewpoint, attitude, behavior, religion, ethics, morality. They can translate the form of the poem into other types of writing — monologues, scripts, paragraphs, or vice versa. They can change a short story into a poem, or translate an ad, a synopsis, or a photograph into poetic shape.

8. After reading poems, the teacher can ask the children for the words they liked, the way the words made them feel, and how the words sounded special. These can be put down on a chart and categorized and classified. They can list their favorite words and phrases, the rhymes they enjoy, the pictures that are the best, the metaphors and the comparisons they will remember.

9. Often a special time for poetry can highlight its inherent value and let children realize that poetry can be a positive and fascinating way to spend time.

10. The teacher can read poems by a single poet, choose poems on a theme, search out poems that somehow fit together by

form, or choose poems from a specific country or a particular culture.

11. Teachers can combine folk tales, excerpts from novels, poems, and songs into a thematic unit to be explored; teachers can read poems of the Inuit or Indian nations, or from aboriginal peoples around the world.

12. The children can take part in the poetry hour by presenting poetry through oral reading or drama, through interviewing authors, or by sharing their own discoveries and delights.

13. You can help children come to poetry by helping them to be more visually aware:
    - Use picture books.
    - Use films.
    - Use study prints that combine picture and poem.
    - Use art books and prints.
    - Use filmstrips of poems and poets.
    - Use signs and photographs to accompany poems.
    - Use the environment as a screen for poetry.
    - Make the pupils tell you what they see; but don't make it a session of right or wrong answers. Use magazine pictures and advertisements with directed activities with poetic language.

14. Give children constant exposure to poetry:
    - Collect anthologies of every kind: riddles, jokes, ballads, funny poems, story poems, theme books, songs.
    - Clip your favorite poems from magazines.
    - Read two or three poems at one time so children can compare and have opinions. Always have more than one poem in case you have misjudged.
    - Make poetry natural in your class — use it often and it will become part of the environment.

15. Have the children respond to poems by:
    - Painting, drama, singing;
    - Talking about the poem;
    - Finding material related to the poem;
    - Reading the poem as a play for partners;
    - Writing a similar poem;
    - Making a word or picture collage from magazines and newspapers;
    - Finding a related excerpt in a book.

Poetry To Be Read Aloud

The teacher is a model for poetry, a medium through which the children can come to these "special words in a special order". The teacher can emphasize the music and the words at the same time. She or he can create a mood: tranquil, funny, or mysterious. The teacher must examine the poem carefully, find how to bring it to life, how to help the child look inside it, catch the meaning of the web of words.

Teachers can read or recite from memory poems to the children on special occasions. Sometimes children should read the poem from their own copy or on an overhead transparency, a chart, or a blackboard. Because poetry is so compact and concentrated, it may be necessary to repeat the poem a number of times so that the children can savor a special word or image, or refresh their memories.

Children can listen to records, tapes, or sound filmstrips that allow them to hear different voices reading the poems with different interpretations of the poems they have heard or read themselves.

> I am a firm believer in reading aloud because, I suppose, I loved it so much as a child. Both roles were wonderful — reader and listener. Truthfully, I think that I liked reading best. It combined the advantage of listening to the fascinating sound — your own voice — with the feeling that whatever you were reading was a gift you were bringing to your audience. Because it was your discovery, you had part ownership.
>
> *Karla Kuskin*

These three excerpts can be read aloud in two minutes, and the word play can tune their ears to the delight of language.

The Kangaroo

Old Jumpety-Bumpety, Hop-and-Go-One,
Was lying asleep on his side in the sun.
This old kangaroo, he was whisking the flies
(With his long glossy tail) from his ears and his eyes.
Jumpety-Bumpety-Hop-and-Go-One
Was lying asleep on his side in the sun,
Jumpety-Bumpety-Hop!

Anon

Rain

The rain is raining all around,
It falls on field and tree,
It rains on the umbrellas here,
And on the ships at sea.

R.L. Stevenson

Rain

Rain on the green grass
And rain on the tree,
And rain on the housetop,
But not upon me.

Anon

We can expose our children to thirty or forty thousand lines of poetry a year, written by craftsmen and geniuses. Our chances of recognizing good writing and later of producing decently crafted writing, are considerably enhanced.

If Rembrandt had never seen another picture, or Rodin had never been exposed to carvings, how effective would their techniques have been?

Added to all this is the sheer joy of poetry. The more we are exposed, and the more we learn how to understand the arts, the greater is the enjoyment.

Reading poetry aloud is a pleasurable activity. It is fun to play around with the sounds of this lovely language.

Hundreds of lines of well-thought-out poetry, falling daily upon the ears, must surely do something to the listener. One effect will be the increase in the listener's vocabulary. The better one can manipulate language, the better will be that individual's ability to think, read, and write.

With daily exposure to poetry the listener gradually becomes sensitized to the one right word for each particular thought.

A Grade-six boy, after exposure to several lines in which the word *glimmers* appears, wrote this of a winter sunset:

> The red ball of the sun glimmered behind the
> black sticks of the trees.

- Most poetry is meant to be read aloud. Not all but most.
- We read aloud for one of three reasons: to inform, to entertain, to persuade.
- Most poetry falls into the entertainment area. Entertainment can be anything from a belly laugh, to being so emotionally affected that one's life changes radically. Poetry can do this.
- Greater appreciation of a poem can often be gained when we read it aloud.
- There is something magic about the sound of words, the tune, the rhythm of the language.

> The moon like a paper lantern
> Is lifted over the hill,
> And below in the silent valley
> Even the aspens are still.
>
> *Bliss Carman*

> Full fathom five thy father lies;
> Of his bones are coral made;
> Those are pearls that were his eyes.
>
> *Wm. Shakespeare*

There is something in *hearing* words spoken that helps to clarify points in discussions. Sometimes we read aloud to ourselves to make things clearer. (Have you ever tried putting together a model airplane, or made a gourmet cake? Maybe reading the instructions aloud slows us down, and thus makes things clearer.)

We must remember that there are usually at least three people involved when a poem is read aloud: the writer, the reader, and the listener.

Our job, as reader, is to recreate in the listener some of the emotions, thoughts, ideas, and dreams that the poet had. We do this through the use of the voice.

We must know what the poem means to us; otherwise we cannot read with any sense. Sometimes there are difficult words, but we can guess their meanings from the context; at other times, we have to look them up in a dictionary. If there are too many that we have to look up, the poem might well be too difficult at this time.

Twas brillig, and the slithy toves
Did gyre and gimble in the wabe;
All mimsy were the borogoves,
And the mome raths outgrabe.

Lewis Carroll

Most of these words are not in a dictionary. Perhaps you could guess their meaning.

The chill rain is falling, the nipped worm
is crawling,
The rivers are swelling, the thunder is knelling.

P.B. Shelley

Nipped has many meanings. We can predict what it means here.

The Crocodile

Hard by the lilied Nile I saw
A duskish river-dragon stretched along,
The brown habergeon of his limbs enamelled
With sanguine almondines and rainy pearl.

T.L. Beddoes

Habergeon stumped us. The dictionary revealed its meaning: a kind of armor.
Almondines means shapes, lozenges, the way a crocodile's skin is sectioned. Are the words here too hard? Or is it worth the trouble of finding their meanings? You have to decide.

Once you have grasped the meanings of the words, the next step is to decide on the emotional tone, the feelings in the poem. It may be that emotional tone is the most important element in reading aloud. When you look over something, prior to reading it aloud, you must ask yourself these questions:
• What does the writer want to do to the listener?
• Is the listener to weep, to laugh, to feel nostalgia, etc.?
• Is the listener to feel anger, pity, delight, mild amusement?
• How does the writer transmit those feelings?

Emotion

How do we get the "feel" of the piece? — by reading, re-reading, talking about it with others. Some poems offer their emotional tone and their meanings immediately. Others need longer wooing.

How can we express the emotions, once we have decided what they are? — anger, joy, love, hate, wounded pride, bewilderment? What is the emotional tone here?

> I think I could turn and live with animals, they are so
>   placid and self-contained.
> I stand and look at them long and long.
> They do not sweat and whine about their condition,
> They do not lie awake in the dark and weep for
>   their sins,
> They do not make me sick discussing their duty
>   to God,
> Not one is dissatisfied, not one is demented with
>   mania of owning things,
> Not one kneels to another, nor to his kind that lived
>   thousands of years ago
> Not one is respectable or unhappy over the whole
>   earth!
>
> *W. Whitman*

This would begin in a happy, lilting fashion:

> Spring is showery, flowery, bowery;
> Summer: hoppy, croppy, poppy;
> Autumn: wheezy, sneezy, freezy;
> Winter: slippy, drippy, nippy.
>
> *Mother Goose*

Of course, not all the lines will sound happy. A change comes with autumn, doesn't it? Those are lovely words: *wheezy, sneezy, freezy* and *slippy, drippy, nippy*. Many times in a poem the emotional tone changes from line to line, and Mother Goose knew how to do it, long ago.

The Golf Course

> The golf course lies so near the mill
> That almost every day
> The laboring children can look out
> And see the men at play.
>
> *S.N. Cleghorn*

At first it looks as though this is just a statement of fact. Who is playing? Who is working? How should we sound when we read it?

Here are some children's rhymes. How should they sound?

> Roses are red,
> Violets are blue,
> What you need
> Is a good shampoo.

> I had written to Aunt Maude,
> Who was on a trip abroad,
> When I heard she'd died of cramp,
> Just too late to save the stamp.
>
> *Harry Graham*

And here is another anonymous piece. Read it with a mixture of emotions.

> As I was standing in the street
> As quiet as could be,
> A great big ugly man came up
> And tied his horse to me.

Sometimes, in a poem, you can say things in a funny way, even though in real life they aren't humorous at all.

> Auntie, did you feel no pain
> Falling from the apple tree?
> Would you do it, please, again,
> 'Cos my friend, here, didn't see.
>
> *Harry Graham*

Pitch

Once we have understood the words and their meanings, and figured out the emotional tone of the lines, the next thing to do is to decide what pitch to use. The human voice is capable of an amazing variety of pitches from the very deep and low tones to high and even squeaky falsetto notes.

The pitch at which we read, how high or low a voice we use, is important. Would you read a ghost story at the same pitch as the exciting description of a hockey player blasting a way down the ice? A good rule of thumb is this: for exciting happy, funny, amusing, exhilarating lines, we usually use a higher pitch; while for mysterious, sad, unhappy, worried lines, we use a lower pitch.

Think of this as the opening line of a poem:

I shall never forget that particular night.

If the poem is to be mysterious or ghostly, the pitch will be lower. The same line, as the opening of a funny story will be taken at a higher pitch. This alerts the listener, and points out what to look for, what is coming.

I know two things about the horse,
And one of them is rather coarse.

Naomi Royde Smith

Methuselah

Methusela ate what he found on his plate,
And never, as people do now,
Did he note the amount of the calory count;
He ate it because it was chow.
He wasn't disturbed, as at dinner he sat,
Devouring a roast or a pie,
To think it was lacking in granular fat
Or a couple of vitamins shy.
He cheerfully chewed each species of food,
Unmindful of troubles or fears
Lest his health might be hurt
By some fancy dessert:
And he lived over nine hundred years!!

Anon

You have to change the pitch in this poem.

Windy Nights

Whenever the moon and stars are set,
Whenever the wind is high,
All night long in the dark and wet
A man goes riding by.
Late in the night when the fires are out,
Why does he gallop and gallop about?

Whenever the trees are crying aloud,
And ships are tossed at sea,

By, on the highway low and loud,
By at the gallop goes he;
By at the gallop he goes, and then
By he comes back, at the gallop again.
                              Robert Louis Stevenson

What changes in pitch would you use in "Windy Nights"? You could use *moon, night, wind, high* as clues to the emotional tone, hence the pitch to use.

Pace

Pace is an important aspect of speech. Usually, a higher pitch will call for a faster pace, and a lower pitch for a slower pace. If you are reading a description of a hilariously funny downhill toboggan ride, the chances are you will read at a fair clip. If you are describing the funeral of a beloved monarch, the pace will be slower.

Governing and over-riding all these instructions is this: variety is the essential element. We never read at the same pitch or pace for long stretches. Monotony comes from montones.

This autumn piece is one in which you would use a lower pitch and a slower pace:

> Now is the time for the burning of the leaves.
> They go to the fire, the nostril pricks with smoke
> Wandering slowly into a weeping mist.
>   *Laurence Binyon*

These lines are about something esentially quiet, rather melancholy perhaps. If we read them in a high, fast voice, the whole feeling disappears.

Notice *wandering* slowing into a *weeping mist*. The mist doesn't really weep. We know that. Then why the word *weeping* and why does it work?

The Squirrel

Whisky, frisky,
Hippity hop,
Up he goes
To the tree top!
Whirly, twirly,
Round and round,
Down he scampers
To the ground.

Furly, curly,
What a tail!
Tall as a feather,
Broad as a sail!

Where's his supper?
In the shell,
Snappity, crackity,
Out it fell.
                              Anon

This one has to start off at a crackling pace. Then it slows down in the middle, and picks up again at the very end. *Whisky* and *frisky* are words that give you the tone.

> The night was thick and hazy
> When the *Piccadilly Daisy*
> Carried down the crew and captain in the sea;
> And I think the water drowned' em,
> For they never, never found' em,
> And I know they didn't come ashore with me.
>
> *C.E. Carryl*

This calls for a fast and rollicking pace, as does the following:

> A capital ship for an ocean trip
> Was the *Walloping Window Blind* —
> No gale that blew dismayed her crew
> Or troubled the captain's mind.
>
> *C.E. Carryl*

On the other hand we need a different pace for:

> Who killed Cock Robin?
> "I," said the sparrow,
> "With my bow and arrow,
> I killed Cock Robin."

or

> Snail upon the wall,
> Have you got at all
> Anything to tell
> About your shell?
> Only this, my child —
> When the wind is wild,
> Or when the sun is hot,
> It's all I've got.
>
> *John Drinkwater*

Pause

A pause can be worth a thousand words. The trick is to discover where the pauses should be.

When we read some words, then pause, then start again, we are phrasing. Phrasing is extremely important in poetry.

The rule is this: you stop where the sense tells you to stop. In most cases the punctuation will tell you quite clearly. What we must avoid is a reading where the end of the line marks a distinct stop, and the whole thing is run together in such a way as to make no sense at all. Many people, unfortunately, seem to feel that they must end-stop all the time — that is, stop at the end of every line, whether it makes sense or not.

Often there is rhyme. It marks the end of lines for listeners, and also tells the reader when to pause:

> The curfew tolls the knell of parting day,
> The lowing herd winds slowly o'er the lea,
> The ploughman homeward plods his weary way,
> And leaves the world to darkness and to me.
>
> *Thomas Gray*

This sort of verse is easy to phrase. The difficulty here, though, lies in its very regularity, which, if we are not wary, will trap us into singsong delivery.

Shakespeare knew how to use the rhymed couplet, so neat and pleasing to phrase. Having no scenery, he had to tell people in the audience when a scene was over. He did it, often, through a rhymed couplet:

> For never was a story of more woe
> Than this of Juliet and her Romeo.

If there is no rhyme, as in free verse, we must use the sense of the piece to tell us where to stop. The same is true for blank verse.

You do not read straight on, as though it were prose. There must be a slight pause at the end of the line, so that the listener will know that there is a line ending. We call this the suspensory pause.

Here is a poem by an anonymous writer. You will have to read it through very carefully before you can put the pauses in the right places, so that it makes sense:

> I saw a peacock with a fiery tail
> I saw a blazing comet pour down hail
> I saw a cloud all wrapt with ivy round
> I saw a lofty oak creep on the ground
> I saw a beetle swallow up a whale
> I saw a foaming sea brimful of ale
> I saw a pewter cup sixteen feet deep

I saw a well full of men's tears that weep
I saw wet eyes in flames of living fire
I saw a house as high as the moon and higher
I saw a glorious sun at deep midnight
I saw a man who saw this wondrous sight.

I saw a pack of cards gnawing a bone
I saw a dog seated on England's throne
I saw King George shut up within a box
I saw the orange driving a fat ox
I saw a butcher not a twelve-month old
I saw a greatcoat all of solid gold
I saw two buttons telling off their dreams
I saw my friends who wish I'd quit these themes.

Emphasis

The weight put on certain words or groups of words can make a tremendous difference in meaning:

- Did *Mary* get the prize? (I knew someone would, but never thought of her getting it.)
- Did Mary *get* the prize? (I knew she had won it, but that is such a scurrilous outfit, I doubted that she would ever actually lay her hands on it.)

and so on . . .

When you look over a piece you are going to read aloud, one of the first things is to decide where the emphases lie. The emphasis won't always be where the rhythm places it. It will always be where it makes the piece sound right.

> Listen! You hear the grating roar
> Of pebbles which the waves draw back, and fling
> At their return, up the high strand
> > *Matthew Arnold*

> Lying on Downs above the wrinkling bay.
> > *Victoria Sackville West*

> The wrinkled sea beneath him crawls.
> > *Alfred Tennyson*

> It was a chilly winter's night;
> And frost was glittering on the ground. . .
> > *S. Barnes*

Solemnly and slow;
Caw; caw! the rooks are calling,
It is a sound of woe,
A sound of woe. . .

H.W. Longfellow

We all like repetition, which is a form of emphasis.

All things I thought I knew; but now confess
The more I know I know, I know the less.

J. Owen

Pronunciation, Articulation, and Enunciation

Pronunciation is the way we sound out the word. There are many words which have several pronunciations, like *either, neither,* and so on. People from one part of the world will say *banana* one way, others will say it another way. These are regional differences and are acceptable.

There are words, however, which people mispronounce. Here are some. You might have a few favorites of your own: February, library, elm, film, government, luxury, coupon, and so on.

Then there are the sloppy pronunciations, like doin', lookin', budder (for butter), liddle (for little), etc.

Articulation usually refers to consonants, while **enunciation** refers to vowels, though the two overlap. Sometimes we make it clearer if we simply talk about **clarity:** saying the words carefully and distinctly.

Try these:

A chubby little sister
Was rubbing in her tub;
A chubby little brother
Came up to help her rub.
The chubby little brother
Fell in there with a cry;
The chubby little sister
Then hung him up to dry.

Anon

There was a rustling that seemed like a bustling
Of merry crowds justling at pitching and hustling;
Small feet were pattering, wooden shoes clattering,

Little hands clapping, and little tongues chattering,
And, like fowls in a farmyard when barley is scattering,
Out came the children running.

Robert Browning

Edward Lear's famous "Alphabet" is a wonderful challenge for *articulation, pronunciation, and enunciation*.

A was once an apple pie,
Pidy, widy, tidy, pidy,
Nice-insidey, apple pie.

B was once a little bear,
Beary, wary, hairy, beary,
Taky carey, little bear.

C was once a little cake,
Cakey, bakey, makey, cakey,
Takey cakey, little cake.

D was once a little doll,
Dolly, Molly, Polly, Nolly,
Nursy dolly, little doll.

E was once a little eel,
Eely, weely, peely, eely,
Twirly, tweely, little eel.

F was once a little fish,
Fishy, wishy, squishy, fishy,
In a dishy, little fish.

G was once a little goose,
Goosey, moosey, boosey, goosey,
Waddly, woosey, little goose.

H was once a little hen,
Henny, chenny, tenny, henny,
Eggsy any? little hen?

I was once a bottle of ink,
Inky, dinky, thinky, inky,
Blacky, minky, bottle of ink.

J was once a jar of jam,
Jammy, mammy, clammy, mammy,
Sweety, swammy, jar of jam.

K was once a little kite,
Kitey, whitey, flighty, kitey,
Out of sighty, little kite.

L was once a little lark,
Larky, marky, harky, larky,
In the parky, little lark.

M was once a little mouse,
Mousy, bousy, sousy, mousy,
In the housy, little mouse.

N was once a little Needle,
Needly, tweedly, threedly, needly,
Wisky, weedly, little needle.

O was once a little owl,
Owly, prowly, howly, owly,
Brownly, fowly, little owl.

P was once a little pump,
Pumpy, slumpy, flumpy, pumpy,
Dumpy, thumpy, little pump.

Q was once a little quail,
Quaily, faily, daily, quaily,
Stumpy, taily, little quail.

R was once a little rose,
Rosy, posy, nosy, rosy,
Blow-sy, grow-sy, little rose.

S was once a little shrimp,
Shrimpy, flimpy, nimpy, shrimpy,
Jumpy, jimpy, little shrimp.

T was once a little thrush,
Thrushy, hushy, rushy, thrushy,
Flitty, flushy, little thrush.

U was once a little urn,
Urny, burny, turny, urny,
Bubbly, burny, little urn.

V was once a little vine,
Viny, winy, twiny, viny,
Twisty, twiny, little vine.

W was once a whale,
Whaly, scaly, shaly, whaly,
Tumbly, taily, mighty whale.

X was once a great king Xerxes
Xerxy, Perxy, Turxy, Xerxy,
Linxy, lurxy, great king Xerxes.

Y was once a little yew,
Yewdy, fewdy, crudy, yewdy,
Growdy, grewdy, little yew.

Z was once a piece of zinc,
Tinky, winky, blinky, zinky,
Tinky, minky, piece of zinc.

Variety of Skills

Finally, a word on variety. It goes without saying that all the skills of reading are used together. You don't say to yourself, ''I think I'll use a little pitch today, and I'll use emphasis tomorrow.''

All the skills — getting the meaning from the words, finding the emotional tone, deciding on the correct pitch and pace, choosing the right phrasing and making the correct pauses, knowing where to place the emphasis, and making use of correct and clear diction — all of these are used together.

Variety is what we seek. Monotony is its opposite, and is an easy trap to fall into, especially in ballads and in strongly patterned poetry.

We gain variety through all the skills mentioned above, as well as through the correct use of volume, and modulation of the voice. Here are a few poems that need an array of skills in presentation:

Night is come,
Owls are out;
Beetles hum
Round about.

Children snore
Safe in bed,
Nothing more
Need be said.

Sir Henry Newbolt

Eight O'clock

He stood, and heard the steeple
Sprinkle the quarters on the town.

One, two, three, four, to marketplace and people
It tossed them down.

Strapped, noosed, nighing his hour,
He stood and counted them, and cursed his luck;
And then the clock collected in the tower
Its strength, and struck.

A.E. Houseman

A Memory Snug in My Mind

I remember a time of coziness,
A time when fire crackled,
A lazy time,
A hot chocolate time,
A slow time.
It was a quiet time
back in the good old days.
It was a family hour,
A time to whisper.
It was an O'Henry time.
A time of tune,
A time of peace.
It was a wintertime.
It was a happy time;
It was a time remembered.

Yasi Javid

Washing

What is all this washing about,
Every day, week in, week out?
From getting up till going to bed,
I'm tired of hearing the same thing said.
Whether I'm dirty or whether I'm not,
Whether the water is cold or hot,
Whether I like or whether I don't
Whether I will or whether I won't —
"Have you washed your hands, and washed
    your face?"
I seem to live in the washing place.
Whenever I go for a walk or a ride,
As soon as I put my nose inside

The door again, there's someone there
With a sponge and soap, and a lot they care
If I have something better to do,
"Now wash your face, and your fingers too!"
Before a meal is ever begun,
And after every meal is done,
It's time to turn on the water spout.
Please, what is all this washing about?

John Drinkwater

When Children Read Aloud

When poems are read aloud, the heart and core of the poem emerges. The rhythm or beat of the poem relates to, and reinforces the message. Whether the poet uses the cadences of natural speech, the formal unit of literary phrases, repetition, alliteration, onomatopoeia, or rhyme and repetition, the children will come to realize that all of these qualities create the effect of the poem.

Although reading aloud is not necessary for proficient reading comprehension, it can stimulate learning. It shows children how they can manipulate a text, and trains their eyes and ears in exploring the rhythms of language. Reading aloud lets children demonstrate their reading comprehension, and encourages students to try out new language styles and patterns. Oral reading also verifies print, helping silent readers to "hear" dialogue.

Reading aloud may involve the teacher reading with the class, the class reading to the teacher, a child reading with a group, a child reading to a partner, or a group reading to a group. When children are reading aloud in groups, several groups may be reading at the same time.

We ask the children to read aloud when there is a contextual reason for doing so. For example:

• reading poems with a partner or a group;
• choral dramatization;
• singing songs in-role;
• reading poems as others move in response;
• reading what has been written as response by individuals or by groups as a reflection after reading or hearing a poem;
• reading the research information that will affect the interpretation of the poem.

Children should read aloud:

- to share actively a range of poems in a non-critical atmosphere;
- to practise the skills of oral reading (pause, pitch, emphasis, etc.) in an interesting manner;
- to bring to life the words of others;
- to expose other children to sources of literature they may have abandoned or never discovered (for example, picture book versions of poems).

Oral reading should lead us to discover:
- what the words mean to the children;
- how they might be spoken;
- how the listener is affected;
- what emotions are involved;

When a child reads to his or her classmates, it should usually be when:
- he or she alone has a copy of the material to be read (unless it is drama);
- the listeners are not familiar with what they are going to hear;
- the child has had come previous individual coaching;
- the child has had time to rehearse the selection.

If you are operating an individualized program, then your individual interviews will provide the opportunity for coaching. Coaching consists of assisting the child with some of the following:
- Is the reading indistinct?
- Is the punctuation followed?
- Is there misunderstanding of the sound value of certain spellings?
- If there is faltering, is it a decoding problem or is the material too difficult (spellings, sophistication of content)?

Other opportunities for practice and coaching can be achieved through group choral reading and the smaller, buzz-group sessions.

Choral Speaking

As the children interpret poetry through choral speaking, they are exploring the voice of the poem. They are finding ways of saying words and phrases that bring them new or deeper meanings. They are learning to respond as a group to the poems.

They can explore the language without fear because they are within the group. The children can all participate, co-operate, and work together to make meaning happen. They can work as a whole class, or in groups, developing appreciation for the poem by making it part of their voices.

Choral speaking, or choral reading as it is often called, means people speaking in chorus, together. The speech choir is like the singing choir, except that the musical modulations of the speaking voice are far more subtle and complex than those of the singing voice.

Over the years, different people have tried to write down the notes for the speaking voice, analogous to those used for singing. Unfortunately, it was found to be impossible. In half a tone in the musical scale there might be several, perhaps scores of intermediate tones in the speaking voice.

Some people think that choral speaking is something newly invented. The technique is an ancient one, and goes back to classical Greece and beyond. Greek drama, especially the earlier style, used a speaking chorus with one or perhaps two actors. The main body of the story was carried by the speaking choir.

Gradually the drama changed, but there was always a thin stream of choral speaking running through the Roman times, the Middle Ages, and later.

It is true that it became popular, once again, in the earlier days of the century, especially promoted by John Masefield, then poet laureate of England.

There are many reasons for speaking poetry chorally:
a) It is easier to speak with emotion in a group, and emotion is demanded in poetry.
b) It is less demanding or inhibiting for most children to speak poetry together.
c) Continuity of tone is much more effective when a group speaks.

To join with others in the voicing of a great poetic
experience is to feel oneself swept into a oneness of life that
is well worth the having.

Harry Overstreet

When children speak poetry chorally there is no doubt that diction improves. Articulation and enunciation have to be done with care when a group speaks, or the slovenly becomes very obvious. After all, most poetry was intended to be spoken aloud.

As Cecile de Banke, a well-known expert in the field, said:

That the expressive and impressive rendition of poetry is impossible without perfection of speech and beauty of voice is obvious . . . a recognition of the value of these . . . will be inculcated in every member of the speaking choir.

She goes on to say:

It is possible to raise the whole standard of speech in a group of 30 people without their being conscious of embarrassment or discouragement.

Little children love chanting and speaking in chorus. With older students, the approach should be that spoken poetry is an enjoyable means of exploring the poem.

With very small children the best approach is the rote system. This works well with nursery rhymes and short pieces. Choral speaking and chanting are not exactly the same thing. Chanting depends on heavy rhythm. In choral speaking we are expressing in sound what the poet wrote down. That means that we must be aware of all the skills used in speaking: knowing the meanings of words, emotional tone, pitch, pace, pause and phrasing, emphasis, articulation, pronunciation, enunciation, volume, variety in the use of the voice, and so on.

Choral speaking by rote might go like this:

i) Read the poem to the children.
ii) Read it again, talking about it, the words, the humor, etc.
iii) Read it again. This time ask the children to join in on certain parts — a chorus, for instance.
iv) Read it again. Now the children join in as much as they can. Sometimes it is useful to go over one or two lines several times, letting them join in.
v) Gradually eliminate yourself, until the children are speaking alone.

A few points: We always have a starting signal, so that we begin together. A ragged attack spoils everything. We can beat the rhythm out in some way. Sometimes we give them "mnemonics", pictures, usually to help them remember the sequence.

> If you should meet a crocodile
> Don't take a stick and poke him;
> Ignore the welcome in his smile,

Be careful not to stroke him.
For as he sleeps upon the Nile,
He thinner gets and thinner;
Whenever you meet a crocodile
He's ready for his dinner.

Anon

After reading this over several times we talk about how we would feel if we met a crocodile, what we would do, what we should *not* do, and so on. Then we take the first two lines and say them over and over. Then the children say them with us. (People are always telling children *not* to do things, so they will have no problems in getting the intonation of this poem right.)

Then we take the next two lines in the same manner. Then we say all four; then gradually complete the poem. These sessions should never be longer than a very few minutes.

We have done this particular piece in a week: read and talked on Monday, practised two lines on Tuesday, added two more on Wednesday, two more on Thursday, and the last two on Friday. Each "lesson" was no longer than three minutes. We stopped while they still wanted to go on. By the end of the week we had the poem, and the children remembered it with pleasure. We always laughed as we really hit the last line. There are as many variants on this technique as there are teachers and children.

The main value of the technique lies in the structure. The children have time to understand what the words mean, then the feeling of the piece. This is very important, as we do not want a mere chanting of words, but an interpretation of what the poet meant. Usually with rote pieces, we begin practice with everybody, a true chorus.

After the children become confident in their powers, we can move on to dialogues, opposite points of view, etc.

Said the Duck to the Kangaroo
"Good gracious! how you do hop
Over the fields, and the water, too,
As if you never would stop."

Edward Lear

A speech choir may speak in *unison*, with solo speakers, in groups of higher and lower voices (sometimes called light and dark voices, which parallel sopranos and altos in two-part singing).

Another technique is *antiphonal*, where two groups alternate.

Then there is *cumulative*, where you begin with a small number of voices, and line by line increase the numbers. This gives a swelling volume and depth and can be very effective.

Here are some poems and verses for very young children to try chorally.

> Oh, Susan Blue,
> How do you do?
> Please may I go for a walk with you?
> Where shall we go?
> Oh, I know —
> Down in the meadow where the cowslips grow.
> > *Kate Greenaway*

> Bow, wow, wow!
> Whose dog art thou?
> Little Tommy Tinker's dog.
> Bow, wow, wow!
> > *Mother Goose*

> Hey diddle, diddle,
> The cat and the fiddle,
> The cow jumped over the moon;
> The little dog laughed
> To see such sport,
> And the dish ran away with the spoon.
> > *Mother Goose*

> I went to the animal fair,
> The birds and the beasts were there.
> The big baboon, by the light of the moon,
> Was combing his auburn hair.
> > *Anon*

These are simple, relatively easy pieces. This does not mean that quite young children cannot tackle and enjoy more complex material. There really is no such thing as a "primary poem" or a "senior poem". It all depends on the sophistication of the children, and that of their teacher.

Once children can read, we usually like working with a script. This can be written on the board, on an overhead, or on paper. We prefer not to work from a book, as we want the children to mark up their poems for future reference.

To begin with, we choose a poem that has a fairly strong rhythm, and is either funny or mysterious.

Everyone has a different technique. This is ours:

i. Introduce the poem. Talk about the subject. Read it to the class.
ii. Read it again, pointing out various important points.
iii. Start the choral speaking by reading the first couple of lines.
iv. Show them how to mark up a script — underlining words to be emphasized, marking pauses, increase in volume, etc.
v. Do the first two lines together in unison.
vi. Now do the next two. Then do the four together.
vii. Keep on doing a bit at a time, and add it, until the whole piece is done.

We talk about marking scripts. Professional readers on radio and television do this. It helps them to remember how they are to interpret.

At first we tell the children almost everything they are to do. Gradually we get them to tell us how we should read. Then they decide on the complete interpretation, once they have enough experience and confidence to do so.

Model 1

Windy Nights

Whenever the moon and stars are set,
Whenever the wind is high,
All night long in the dark and wet,
A man goes riding by.
Late in the night when the fires are out,
Why does he gallop and gallop about?

Whenever the trees are crying aloud,
And ships are tossed at sea,
By, on the highway, low and loud,
By at the gallop goes he;
By at the gallop he goes, and then
By he comes back, at the gallop again.

Robert Louis Stevenson

i) Read the poem, talking about the things heard, etc.
ii. Re-read, with further talk about how it should sound, how you can get the spooky effect the poet desires.
iii. Read the poem again; then do the first two lines. Telling the children which words to emphasize: *moon, stars, wind, high.* I let them underline these words.

iv. Read again, then have all read lines one and two together, aiming for the effect wanted.

v. Do the next two lines: talk about how they should sound, mark them, and say them.

vi. Now do all four lines.

vii. And so on.

It might be claimed that this is a very mechanical way of tackling a poem. Our answer is: most of us thrive within a structure, and this very structured approach will gradually change, as you become more at ease. As soon as possible, have them tell you how it should be done.

One other point: pauses are immensely important. We can mark pauses with a vertical stroke after the word.

Start doing everything in unison. Once the students are experienced. Use solos for certain lines, groups for some parts, light and dark voices, boys and girls, cumulatively, and so on. How you divide the poem depends on how you feel it will be best interpreted.

Model 2

> Rumbling at the chimneys,
> Rattling at the doors,
> Round the roofs
> And round the roads
> The rude wind roars
>
> *Anon*

> Grumbling, stumbling,
> Fumbling all the day;
> Fluttering, stuttering,
> Muttering away;
> Rustling, hustling,
> Rustling as it flows,
> That is how the brook talks,
> Bubbling as it goes.
>
> *Anon*

These are good warm-ups, to get the tongue loosened. Do the poems in unison, then make up some of your own poems and patterns of choral speaking.

Model 3
Wolf

I heard him howl in the dark . . .	
Night had blotted the burnt gold of the wheat,	*blotted*
Night, drowsy with brooding silence, and sweet,	*brooding silence*
Sweet with faint wine of the fading rose,	*faint wine of the*
Where he came from, or where he went, who knows?	*fading rose*
The four stealthy feet	
Slinking by the cabin made no mark;	
But out on the ridge, beyond the cattle barns,	
Baffled, he paused. . . he uttered his voice to the stars:	*Baffled*
And I lifted the blind in the dark,	
(My spine tingling, my skin creeping), and high	*all the i sounds*
Picked out in silver he stood against the sky,	
A deathly shadow with emerald eyes burning:	*emerald eyes*
And again he uttered his cry . . .	*burning*
And cowed by the clear sword of coming dawn,	*cowed, clear*
Slowly he dropped his head, and slowly turning,	*sword*
Crossed the ridge, and was gone.	

Anon

This is a great "atmosphere" piece. It lends itself to unison choral speaking.

Model 4

Shiloh. . . A Requiem

Unison Skimming lightly, wheeling still,
The swallows fly low
Over the field in clouded days,
The forest field of Shiloh —

Group 1 Over the field where April rain
Solaced the parched ones stretched in pain
Through the pause of night
That followed the Sunday flight
Around the church of Shiloh —

Group 2 The church so lone, the log-built one,
That echoed to many a parting groan
And a natural prayer
Of dying foeman mingled there —

Solo	Foemen at morn but friends at eve —
Solo	Fame or country least their care:
Solo	(What like a bullet can undeceive?)
Solo	But now they lie low,
Unison	While over them the swallows skim,
	And all is hushed at Shiloh.

Herman Melville

Model 5

Each child can call out a flavor in this poem as the class begins and ends chorally:

Bleezer's Ice Cream

I am Ebenezer Bleezer;
I run BLEEZER's ICE CREAM STORE,
there are flavors in my freezer
you have never seen before,
twenty-eight divine creations
too delicious to resist,
why not do yourself a favor;
try the flavors on my list:

COCOA MOCHA MACARONI
TAPIOCA SMOKED BALONEY
CHECKERBERRY CHEDDAR CHEW
CHICKEN CHERRY HONEYDEW
TUTTI-FRUTTI STEWED TOMATO
TUNA TACO BAKED POTATO
LOBSTER LITCHI LIMA BEAN
MOZZARELLA MANGOSTEEN
ALMOND HAM MERINGUE SALAMI
YAM ANCHOVY PRUNE PASTRAMI
SASSAFRAS SOUVLAKI HASH
SUKIYAKI SUCCOTASH
BUTTER BRICKLE PEPPER PICKLE
POMEGRANATE PUMPERNICKEL
PEACH PIMENTO PIZZA PLUM
PEANUT PUMPKIN BUBBLEGUM
BROCCOLI BANANA BLUSTER
CHOCOLATE CHOP SUEY CLUSTER
AVOCADO BRUSSELS SPROUT

PERIWINKLE SAUERKRAUT
COTTON CANDY CARROT CUSTARD
CAULIFLOWER COLA MUSTARD
ONION DUMPLING DOUBLE DIP
TURNIP TRUFFLE TRIPLE FLIP
GARLIC GUMBO GRAVY GUAVA
LENTIL LEMON LIVER LAVA
ORANGE OLIVE BAGEL BEET
WATERMELON WAFFLE WHEAT

I am Ebenezer Bleezer;
I run BLEEZER's ICE CREAM STORE,
taste a flavor from my freezer;
you will surely ask for more.

Jack Prelutsky

Model 6

This poem lends itself to cumulative participation:

An Animal Alphabet

Alligator, beetle, porcupine, whale,
Bobolink, panther, dragonfly, snail
Crocodile, monkey, buffalo, hare,
Dromedary, leopard, mud turtle, bear;
Elephant, badger, pelican, ox,
Flying fish, reindeer, anaconda, fox,
Guinea pig, dolphin, antelope, goose,
Hummingbird, weasel, pickerel, moose,
Ibex, rhinoceros, owl, kangaroo,
Jackal, oppossum, toad, cockatoo,
Kingfisher, peacock, anteater, bat,
Lizard, ichneumon, honeybee, rat,
Mockingbird, camel, grasshopper, mouse,
Nightingale, spider, cuttlefish, grouse,
Ocelot, pheasant, wolverine, auk,
Periwinkle, ermine, katydid, hawk,
Quail, hippopotamus, armadillo, moth,
Rattlesnake, lion, woodpecker, sloth
Salamander, goldfinch, angleworm, dog,
Tiger, flamingo, scorpion, frog,
Unicorn, ostrich, nautilus, mole,
Viper, gorilla, basilisk, sole,
Whip-poor-will, beaver, centipede, fawn,
Xantho, canary, polliwog, swan,

Yellowhammer, eagle, hyena, lark.
Zebra, chameleon, butterfly, shark.

Anon

Model 7

Chants and cheers offer immediate opportunities for joining in.

Crackers and Crumbs

Crackers and crumbs
Crackers and crumbs
These are my fingers
These are my thumbs
These are my eyes
These are my ears
They're going to grow big
in the next ten years.

Sonja Dunn

Memorization

To memorize or not to memorize, that is the question. There is no
doubt that the hatred, or at least indifference, many adults feel
towards poetry is connected with the fact that they were forced
to memorize vast chunks of poetry when they were younger.

This was done because of a mistaken belief that memorizing
poetry would somehow increase the child's ability to memorize,
or remember, other really important things, such as the dates of
battles and mathematical formulae. We now know that the carry-
over there is minimal. If you learn how to memorize poetry you
will increase in ability to memorize poetry.

> Not the poem which we have read, but that to which we
> return, with the greatest pleasure, possesses the genuine
> power . . .

S.T. Coleridge

And, if we want to return, how much easier and more pleasing
if we can find it in a memory bank, stored with interesting and
fascinating lines.

Should we ask children to memorize poetry? Yes. But if we
do, there must be strong reasons for doing so.

Here are the simple criteria:

1. The memorizer must understand the basic meaning of the piece, as well as its emotional tone, so that when saying the poem, he or she says it well.
2. There must be some degree of choice. After reading four or five pieces, the memorizer picks a couple of lines he or she wants to learn. ("Off by heart" is the expression. It suggests that some love should surely accompany the learning.)
3. The learner must want to do it.

Quality is essential, not quantity. Two or three lines learned from love of them may well be far more valuable to a person than whole reams forced into the memory bank.

The memorizer must understand the poem:

How often, in the olden days, were entire classes forced to memorize some poem from a reader. Possibly a quarter of the class understood what it meant. No account was taken of individual differences.

Some children thoroughly loathed the experience, because the threat was often made: "Those who haven't learned this week's memory work get no phys.ed. and no art until they do." The ultimate horror, often a favorite at higher levels, was the writing out of the piece, complete with all the necessary commas and semicolons.

If the poem has been discussed, the word pictures considered, and the way the poet used words and techniques has been talked through, then the child has a good chance of understanding it.

The memorizer must have a choice:

If we read hundreds of poems with our children, talk about them, discuss the techniques and the ways the poets work, and the children understand the poem, then there is a chance for the child to select some favorite parts and want to remember them.

The technique might be roughly this: read five poems about dogs. As each poem is discussed, the children pick out lines, phrases, or words that appeal to them. They might read them aloud to you or to their friend. Once you have read three poems, you ask them which poem they prefer. Then ask for a line or so from that poem that really appeals to them. These lines could then be memorized.

The memorizer must want to do it:

This is the task of the teacher — to make the children want to do it. The teacher's real enthusiasm and interest in the poems, along with the feeling of freedom to discuss, argue, disagree, question, take and give advice — all these build the atmosphere where the children are willing or even eager to learn some chosen lines.

Quality is what matters. The interesting thing is that once children are encouraged to memorize this way, they usually do far more than most of us would ever demand.

How do we do it?

Young children are quite used to memorizing poems as they join in the call-and-response chants of parents, the songs of primary classrooms, the verses of recess games, the fun of rhymes in Big Books.

With older children, we teachers can use a more formal approach. The child chooses a couple of lines. We ask him or her to read the lines to us. We admire them, and the way the child has read. Then we ask him or her to read them again. Once more we praise the reading, and yet again. By now the child can probably say the lines without looking at them. They have been memorized through repetition.

Whenever we teachers ask children to memorize, we must be willing to listen as they speak the lines. We must show delight. When we trust each other utterly, we might even suggest improvements in interpretation.

Another technique shows them the complete poem, and gradually reduces the clues, until they can say the whole thing.
Step One: Show the poem and discuss it.
Step Two: Show the whole poem, read it aloud. Read it again. The students read with you.

The Eagle

He clasps the crag with crooked hands;
Close to the sun in lonely lands,
Ringed with the azure world, he stands.

The wrinkled sea beneath him crawls;
He watches from his mountain walls,
And like a thunderbolt he falls.

Alfred Tennyson

Step Three: Rub out certain words. The students read it again, filling in the missing words.

> He clasps ----- crag with crooked hands;
> Close to the ----- in lovely -----,
> Ringed with the azure world he stands.
>
> The wrinkled ----- beneath him crawls;
> He watches from his mountain -----,
> And like a ----- he falls.

Step Four: Continue eliminating words as we re-read:

> — clasps the ----- with crooked -----;
> Close to the ----- ----- lonely -----,
> Ringed with the ----- -----, he ----- .
>
> The wrinkled ----- beneath ----- -----;
> He watches from ----- ----- -----,
> And like a ----- ----- falls.

Step Five:

> ----- clasps ----- ----- crooked -----;
> Close ----- ----- ----- ----- lonely -----,
> Ringed ----- ----- ----- -----, ----- -----,
>
> ----- wrinkled ----- ----- ----- -----;
> He watches ----- ----- ----- -----,
> And like a ----- ----- -----.

Step Six: eliminate every printed word, and say the poem.

The speed at which you work will depend upon the class.

Also, this would be done with either the whole class, or with a group which has chosen this poem instead of another.

A variant of this technique is to read a line, read it again, read it again, cover it, and say it. Then do the next line; and so on.

One of the most pleasant ways of memorizing is through choral speaking. Here we all learn not only the words together, but the interpretation.

Memorizing can be pleasant and highly profitable. The teacher, of course, should memorize most of the poems he or she is going to teach. Being able to say the poem — even if there is no copy in front of everyone — is a great advantage.

Drama and Poems: A Natural Relationship

Drama can bring meaning to the poem, and the poem can provide a context for the drama. We have used drama with poems in three basic ways:

1. as an introduction to the poem where children can explore the issues and ideas embedded in the poem, and prepare for the subsequent reading, so that they may bring a wider perception to the poem;
2. as a follow-up activity to the poem, where poets' ideas and feelings bring forth suggestions for the dramatic exploration;
3. as a means of bringing depth and understanding to the continued interpreting of the poem, so that the children find new levels of meaning each time they read the poem aloud. Poems offer children words that can be read orally over and over again, and the opportunities for making new meanings grow with each reading. If drama can create contexts, situations, and roles that encourage understanding of the words, then poems and drama can be mutually supportive in helping children grow.

Poems can be a starting point for dramatic improvisation, and dramatic work can lead to a greater understanding of poems. Drama becomes a tool for the exploration of the ideas, relationships, and language of the poem. Drama can enhance the child's understanding of what is to be, or has been read. The very act of dramatizing some element of the material that has been read extends the child's mental and emotional grasp of the poem. Children explore the situations, characters, and problems in their poems and reveal their private comprehension in-role. Through the subsequent interaction with the teacher and other children, these personal meanings are expanded, adapted, clarified, and altered until the many levels of meaning within the poem become available to the students.

The use of a situation from a poem as a beginning point for drama may deepen and enrich the dramatic experience. The complexity and subtlety of mood and language may provide potential for stimulating the children's dramatic imaginations.

As well, drama offers opportunities for children to develop their powers of oral interpretation. While in-role, they can read aloud poems and songs, or their own compositions, and can explore various interpretations of them. Working in small groups, children can select the interpretation they wish to give the words, and even devise ways to express the text in dramatic terms, establishing the poem in space, making specific recommendations about tone, volume, pace, and exploring how the words should be spoken.

The teacher must consider the poem carefully for dramatic possibilities — for issues, concepts, or problems that might absorb the children's attention. The poem may be told or read by the teacher, or read silently by the children, either before or after its use as a source for the drama. Children may enact incidents from the poem, extend the action of the poem, elaborate upon the details of the poem, or invent their own drama from the concepts found in the poem. The teacher should continually help the children to return to the poem for further inspiration while they are devising their own improvised responses.

Overheard on a Saltmarsh

Nymph, nymph, what are your beads?

Green glass, goblin. Why do you stare at them?

Give them me.

No.

Give them me. Give them me.

No.

Then I will howl all night in the reeds,
Lie in the mud and howl for them.

Goblin, why do you love them so?

They are better than stars or water,
Better than voices of winds that sing,
Better than any man's fair daughter,
Your green glass beads on a silver ring.

Hush, I stole them out of the moon.

Give me your beads, I desire them.

No.

I will howl in a deep lagoon
For your green glass beads, I love them so.
Give them me. Give them.

No.

Harold Munro

The poem "Overheard on a Saltmarsh" is a perfect vehicle for dramatic exploration, because it is full of the tension between two speakers — Nymph and Goblin. Even when reading it silently, the voices seem to fill the room.

The children can read the poem aloud, bringing their own interpretation to life, and exploring the different contexts they develop for the reading. This improvisational activity that surrounds the attempts at interpreting the words, gives the children opportunities to work in-role as they solve the problems of finding the appropriate voices and meanings, and can lead to the full-fledged situation for drama. The drama informs the reading, and the poem suggests the drama. There are many different ways to involve children in using drama with this poem:

- the children can work as partners, alternating the roles of Nymph and Goblin as they read the poem aloud several times;
- the partners can suggest and select a setting for their dramatization — a marsh, a jungle, a cave, a playground;
- they can experiment with levels or space as they read, such as one partner standing and one lying down;
- they can try whispering, shouting, or singing the lines;
- the whole class can read one part chorally, while the teacher in-role or a student reads the other, and then the roles can be exchanged (this will add great strength to the interpretation);
- the readers can extend the dialogue, adding new words while remaining in-role, continuing the situation until resolution occurs. The sets of partners can discuss each ending with the rest of the class and examine the differences;
- the children can explore the reason for the nymph and the goblin fighting over the green glass beads.

One class decided that the beads contained the power necessary to leave the earth: they had been stolen from the moon. The goblins then had to devise a plan to obtain the beads from the nymphs. Another group used the poem as an analogy of two groups who were in conflict over a holy object and built an entire playmaking session around that premise. They finally read the poem at the conclusion of the drama as a requiem for the loss of the icon.

The poem gives rise to strong ideas about the voices inside the poem, and these voices promote the exploration of ideas that are developed through drama.

Many aspects of poems can be effectively paired with drama:

- monologues, where the voice that is evident and the unseen audience provide sources for role-playing by the children;
- dialogues, which can act as minimal script for the children to interpret, in pairs in small groups, or as a whole class divided into parts;
- chants, cheers, prayers, invocations, and songs where the children's voices can be raised together as a village, a tribe, a society;
- situations, so intense and concentrated, that role-playing and improvisation present ready avenues for exploration;
- reflective poems that can add to the understanding after the drama. Children can read or listen to poems that contribute to the meanings explored in the drama, or find poems that speak to the drama, then share them or copy them in their response journals;
- poems written by the children can be used within the drama to further the action, or to cause the group to ponder what has happened before continuing with the apparent action. The poems can form proclamations, summaries, or rituals.

Some of the following teaching strategies that can be used effectively by teachers to blend drama and poetry:

Sound Exploration

Sound exploration involves the creation of sounds, rhythms, and music, and complements dramatic exploration.

The pupils create, select, and organize sounds, language, and music in order to explore the spectrum of sound and the potential of the human voice for producing a range and variety of sounds. Sound exploration should be carried out as a part of the dramatic context that is being explored. For example, a chant can accompany the sight of the sea creature; a rhythmic beat can encourage the hunters in the jungle; a "sound track" can complement the report of the robot search team on the strange planet Earth.

Narration and Mime

Narration and mime can be used with the poem. The children may enact the poems together, each creating his or her own response, or the children may work in pairs or small groups. The teacher can read the poem as the children go through a series of mime activities, building-in opportunities for individual choices or decisions. The teacher reads the poem, and the children mime the action, interpreting the words through their movement. This activity works well with beginning groups and as a warm-up for experienced groups. Poems may be chosen to complement a particular aspect of the curriculum.

Tableaux

Tableaux are "frozen pictures" created by the children in response to a theme or situation. Their use allows children to focus on one significant moment. In addition, children learn to contribute to a group effort, and gain experience in exploring poems and in presenting situations from different points of view.

Dance Drama

Dance drama is movement that can interpret a poem. The patterns and rhythms of dance blend with the essence of the poem, so that the action and feeling are conveyed through movement. Dance drama emphasizes expression rather than form.

Dance drama can be simple, with each child creating a response independently; or it can be more complex, with groups of students sharing a poem through stylized movement. Dance drama can be supported by music, sound exploration, an accompanying poem (either read or narrated), a chant, or costumes (e.g., masks or capes).

Choral Dramatization

In choral speaking, the children explore the sounds and rhythms of language as they interpret poems, songs, chants, and excerpts from children's literature. However, many children need an extra incentive to enjoy the experience of choral reading; dramatization of the selection can provide this, helping the child feel the music and meaning of the words. Selections with the strongest appeal for the children will probably be those that enable them to form clear mental images of what the words are saying.

As children gain experience, they may interpret more complex selections, using sound and movement, and tableaux.

Scripts

Although there are few scripts per se for children to read aloud (writers of children's literature generally choose other genres for their writing), poems written for children are an excellent source of good dialogue that may easily be adapted for oral reading activities. Children can work in pairs or small groups, reading the dialogue silently and then aloud. The teacher asks the children to change roles, introduces new settings or new tensions, or changes the time period, and helps the children dramatize the selection so that they can discover new meanings in the text.

Poems can be created from the improvised drama — transcribed from tapes or from memory by those who were involved in the drama. These scripts can be read aloud by other groups.

Poems are excellent sources for dramatic exploration. The ideas contained in the poem are minimal scripts. The interpretation can be carried out through improvisation and role-playing. The ideas, the concepts, the feelings, the voices, are all avenues for drama. The words themselves can be used as scripts. The children can find the voice within, decide upon the speakers, and interpret the poem orally. They can use movement, mime, and sound exploration to accompany their work.

Summary

Drama can:
a) broaden the child's experiences, both active and symbolic, before he or she reads poems.
b) motivate the child's need or desire to read the poem.
c) prepare the child for what is to be read.
d) intervene in what is being read, so that new understanding can be brought to the poem.
e) examine what has been read in a new light, with a view towards building new expanded meanings in a collaborative, interactive mode.
f) make immediate and vital poetry that seems at first to be without contemporary application.

g) help children discover the poem — its challenge, its beauty, its caring, its healing, its joy, its power of revelation.

h) help children develop skills of oral interpretation. While in-role, they can read aloud poems and songs. While reflecting about the drama experience, they can share poems in the journal writings.

i) give children opportunities to reveal their private comprehensions in-role so that through interaction these personal meanings can be expanded, adapted, clarified, and altered.

j) build curriculum connections, because drama and poems are the stuff of learning.

k) motivate children to do both parallel reading and further reading, using other genres, reference materials, and related writings.

l) stimulate children to write their own poems, in-role, as reflection, or in appraisal. Children can do research and background writing as planning and preparation for the drama, or to find new directions as the drama develops.

m) build a sense of poetry — words, shapes, syntax, style, structures, and author's voice.

n) find or restore voice to the poem.

Presenting Poetry

The goal of teaching poetry is the exploration of words, ideas, roles, physical and verbal interactions, feelings, and attitudes. Just as in art class, the goal must not be the showing of the work. There may be reasons for sharing, but exploration and learning come first.

Sharing is the interaction that occurs when individuals or groups communicate with others. Through the free exchange of ideas, children discover and/or clarify what their assumptions are, see different points of view, become aware of their own, and begin to understand poems they are listening to, reading aloud, or dramatizing.

There may be times when children wish to take a particular activity out of the classroom environment to share it with a wider audience. When children are placed in performance situations, the point of view of the audience becomes the major consideration rather than the development of the children's own feelings and relationships. This type of sharing should occur only when the children are prepared and ready, and when the exploration and learning have been wholly satisfactory.

When planning to share the work of the children with others, the teacher must consider the following:

   i. the purpose for the sharing, and what impact the sharing will have on the poetry exploration;
  ii. the social health of the group, and whether the students wish to share the work (e.g., should beginners be encouraged to show work or should they concentrate on themselves and their own group?);
 iii. whether or not to explore informal ways of working with an audience (e.g., informal demonstration for discussion or observational purposes, on-the-spot spontaneous sharing during the lesson, or sharing work with others who are carrying on a similar exploration);
  iv. the advantages and disadvantages of setting up situations where volunteers can do the sharing, such as a group assignment.

Presenting poetry involves sharing work with others who have not been engaged in the process of exploring and learning. It might involve showing the work to another class in the same school or to students working on similar activities but at different times and places. It should be remembered that different classes work differently and need different evaluation criteria; the teachers of both the spectators and the participants must take this into account in any type of presentation.

Some polishing and refinement may be necessary, because the emotional risks to the children are greater in more formal situations.

Performing is a formal event, a way of sharing work with an audience that is outside the creative process and that sees and evaluates only the finished product. Therefore, the material must be polished and practised for the sake of the audience. Children who are growing and learning at various stages of development should not be put in the high-risk position of trying to please an audience.

Poetry is meant to be enjoyed. It might have some other uses, but the main thrust is pleasure, as in music and the other arts. One way we can enhance this pleasure is by sharing poems with others.

This can be done in several ways:

1. The teacher finds a poem he or she particularly likes and simply reads it to the children.

2. The child finds a poem in a magazine or a book, likes it, and reads it, either to the teacher alone, or to the whole class.
3. Working in pairs, children read their poems to each other.
4. After we have read and studied several poems by A.A. Milne, we have an in-class concert. Some student acts as chair person, the program is arranged, and everyone takes part. Some read whole pieces, while others simply read lines they have liked, and tell why they made that particular choice.

   Another part of this kind of performance could be a short reading by one or more students about A.A. Milne. Once we have 30 or more of his poems we become interested in his biography — *not before*. We have a television-style interview of the poet, with one child playing Milne, and another the interviewing announcer. Poems inspired by Milne and written by the class are included in the program.
5. This kind of program could easily be exported to another classroom within the school.
6. A Grade 4 class could build a similar type of program for the Grade 1 children to see and hear. This could include poems that particular Grade 1 class likes.

A Model for Presentation

The program is well-rehearsed beforehand and involves the whole class. If there happens to be a piano player, an accordionist, a guitar player in the class, by all means involve them. Children are used to background music in television, and background music can often help the poem have a greater impact upon the listener.

The whole class can be on stage, at various levels. Use platforms and boxes to create interesting patterns — some seated on the floor, others on the platforms, or on chairs at different levels. The backdrop could be a mural, done by the children and indicative of the theme of the performance. Music plays (if you have no musicians, use tapes). Chairperson (or two or three, as you wish) introduces the program and tells the audience how much this class has enjoyed the poems they are about to present, etc. Begin with a choral-speaking number. Keep it light and amusing. (Later, we can do some mysterious and serious material.) Then have two or three single readers. They introduce their poems, tell why they chose them, talk a little about them, then read. Sometimes this can be accompanied by music.

For variety, sing a couple of songs. Good songs, after all, are poetry. Do more choral speaking and more solos. You could include some "interviews" with poets. Include poetry written by the children themselves. Many of the "readings" will have been memorized.

The poems could be projected on an overhead. This gives the listeners a visual aid as well. This might be very important when the children are reading poems they have written.

Lighting can make a difference. If you have colored lights, they can be used to suggest moods — blues for sadness, reds and oranges for joy, etc. A spotlight on a speaker is good. A film-strip projector can be used as a spotlight. It can also be used to create mood backgrounds. Draw a colored design on a blank slide, then project it — out of focus — on the back wall. This can give all kinds of interesting effects.

The whole program should be smoothly organized, and should not be longer than 15 minutes. In this way, the interest is sustained, and everyone goes away wanting more.

Poets in Schools

It is becoming a more common practice to bring poets to schools for periods varying from a single day to a week or more to work with children and teachers interested in writing and in reading poems. These programs offer many children the best opportunity they may have to learn how to work most effectively with language and with writing. If language learning includes exposure to, and writing of poetry, children will be able to use language more appropriately and more effectively.

> Visiting poets who are to be with students for short periods, let us say for periods of from three to five days, which is their usual tenure in a given school district, need to provide students with a structure which will make it possible for them to produce a substantial quantity of writing in a brief time span; and then they must allow, within the structure they provide, the freedom that students will require in order to write freely, authentically, and with conviction. Finding the balance between freedom and discipline is challenging; the visiting poet is the fulcrum upon

which the balance rests and by which it is achieved.
R. Baird Shuman

Poets in the schools can build in children an enthusiasm for words and for language structure which will increase their eagerness to experiment with language and to play in the future with style, sound, and structure. They can also give gentle nurture to students' self-confidence in working with words and interpersonal ideas and feelings. Thus, they can encourage students to develop a heightened ability to observe and react to their surroundings and to their inmost feelings. They can help each student to define his or her personal space and to function with it, ever seeking simultaneously to expand it.

When we invite poets into our schools, we make it possible for children to meet writers who are concerned with the real world around us. Rather than view a poet as someone who lives only an aesthetic life, children may come to understand that the genuine poet is concerned with life today, and that words and patterns of words are the poet's medium of expression. Poets manipulate and manufacture words to make public their private meanings. The Welsh bards called themselves the "carpenters of song". It is important that we teachers be aware of the continuity of poetry and that we consider the significant poets of our time along with their predecessors. Thus we neither put down the tradition of the writers of the past, nor undervalue the free-verse style of so many contemporary poets in the children's minds. In pre-literate times, poetry was a vital form of language. Prose is a by-product of the printing press, but the oral poets required memory to share their work.

The school should take advantage of programs that place practising artists in the classroom for direct involvement with the children, so that children and teachers may learn new techniques and develop commitment. Planned carefully, such visits can inspire follow-up activities in the schools.

Learning Out Loud

Poetry is earprint. It longs to be said aloud. It plays with language and with the sounds and the rhythms of language. Very young children know about poetry. They clap alone, sing along, and join in with rhymes that are hundreds of years old. We can bring poetry to the ears of our children in many ways.

It is the constant ear training that will bring children to see need for poetry. This happens not through being told what poetry is, but through finding poetry in your own time and space. Children who are exposed to much poetry will become critical, creative, and compassionate about language. Children who have experienced poems through the ear will meet them in print much more easily and, perhaps, seek them out throughout their lives.

Beware

We need no reason
to teach
a poem
other than
the poem is
and I am
and you are

Poems hover above
teaching goals
like will-o-the-wisps
and dragonflies
darting here
landing there
motionless in the air
on their own
controlled by forces within
and we without
can only wonder

D. B.

1. We can read poetry aloud, at various times during the day, quiet times, and fun times. We can use curriculum-based readings, reading three or four poems at one time with no comment, reading three or four poems by a particular poet, using poems as our source for dramatic exploration or for discussion, looking at the content of the poem as we share it, and putting it on the overhead so we can all join in the reading of it.
2. We can have tapes and records and films of poets reading their own works, and of actors reading poems. We ourselves can make those tapes, as can our children for each other. The act

of tape-recording a poem is a special kind of learning. It demands very keen reading and careful observation, as well as subtle interpretation. There can be no more useful practice for a child orally interpreting a perfect piece of poetry. We can add music under their reading, and we can add sound effects.

3. We can have children read aloud the poems they've written themselves, poems they've patterned, or poems they've created. By bringing their own words to life through oral interpretation, children come to hear the sounds of language. A new kind of life enters the words they write when they share those words with someone else.

4. We can investigate having children read children's writings other than their own. They can work in pairs reading each other's work, or reading each other's work together. They can also present a poem written by a child as a choral-speaking selection.

5. Children can read poems they have discovered themselves. By having many anthologies in the school library and the classroom, children can bring to the attention of others the poems they themselves have enjoyed. This gives them a reason to read aloud, in that they are sharing what other people have not seen.

6. The class can read poems chorally, from overhead transparencies, from charts, from textbooks, from wall charts, from blackboards, and from handouts. A class can have its own choral-speaking file to take out at various times during the year for themselves or for guests. They can think of reading aloud as normal, and the cadences, rhymes, and the language of poetry will give them strength in all aspects of language.

7. They can make poems together — group poems, list poems, collective poems — and then use these as the basis for their oral reading.

8. They can find poetry in daily life, in advertisements, in travel brochures, in novels, in letters, and in diaries. They can begin to notice things especially suited to poetry.

9. Bulletin boards can display poems or poetical language that children have discovered. The pieces are grouped by theme, by form, and by idea.

10. Children can bring into the class songs that are poetical. They can share lyrics, sing the songs with the class, and play tapes and records of the songs. They can separate the lyrics from the tune to see if they stand on their own as poems.

11. Poets can be invited into the classroom to read their own work. Songwriters can play their own songs and accompany them with guitars, piano, or whatever instrument they choose.
12. Older students can present poetry they have created or anthologized into classes of younger students.
13. Booklets of poetry prepared by the school board can be used the next year as sources for oral reading.
14. Friday afternoon can be a sharing time where children can read their own poems and bring in poems they have found, and where the teacher can share poems he or she enjoys.
15. A class of older students can prepare a poetry reading for younger students (they might want to involve them in a "join-in" activity).
16. The children can translate the poem into a visual representation — a painting, a sculpture, a cartoon.
17. Several groups can be given the same poem, and explore it orally apart from each other. When the groups come together, they can explore the various interpretations aloud, and can come to understand the many possibilities open to readers of poetry.
18. The child can use the poem as a starting point for writing about the poet's intent, the voice of the poem, the unseen audience, the questions that arise, and the feelings that are revealed.
19. Choose the poems for your children carefully. Every class has a different chemistry, and requires a special selection of poetry if you are to build successful teaching moments. Even from day to day, a class' attitude alters, thus, an effective teacher must consult the needs of the children.
20. If children feel that poems should always have an identifiable rhyme, it may be that they have experienced only one mode. We should expose our children to a variety of forms and language, so that their poetic backgrounds are enlarged and their frames of referenece are increased: poems of various length and format, some readily comprehended and others that stretch the mind, some with available language, others that build up layers of meaning. As well, some favorites can be selected from poems of the past, while contemporary or modern poets can be read for a balanced diet.
21. A "poetry zoo" can be created. The children can build box cages for each creature and fill them with appropriate poems.

Artwork can be added to create the "poetry zoo".
22. Poetic dictionaries can be collected by individual children or by groups. As special phrases, words, or passages that hold a poetic quality are read in books and magazines, they can be recorded in the poetic dictionary for use in writing.
23. Art prints, photographic ads, and original art can be used to complement specific poems. Members of a group can pore through anthologies to select the poem that best fits the visual.
24. A character from a novel or a picture book can be represented by a particular poem chosen carefully to suit the character.
25. Children can choose a "Poem of the Week" or month, or for a special occasion. This poem can be written in a special fashion by volunteers and displayed for the class. When a child has a birthday, the class can create a group birthday card by selecting a special poem in honor of that child. As well, a "Poet of the Month" can be selected and each day a selection by the poet can be shared. Information about the poet's life or background can be included — photographs, records or tapes, and biographical details.
26. A weather calendar can be extended by having the children find a poem that represents the weather of the day. The poems can be copied and placed in the *Weather Book*. The seasons can be welcomed and abandoned with a selection of poems and songs.
27. Read poems to the class in two ways: 1) where the children do not have a copy of the poem in front of them; 2) where the children do have a copy of the poem in front of them. How are the responses of the children different in each mode?
28. We can let the children browse at their own pace through a book of poems.
29. In small groups, the children can read poems to each other.
30. The children can create their own programs of poetry to be read aloud or to be taped for others to listen to.
31. The children can choose poems they have enjoyed, to be read again by the teacher.
32. The teacher reads aloud to the children poems that he or she recently read and enjoyed.
33. The children can begin by filling in blanks in poems they have heard before or that involve simple predictability. The reverse process can also help children learn poems, as you cover words

or phrases that children are reading aloud, until eventually they have memorized the whole poem.

The Bird

The bird you captured is dead.
I told you it would die
but you would not learn
from my telling. You wanted
to cage a bird in your hands
and learn to fly.

Listen again.
You must not handle birds,
They cannot fly through your fingers.
You are not a nest
and a feather is
not made of blood and bone.

Only words
can fly for you like birds
on the wall of the sun.
A bird is a poem
that talks of the end of cages.

Patrick Lane

5
When Children Write Poems

Tinkering

I love beginning with
a clean sheet and
laying down each grease-black
cog and bolt and link
aligning positions
adjusting tensions and
checking for wear.

I love finishing in reverse order and
picking up each clean, oiled
sprocket, nut, and washer
spinning the wheel
and hearing only the whirr
of everything in place.

Diane Dawber

Children as Poets

While children may not be poets, they share many of the qualities
that poets possess. Their feelings are out front. They love word
play and they respond naturally and without guile. If they have
the opportunity, they will enjoy expressing themselves in poetic
form using poetic language, very close to that the poet uses. There
are three basic ways to have children write in poetic fashion:
1. Give them poetic patterns and structures on which to hang their
   own ideas.
2. Have them use poems as forms for expressing thoughts and
   feelings.
3. Restructure what they have written into a more poetic frame.
   The poems written by children may not possess the true literary and artistic value of good quality poetry, but they do demonstrate their ability to use language to shape ideas into emotions.
Sometimes the impact of their writing is as strong as that of many

"real" poets. The simplicity of their prose pieces in free-verse style can create a poetic sensibility. Balanced by the children's reading and listening to the poetry of accomplished artists, their own writings take shape and value as responses and modes of expression. Myra Cohn Livingston questions the validity of children as poets. She feels it is a myth to call the child a natural poet: "Children may have the intuition of the poet, but that natural fresh vision may disappear as they become hampered and hemmed in by style and technique." However, for children, writing poetry has a special value.

> More self-conscious and more self-possessed. They begin to perceive the discrepancy between the thing made, its order and purpose, and the meaningless dissonance of life in this place. They see discrepancy between things as they are and as they might be. Children must learn to look ahead, try out the possibilities of feeling and form, work with the unexpected, the chance to examine their own habits of perception, of thinking and feeling. Writers must be seen as real individuals to whom things matter and matter to us. They must never lose the sense of possibility. We will find aggression in their work, conflict, things that disturb us, perhaps gross or violent items. They will be playing with words and with their ideas and their feelings, and their hands make it dirty. Perhaps poetry gives us this strange freedom-and-control mixture and helps us live with the tension of life, managing our own worries with feeling and fantasy. The question may not be, "Will they speak their minds? but will they use their minds at all?
>
> Michael Rosen

If we want children to develop a sense of self, then poetry is a medium we need.

Children should have the opportunity to create their own literature. As creators themselves, they become more appreciative of the efforts of others. The more children write, the greater the need for input, and the deeper the children become involved in the search for meaningful language. But being creative isn't easy — especially in print. Children require many frameworks and stimuli to assist them in getting started. Poems, songs, and chants contain strong rhythm, refrains, and repetitions that the children can borrow and adapt for their own writings. When literature is a stimulant, the children need not borrow the content — they can absorb the characters, settings, story ideas, and patterns which they can recombine. Reading aloud in groups, dramatizations, and discussion are vital if children are to acquire vocabulary, styles, and language structures. One of the best ways to enjoy reading poetry is to write poetry. It will not be easy:

> *The poet does not get a free ride on the wings of imagination.*
>
> David Swanger

At this point it might be asked, "What is the purpose in attempting to write verse or poetry? After all, the majority of us never will become great poets." True enough, and the majority of us will never become Rembrandts or Picassos, but we see nothing amiss in taking *art* lessons. We reason that the creative urge is present in all of us, and that exposure to materials and practices will give pleasure, plus a more real appreciation of the accepted artist. The same is true for writing verse or poetry. Admittedly, the earliest efforts of most writers will be bumbling and derivative. This does not mean, however, that the writer is not learning things of immense value. If you can write a three-line poem, putting across an idea or emotion succinctly and clearly, then you are developing an ability to control language, an ability that will make your longer and more formal pieces much easier to write and to read. It must also be remembered that there is a difference between *writing* and *learning to write*. *Learning to write* precedes *writing* . . . a paradox really, because the *learning-to-write* stage demands much *writing*, and even when a person has embarked upon *writing* a serious poem, he or she must constantly keep up the *learning-to-write* skills, and daily play with words, groups of words, and the mechanics of language.

> *The poet and the scientist. . . both are willing to waste effort. To be hard on himself is one of the main strengths of each.*
>
> *Each is attentive to clues, each must narrow the choice, must strive for precision.*
>
> Marianne Moore

Isn't that what we do in all our writing?

The word *poetry* comes from the Greek word *poiein*, which means *to make*. Why should children be encouraged to write poetry, to *make* poems? Here are some of the reasons:

1. We all like to make things. When we are very little we love to make mud pies, and later on airplanes. We love drawing and painting. We like to make things.
2. We all like order, structure, and organization. This we must have when we write poetry. We enjoy it in games, so why not in the game of putting words together?
3. We all like jokes: a joke is a game with words; a poem is a game with words.
4. We all love slang. Poetry and slang are very much akin, in that each uses language swiftly, vividly, and often in an unorthodox fashion.
5. We like sharing our ideas with others.
6. All humans are emotional creatures. We like to laugh and cry, feel happy, sad, or nostalgic. Poetry allows us these experiences better than any art form, for we can express all these things in words.
7. We are all rhythmic creatures, from the beat of the heart to the intake and output of breathing. Rhythm is a part of poetry.
8. The more we mess about with words, the more intrigued with words do we become. The more words we have at our disposal, the better we can think, thus the better we can write.

> The sparkling blue pond, oval shaped,
> Was disturbed by the storm.
> The bright forest became dark.
> > *Wendy* (age 10)

> The snow passed by.
> The taste of it was shivery.
> > *Shahid* (age 9)

> O cold gray sky
> Witness of the hush
> Of early morn,
> Slow suffused with flush
> Of faintest pink,
> Awaiting those rays
> Which herald in
> The sun with gorgeous blaze.
> > *Mary Craven* (Age 14)

In the time of drastic budget-cutting and a new emphasis
on "Back to Basics", people often ask me "why poetry?"
Is it just a frill, one of the niceties we can just as well do
without? It has been my experience that poetry is a basic
tool for communication, a tool which belongs to us all; use-
ful because it helps us to say what we need to say in the
fullest and most authentic way we know.

Beyond Words

David was twelve years old. A silent, worried child who found
a vehicle for expressing his own fears:

Alone

On a window sill
three feet by one
Five stories up
The window is locked
People stare, laugh
But none try to help.
Different, very different,
Not like people at all.
I know their habits.
I watch always.
Their stares never cease.

This six year old found a metaphorical truth in his ideas and
arranged the words on his paper to look like a poem.

Trees

Two big, old trees
Stand
Out in our lawn.
It is boring
To hear them groan.

Morna, at seven, writes her poem with wordwise understanding.

Unicorn, unicorn,
In the woods
Where are you?
The sun shines high
In the sky
But where are you?

Maiden, maiden,
I am here.
I'll come to you,
By the lake
In the moonlight,
I'll wait for you.

When Jay, at seven, wrote his first poem, he wanted to "write like a poet does."

The Father
sits
and
waits
for
the son.

Six-year-old Susan had feelings to express, and her composition gave her the format for, and the satisfaction of clarifying her feelings.

I love my mother and father.
And they love me.
When you love people,
They look nice.

William, at eight years, is able to choose words wisely:

Oh Grizelwump
with your icy smile
slither and squirm
away from here
I have no use for your
wizardry.

Ideas for Writing Poetry

Children can write poetry from their own lives and their relations with people — parents, adults they know, relatives, siblings, friends, enemies, neighbors, new babies, and new neighbors. They can write poems about their schoolroom — activities, games, favorite subjects, speakers, weather, the teacher, the custodian, and the principal. They can write about the environment — things that grow, animals, insects, birds, lakes, rivers, mountains, seasons, weather, and clay. They can write about special occasions — Christmas, Thankgiving, Valentine's Day, the last day of school, the first day of school, Groundhog Day, the first snowstorm, and the first warmth in spring. They can write about buildings — old, new, tall, small, beautiful, and ugly. They can write about bridges, factories, machines, people at work, and transportation. They can write about the rural experience — the country, farms, fields, orchards, crops, farm animals, woods, forests, streams, lanes, and footpaths.

Most of all, they can write about life, family, what they do each day, and what they see. Ask: What surrounds them? What touches them? What angers them? They can make sense of their feelings with this art form called "poem". They can respond to any stimulus and shape the content with poetic structures.

Children can write from their personal experiences that may be immediate, fresh in their memory, remembered from yesterday or yesteryear, or imagined experiences where they were transported into new countries, new realms, new families, new situations, and new dreams. Vicarious experiences may be as powerful as immediate ones as sources for writing poetry. Books, novels, short stories, and folktales can suggest ideas for poetry and even offer words, phrases, and rhythms that they can manipulate and make their own. When a picture book that is an illustrated version of a poem is used with the class, the children may want to make their own illustrated versions of poems they have read or written.

The poem must not be presented as an item to be marvelled at, nor as a model for composing only. As well, the children must choose the poems and find the reasons for wanting to read them, and they must be aware of occasions when the writing of poetry is useful and significant. Writing poetry is a natural adjunct and complement to reading poetry. However, the two are not necessarily two sides of a coin. An understanding of how a poem works is built up over time. As children play with words in their own writing, explore form, and read the writings of others in class, they begin to understand the impact of form on writing and the use of poetic structure for making particular meanings.

Patterns For Poems

Kenneth Koch uses the approach of having children read "adult" poetry in class, discuss it, and then write, using that poem as a model. Like the experience of having an artist in the classroom, it is one method of having children begin to look at poetic form as an avenue for expression. It may not be the way a poet writes. Similarly, the difficulty with rhyme leads many teachers to eliminate its use when children write poetry. Children's own verse, from playground to nursery rhymes, is full of rhyme and strong rhythm, so we are asking children to listen to their own natural lore and yet to write in a contrary mode. The problem for children may not be in finding topics to write about, but in noticing how words work and attending to those words. In that way the children will be enabled to put their messages down in a way that gives a very particular type of satisfaction. Somehow, the children collaborate with the forms of poetry in an attempt to express their ideas and feelings. It may be then that children must find things they want to say for which poetry is a workable mode.

Children may be given a topic, then asked to list words suggested by that topic, and then turn them into descriptive lines. They may be asked to use specific patterns, word count or syllable count, to fit a certain metre or rhythm. All of this may be craftlike, as in making a plasticene ashtray, but have little to do with art. However, sometimes, we need to play with that plasticene, with its texture, its density, its shape-making possibilities, before we can release our own feelings into it. Sometimes, patterns are a way to begin, but they must never be seen as emotionally committed poetry. Poetry usually doesn't spring from satisfaction with things as they are, but rather from our doubts and desires and our fears. It searches out new possibilities; it would change things. But allowing children to follow any feeling or thought to see where it might lead is too experimental, too risky. We must help children consider and develop their feelings, not merely list them. We try to understand our feelings, to step aside, to look in the mirror, to reflect. The teacher of poetry accepts first and helps second. Much of the language of children's poetry is sparked with spontaneity, naturalness, and informality. We can free children with form by giving them patterns and shapes on which to hang their words, arrangements of print to hold their feelings and ideas.

There are many formats and shapes for children to use in placing words in their attempts to write their thoughts and experiences within poetic structures. Good teachers always remember function before form; but sometimes children need shape and pattern to assist in their struggle to mold ideas. Here are a few formats to try:

Acrostic Poem   Free Verse
Autobiography   Haiku
Ballad   Limerick
Cinquain   Narrative Poem
Comparison Poem   Nursery Rhyme
Concrete Poem   Riddle
Description   Shape Poem
Dialogue   Verse
Found Poem

Poems that children read can represent patterns for them to use in their own writing. Because a poem is such an intense and compressed art form, the very way the words are placed on the paper may encourage the child to think in those patterns. That is not to say the child should be a slave to the difficult form in poetry, or of worrying about word or syllable-count instead of making meaning. Form can give children a sense of control and a sense of the economy of poetry. The main goal of putting down thought that explores the writing of pattern poems may be a precursor to revealing feelings and ideas through poetry.

By presenting poems written by good poets as well as by other children, children can use patterns, concepts, and elements that touch them, engage their interests, or draw attention to form. They connect outside print to inside ideas. Even poets find that their own writings are often triggered by poems by other writers. Poems can evoke in children the urge to write, to create an original poem. Starting with the pleasure, entertainment, and satisfaction of reading good poetry, the children respond to imaginative wanderings or empathetic experiences. Sometimes the feelings that emerge as the poem is read will act as a catalyst for the child's own emotional release or clarification. The ideas that a poet has explored can suggest routes for the child's own wonderings and wanderings.

Some children may feel like imitating the complete poem because of the powerful emotional experience they have undergone while reading it. On the other hand, the response to some poems may be stored up and released at a later date, in which case the teacher may not know the stimulus for the writing.

Reading poems written by other children may cause the readers to want to join in and write their own. However, we must see what children have written as a developing process rather than polished works of art to be examined critically.

Poems that act as models and sources for the children's own writing often have an immediate appeal — the emotional connection, the poetic pattern, and the techniques the poet used. Because it is a model, the poem must stand up under several readings, so that the child/author can internalize what is needed for the new poem to be created.

Still More Words

A good way to start is with words. Loosening up the muscles, we start writing lists of words; write a list of *happy* words: mirth, sunny, laugh, fun, pleasure, delight, merry, cheerful, jolly, jollification, joy, smile, glad, guffaw, jocular, jocund, optimistic, etc.

Then write a list of *sad* words, *country* words, *loud* words, *quiet* words, *big* words, *little* words, *old* words, and *new* words.

Then try this: Write as many words as you can think of for *green*. There are many different kinds of green, aren't there? Do the same with red, pink, blue, black, and yellow.

Take one word, and then write down as many words or groups of words as float into your mind in connection with that word. This is a sort of stream-of-consciousness technique. You don't concentrate, but just jot down anything that floats to the surface. Some of the words may seem to be odd. That doesn't matter. For instance, for *summer*, one class wrote:

the beach/ice cream/hot sun on back/swimming/noises of pool/ shout/shriek/roses/smells/lilacs. . .etc.

Poets use words. The more words we can come up with, the greater the pool we have from which to select. After doing summer, try these: winter, ghost, spring, snow, fog, witch, hockey, etc. You might not go any further than this. On the other hand, you could try arranging the words and groups of words to form a free-verse poem.

> Summer,
> The beach, the noisy swimmers in the backyard pool,
> The hot sun pouring down my back,
> And the scent of roses.

You don't have to take this second step.

Simply getting used to jotting down the associated words is a very good exercise. Try doing this with Christmas — holly, ivy, snow falling, presents, turkey, eating too much, smells, sounds, etc.

Poets, as we know, are very fussy about the way they use words. Poets are very specific. We, too, must demand much of ourselves. Play with these words. Talk about the subtle (or not so subtle) difference in meanings here — crowd, group, multitude, mob, legion, host, bevy, pack, bare, nude, naked, in the buff, in the nude, starkers, unclothed, au naturel, etc.

Is there any difference among *fixed, immobile,* and *static?*

Which of these words are what we called PURR WORDS, and which are GROWL WORDS? — leader, master, fuehrer, boss, slavedriver, policeman, flatfoot, cop, pig, detective, shamus, private eye, gumshoe.

Which residence words would you use with which persons? — dwelling, home, edifice, building, dump, pad — writer, hack, drudge, scribe, poet, reporter.

Some of the words above are PURR WORDS (warm-fuzzies), while others are nasty GROWL WORDS. Are any of these neutral words? Will everyone in the group always agree?

Some words are more romantic than others; they have more emotional connotation than others. Words must always relate to the specific subject or mood. Which word would you use here:

The pirates swaggered into the: *pub, tavern, inn, dump, motel.*
The knight galloped up on his: *nag, plug, stallion, steed, charger.*
The man was: *old, ancient, rotting, decaying, aged, an antique.*
She was: *fully grown, pubescent, gross, overblown, fat.*

The chosen word will produce the desired effect.

Try finding the *one word* that describes: the room you are in, the town you live in, the car you have just bought, the car you wish you had not bought, the person with whom you have just fallen in love, the person with whom you have just fallen out of love, etc.

Try describing any of the above in as few words as possible. Then try writing a headline for a nursery rhyme in as few words as possible:

• for Jack and Jill: PAIR CLIMB — FALL
• for Humpty Dumpty: EGG BREAKS, KING'S MEN SCRAMBLE
• for Tom, Tom the Piper's Son: YOUTH PINCHES PIG!
• for Wee Willie Winkie: NOSEY LAD ABOUT TOWN

When you use words, remember that the writer's personal

experience will affect the chosen words' meanings. Pluto may be a planet, or a Greek mythological character. Beware that to many children he is Mickey Mouse's dog, and therefore, funny.

Writers

We try to push our words
Into phrases that will
Unlock the truths we know
Are hiding in the general mind
One step more, can we take
The world that one step more
For which it waits unknowing?
But the safe is held secure
By its hidden combination
Dynamite's no avail.

Yet there are those times
When the searcher stops his search
And the door swings open
As he no longer tries to push —

Or the key falls into his lap,
In a private moment.

Laura Baldwin

Sometimes just playing around with words can produce a "list poem." From words and groups of words suggested by children in one class, we made this poem (nothing added).

Black cats
Goblins
Pumpkins
Kids dressed up
Lots of gooey candies
Trailing up our street in the dark
Halloween!

The major thrust should always be the joy of manipulating words.

We are . . . misguided when we expect great truths or profound ideas from poetry, and measure the worth of any poem by these criteria.

Suzanne Langer

Poets are always comparing one thing with another:
- She ran like the wind.
- He sank like a stone.

Try finishing these:
- His voice sounded like . . .
- He sat there, eating his dinner like . . .(a starving piranha).
- He yawned like . . .
- The old car clattered along along . . .

and so on.

Another way of comparing things is simply to take a color, and illuminate it, thus:
- Red — as red as the maple leaf in the flag.

To begin with, most children will only add one word if you say, "Complete: As red as . . ." — "As red as blood."

This is not very original, but it must be accepted at first. Gradually we will work towards more interesting, original, and specific writing. One method is to force more and more specificity all the time. From "as red as blood", we can go on to demand, "Tell me where."

— "As red as blood dripping from a wound."
— "Now tell me where and when."
— "Blood dripping from a wound after a terrible battle."
— "Now tell me some more about the blood, use some interesting adjectives."
— "Rich red droplets of blood,/dripping slowly from the jagged wound,/after the terrible battle."

And so on.

The trick is to demand more and more. Using the word "blue", we could go from "as blue as the sky" to "as blue as the night sky" to "as blue as the star-sprinkled, velvety night sky stretching there above us". Try the same progression with all the colors: red, blue, green, yellow, pink, orange, etc. You could try the same progression with old/young, big/small, fresh/stale, etc.

Riddles

From here, the poem as a riddle can be explored. All poems are riddles to some extent.

Thirty white horses
Upon a red hill.
Now they stamp,
Now they champ.
Now they stand still. (Teeth)

In marble halls as white as milk,
Lined with a skin as soft as silk,
Within a fountain crystal clear,
A golden apple doth appear.
No doors there are to this stronghold,
Yet thieves break in and steal the gold. (an egg)

Encourage the children to make up their own riddles. They don't have to rhyme.

Personification

Personification is a powerful poetic tool. For example: The electric mower in the garden howled.
Or this: The refrigerator in the kitchen
— moaned and muttered.
— groaned and whinnied.
The wilder the comparisons, the better. Sometimes you can do it the other way; instead of comparing non-living creatures with living, try the other way: The vacuum cleaner danced across the room.

Stream of Consciousness

This time, let your mind idle. Here are the instructions: "Just sit there, and listen. Write down all the noises you can hear, both inside your head and outside." (ticking of a clock, person talking in the hall, hearing footsteps by my desk, pump and wheeze of my heart, etc.) Then, the other senses could be used (smell, touch, taste, etc.).

Completing Something
Another way of using language, playing with words, is to complete something already written, and follow a pattern. Here is an example:

Kids flying out of school:
A hundred popping champagne corks

The second line illuminates the first. The writer could take the first line and complete it differently:

> Kids flying out of school:
> happy bees swarming

Remember, these are all exercises. Just as a person who wishes to become a competent pianist will do scales every day, to exercise the muscles and responses in his or her hands, so the writer must exercise with words and putting them together. At this point, we are not writing for publication.

The next step might be *definitions*. Example:

> Loneliness:
> The old man on the park bench

The first line (word) expresses the idea, the second line illuminates it. Try these:

> love, anger, home, history, dog, lion, elephant, enemy, etc.

> Hate:
> that dark brown, bitter taste

Cliché to Newness

A cliché is a tired old expression, like *as old as the hills*. At one time it was new and bright. Someone created it. Now it is old and tired. Try to refurbish these clichés into new comparisons that make us sit right up and say, "Yes, I never thought of it that way before, but that's right." Example: *as old as the hills* could become *as old as last Friday's doughnut*. Try these:

- as stubborn as a mule
- as sly as a fox
- as dead as a doornail
- as straight as a pin
- as dumb as an ox
- as white as a sheet
- as blue as the sea
- as red as an apple
- as black as pitch
- as clear as a bell

There are many more.

More Words To Play With

Write down one word for:
- the sound of rain on the roof
- the sound of a train in the night
- the sound of a hammer on metal
- the sound of a tennis game
- the sound of the sea (or a river)
- the sound of a milkshake's final drops.

Then, as with the colors earlier, expand, to tell where and when, and with some added adjectives to make the whole thing more colorful:

> As I lay in bed,
> the rain pattered on the roof above my head
> like a thousand tiny animals
> scuffling and pittering about.

Verbs are Important

Write down as many verbs as you can for the way a tiger moves: glides, shambles, slinks, slides, creeps, etc.

Do the same thing for a whale, a dog, a cat, a heavy caterpillar-tractor.

Movements which are less obvious come next. Write down as many words as you can think of for the movement of a fog, a snail, the grass, and so on.

Begin, as many will, with single words, the next step is to add to the one word to make it more interesting.

Slinks. . . the tiger slinks. . . becomes,

> the smoothly muscled tiger
> slinks silently and dangerously,
> through the deep green,
> of the jungle twilight.

Don't worry about over-writing. It is easy to pare down, and that is part of the process, as well.

Free Verse

Those lines about the tiger, above, are free verse. Expose children to many free-verse poems, so that they can see what it is all about. Point out that free verse has a rhythmic pattern, but that it is less obvious than in other styles. Some prose is so rhythmic that it could be written as free verse. For instance:

> Off ran Dingo — yellow dog Dingo — always hungry,
> grinning like a coal-scuttle, — ran after Kangaroo.
>> *Rudyard Kipling*

This could be rewritten as a free-verse poem quite easily:

> Off ran Dingo —
> Yellow dog Dingo —
> Always hungry,
> Grinning like a coal-scuttle, —
> Ran
> After
> Kangaroo.

Several examples like this could be found. Now we might try a simple free verse, taken from this sentence:

> Twinkling stars in the blue sky look beautiful.

becomes

> Twinkling stars
> in the blue sky
> look
> beautiful.

Dividing it into free-verse form makes the rhythm stronger, and somehow points up the meaning and the emotions.

Here is one taken from what a little child said:

> Today
> I took
> All my toys
> And dumped them
> In the bathtub
> Because
> I was so hot
> And the water was
> so cooooooooooool !

Free verse of this kind is pleasing to write. There is some degree of control and structure, but freedom to put down personal ideas.

Primary Teacher

Miss Waite taught me.
Miss Waite smelled of lilac
Chalkgrained fingers *kindhanded* me
Through the year.
As the letters on the blackboard,
Squat, square, multicolored, real,
Jumped and danced in the sunshine of her smile.

[made-up words are interesting]

A *clatter* of geese
fantastically waddling
over the *jade silk lawn.*

[clatter — perfect word; and all the connotations of — jade]
David Gascoigne

Often it is advisable to give an opening line, and a situation; for example, *looking out of the winter window.* Have the writers actually look out, see what there is, pointed out by you: the snow-covered sidewalks, the colors of the snow, on roofs and trees, footprints in the slush, some sounds, the snowplough roaring and sucking, chains rattling on a passing car, and so on. This becomes:

Looking out of the winter windows:
Pockmarked footprinted brown slush sidewalks,
Christmas-card clean snow on roofs,
And the dinosaur snow-sucker
gobbles up our street.

(a group poem)

Another way of helping writers into free verse is to present them with a very definite pattern, from which they can expand. Write down the numbers 1,2,3,4,5. We are going to do a five-line piece.

Here is the situation: You are sitting alone in a deserted farmhouse. It is night. The wind howls around the deserted place. Strange noises are heard. You are uneasy, or maybe frightened. Line one: Write down *one word* to describe your feelings of being by yourself. . . if could be *alone,* or any similar word.
Line two: Write down one word describing something you hear, or your reaction to hearing something.

Line three: write down one word describing something you see, or think you might have seen.
Line four: Write down one word describing some action, either by you or by something else.
Line five: write down one word to wrap the whole thing up.
The piece might look like this. The title is "Deserted House."
1. alone
2. whisperings
3. shadows
4. gropings
5. exit.

The next step is to expand one-word lines. Sometimes comparisons help: as alone as, or lonely as (play with these).
• As alone as a ruined church tower
• As alone as a ghost town
• As lonely as a howling wolf. . .etc
Then do the same with each one-word line: expand it, with comparisons, telling where or when, and we come up with:

Deserted House

As lonely as a lost soul in a deserted chapel.
What are those whisperings, silences, whisperings?
A shadow of a shadow skitters across my sight.
Leap up, heart pumping, thumping:
And regain the safety of outside.

Charlie (age 10)

Another topic could be along similar lines — "The Haunted House". Mysterious and spooky pieces are much easier to write in this way than happier ones; although later a similar scheme can be used for lighter approaches.
• The deserted graveyard
• The ghost in the attic
• The shark and the castaway
The five-line format can be changed to four or six, as you wish. The point is that this structured approach helps the uncertain writer. Encounters with animals and assorted strange beasts can be productive aids.
Here is one on a snake: title — "Snake".
Line One: a word (or groups of words, if by now you have done quite a few of these) describing your feelings. You have been going

blithely about your business and are suddenly aware of a snake under you foot!
Line Two: Use a word, or a group of words, telling about its body.
Line Three: Use a word or words telling about the way it moves.
Line Four: Use a word or group of words telling something about its color or any sound it makes.
Line Five: Use a word or a group of words wrapping up the whole thing.

And so we have a piece like this:
1. Soft, squishy beneath my moccasined foot,
2. This long, slithery, dusty, beady-eyed string
3. Darts in coils away from me,
4. A greenish brown shadow on the hard ground.
5. And I remember Eve.

Once the writer has mastered a few of these, it is a good idea to ask for a more interesting title. After all, "Snake" is not too thrilling. Sometimes a title which slightly mystifies the reader is a good idea. It makes the reader want to read on. Incidentally, after and during this exercise, the reading of D.H. Lawrence on snakes, and Emily Dickinson on the same subject, will often stimulate new lines.

Another structure is this:
Line One: what it looks like
Line Two: what it sounds like
Line Three: what it smells like
Line Four: what it feels like
Line Five: a wrap-up, something to end the piece, and not leave us hanging in the air.

Some possible subjects: *snakes, tigers, lions, ghosts, space creatures, etc.*

Tiger

What's that strangled cough?
A lithe, flickering shadow
Slips, silent as a striped ghost,
Black on yellow in the jungle's green,
Burning bright!

Fred (age 14)

We are gradually moving towards using the senses. Another structure, which follows nicely after these, is the "senses" poem.

Many, many writers tend to use only the sense of sight, with a nod in the direction of the sense of sound, perhaps. A writer must learn to use all the senses.

Here is a suggested pattern:

Teacher: In line one, I want you to write down one word or a group of words, describing the most gorgeous sight you have ever seen.

(Much discussion has taken place beforehand, about beautiful sights, such as sunsets, dawns, little puppies, new cars, etc. It is wise to remember that one person's meat might conceivably be another person's poison.)

Teacher: I am going to give you an opening line. You write your word or words under it. Here is the opening line:
To me, the most beautiful sight in the world is
Write your line under it.
And we come up with *A little puppy.*

Teacher: That is fine, but could you expand it. Tell us where it is and what it is doing.

Writer: How about this: *A frisking, laughing little puppy, taking over my room.*

Teacher: Great, let's see how they look together:
To me the most beautiful sight in the world is
A frisking, laughing little puppy, taking over my room.
That look's good. Now let's add two more *sight lines.*

Writer: (after some time to work on it) I have a couple here:
The red gold of a summer day dying across the lake;
My granny's smile when she sees me come through the door

Teacher: Fine. Now, let's see if we can do the same thing with the sense of smell. (Much talk about the smells we like: *scents, perfumes, odors,* and other words to use for smell.)

Writer: I have one.

Teacher: Let's hear it.

Writer *Bacon in the pan*
We work this one over, adding interesting details as to when and where and we end up with this line:
Tangy, smoky, sizzling, early-morning campfire bacon

Teacher: Good, Now let's put it together: I'll add the line to start the smell section: *I like the smell of.* Here is the whole piece.
To me, the most beautiful sight of all is

A frisking, laughing little puppy taking over my room,
The red gold of a summer day dying across the lake,
My granny's smile when she sees me come through the door.
I like the smell of
Tangy, smoky, sizzling, early-morning campfire bacon.

and we have done a couple more, as well,

The crisp, clean brand fresh perfume of my Dad's new car,
New cut grass in the hot summer morning, etc.

The other senses follow. Working with a few writers, each contributing in this way, a complete *senses* poem can be put together quite rapidly. After awhile, the teacher says, *"I like the smell of"* sounds rather weak to me. Can you give me the same idea again, only making it more interesting?

Writer: Sure, here's one: *The perfumes that are sweet to my nostrils are*, and so on.

Some young writers put this together:

I love the smell of
Crisp, crackling bacon, sifting up through the pine trees;
The green, deep, whispering pines themselves,
Silhouetted against the silver lake;
And the look of
Fluffy new kittens, little black balls of dancing fur;
The smile in the eyes of my friend;
The sound of
Bells at Christmas, and carols in the frosty night;
The rumble, rumble, gurgle of my dad's motorboat;
The feel of
A crisp, green, new dollar bill;
Guck running down my chin as I bite into an enormous
   hamburger;
The taste of
The first delicate, white, new potatoes;
Deep, sinful, rich, dark-brown, chocolate fudge.

(Grade 6 class)

After working in a group, the writer can try a solo. The pattern, the structure, is what makes the writer comfortable.

Haiku

Another structured type of poem is what might be called the Word

Haiku. Haiku proper is based on syllable count. As a lead-in to the concept, try some word haiku. That means that there are three lines, with five words in the first line, seven words in the second line, and five words in the third line. (This parallels the real haiku which has five, seven, and five syllables.) Give the children the first line, and have them complete it:

> My little dog barks, jumps:

They add the second and third lines:

> Such a laughing, merry, friendly, smiling fellow:
> How I do love him!

After you have done several of these, you could have different patterns, such as:

three words	Such a day
four words	Blue sky, white clouds,
three words	I like spring.
two words	I know
four words	You hate it here,
two words	But, wait!

The pattern can be varied. The whole idea is to show the writer that there is *some* structure here. As in this:

two words	At night
four words	when I go out
six words	I see that bright, shining moon
four words	Behind silver clouds, hiding,
two words	So beautiful,
one word:	Alone.

Haiku is based on *syllable count.*

Line one: five syllables	Through the autumn day
Line two: seven syllables	Red leaves, yellow, fall from trees
Line three: five syllables	Lining my roadway.

A good way to start is to give the writers the opening lines, or line, and ask them to complete the pattern. For instance, "A Haiku on Snow" has the opening line: *From the winter sky.* The writers finish it. Encourage the beating out of the syllables, the overemphasis on the syllables. Encourage the writers to jot down lines. The idea is the most important thing; and if there are too many syllables, then a little judicious pruning will do the trick. Often it is necessary to show the writers that lines do *not* need to endstop, and that the idea can carry along over more than one line. It is also good to point out that little words like *the*, *a*, etc., may often be eliminated. Haikus are rather like Japanese or Chinese ink drawings: a few lines suggest far more than a fully delineated series of details. Thus, the haiku above, while it tells of the falling of the leaves, really suggests more; the end of the year, the end of a cycle, the end of life perhaps.

On Snowflakes Falling

The falling snowflakes
each one a cunning work of art,
I look at them in amazement.

Line One has the right number of syllables; Line Two has too many — 8; Line Three has 8 as well. The required pattern is 5,7,5. How can I reduce Line Two to seven syllables? How about: *Each one cunning; work of art!* Then Line Three must be reduced to five. Let's try *Look there! Amazement!* We know who is filled with the amazement. We don't have to hit the reader over the head. So, now we have:

The falling snowflakes
Each one cunning; work of art!
Look there! amazement!

One further improvement: the word *the* in line one is a weak word, impersonal. How about *Those falling snowflakes*, or, better still, *My falling snowflakes*. So, the Haiku now reads: (Title: always give it a title. Sometimes a simple one like this, or sometimes a more quizzical one to make the reader wonder.)

My falling snowflakes.
Each one cunning; work of art!
Look there! amazement!

Here are some professionally written haiku from various times:

Stubborn woodpecker . . .
Still hammering at twilight
At that single spot.

Issa

At this dreary inn
A hound keeps wailing . . . like me
Lonely in the rain?

Issa

One man, single fly
Buzzing alone together
In a sunny room.

Issa

The delightful thing about Haiku is that they can be written on any subject at any time. Also, even the youngest child can do it. Originally, as we know, the Japanese Haiku were all written on subjects involving nature. Equally, we know that the very strict 5,7,5 syllable count is not absolutely necessary. On the other hand, it is a pleasing constraint. Having a very specific number of syllables in each line makes it more structured, and we all tend to move more freely within a structure. It makes us feel better.

On the Difficulties of Writing

Hey there! You old words!
Jumping, twisting, burning bright!
I love you all; but . . .

There are two other advantages to the haiku: i) it is written and polished over a short period of time. Beginning poetry writers are apt to get very frustrated and unhappy if they tackle anything too long. With haiku there can be almost instantaneous response. The teacher can also look at each writer's piece and offer instant advice, criticism, approval; ii) brevity, as someone once said, is the soul of wit, and if writers can learn to control their language to the point at which they can express fairly complete thoughts and ideas in brief form, they are acquiring skill which will stand them in very good stead later on. (Did any skill ever *sit* in good stead, I wonder? Or stand in *bad* stead?)

Get into the habit of writing at least one, and possibly two haiku every day. It is usually easier for the writer if the topic is given. Often the opening line can get the engines primed. Always tell the writers to ignore the suggested opening line if they so desire.

It is essential that writers be presented with all kinds of daily opportunities to juggle words, rhythms, syllables, and so on, so that they gradually learn to *control* language. The thought behind most student haiku will possibly not go very deep, but this does not matter. Here we are doing further daily exercises. Occasionally a gem will pop up unexpectedly. That is serendipity, and not a goal to be pursued. "Daily, Daily, and Many Times a Day" is the motto. Here are a few possible opening lines for

Fall:
- Cooling afternoons
- How crimson those leaves!
- Evenings darken down
- Night comes sooner now
- Whirling, windswept leaves, etc.

Winter:
- Snow comes sifting down
- A blanket of white
- Freezing morning house
- Snuggled under quilts
- Bare, empty, landscape

Rain:
- Gauzy grey curtains
- Bashing down like nails, etc.

Three of these might be completed something like this: (Sometimes you can give the writers the first and second lines, or even the first and last lines, if they really lack confidence.) From *How crimson those leaves* we get:

> How crimson those leaves!
> How black and empty those boughs!
> From houses — wood smoke!

The title could be "How Crimson Those Leaves", or it might be "Fall Scene End of the Year, Summer Gone". Encourage titles which will make the reader think.

From "cooling afternoons", another autumn line, we get:

> Cooling Afternoons,
> Setting sun huge orange ball
> Low on horizon.

The title could be as in the first line, or it might be "Fields in Autumn, End of an October Day". It is a good idea to try for as specific a title as possible, bearing in mind that haiku are personal poems. One more line, *"snow comes sifting down"*, becomes:

> Snow comes sifting down
> Covering houses, haystacks,
> Fields, with white blankets.

Possible titles: "First Snow", "Scene From My Winter Window", "White Coverings".

Earlier, the idea of copying, or borrowing, was mentioned. As long as the borrower admits the borrowing, this is a good technique. Here are some haiku in which the writers very obviously borrowed. Recall the poem "The Mist and All" by Dixie Wilson:

I like the fall,
The mist and all,
I like the night-owl's
Lonely call —
And wailing sound
Of wind around.

I like the grey
November day,
And bare, dead boughs
That coldly sway
Against my pane.
I like the rain.

I like to sit
and laugh at it —
And tend
My cozy fire a bit.
I like the fall —
The mist and all.

Here is the Haiku:

I do like the fall
And those grey November days,
The soft mists, the rain.

November's here now!
Grey days, dead boughs coldly sway
Against my window.

Obviously something was borrowed here, and the haiku is stronger because of it.

An older writer, after relishing parts of Gray's "Elegy", picked out the line: Now fades the glimmering landscape on the sight.

Glimmering landscape:
Black tree trunks. Crimson red sun.
Streaks of dying day.

One of the duties of anyone trying to help others to write is to encourage and, equally, to point out occasional unknowing plagiarisms. We all do it. After reading and enjoying certain lines and phrases, we sometimes incorporate them so easily into our own repertoire that we are unaware that we are doing so.

Tanka

The next step would be to write the Tanka. This is a five-line poem, again based on syllable count. This time the count is 5,7,5,7,7, and is not as easy as it might appear.

Fall Maples

Bronze on azure sky,
These blackboughed maple giants
Burn through afternoons
Warm with end of summer sun
And loud with squirrel chatter.

My Enemy

How fat he; sloppy,
Jowly, slovenly, obese,
With saggy, wrinkled,
Dirty, ancient, greasy clothes,
And that nasty, leering eye.

The first line is given. The children complete the tanka from:
- This bright new morning.
- Thunder! Forked lightning!
- When I look at you.

Sometimes give the children haiku, and have them add the two lines to make it into a tanka:

Glimmering landscape:
Black tree trunks. Crimson-red sun.
Streaks of dying day

they add:

Crows winging their way homewards.
Smoke rising from evening fires.

Cinquain

Once you have tried a few haiku and tanka, and even a few linked haikus, and a few linked tankas as well, you might look at the *Cinquain*. There are various forms and concepts of the cinquain. All do agree, however, that it consists of *five* lines, and deals with syllable count. One form which is very popular goes like this: (num-

ber of syllables to each line): two, four, six, eight, two.
The first cinquain could be about that most fascinating topic: ME

2 I am
4 A kind person
6 With blue eyes, yellow hair,
8 And a great big, wonderful smile
2 for you!

As for instance, "Sorry":

Sorry
I said those words.
I really didn't mean.
To hurt your feelings. Honestly!
Forgive?

or "My Dog"

My dog,
A funny mutt
Of mixed and mixed-up breeds
Dances, smiles, laughs when I come home
Each night.

There is really no limit to the syllable arrangement you can use for a cinquain. The 2,4,6,8,2 form is popular, but how about 1,2,4,8,1?

Runners by the Lake

We,
Running
By water's edge,
See flickering shadows of trees
Dance.

Or you could try this syllable pattern: 3,6,9,6,3:

The Journey

Happily
We set out that fine day
Knowing that for us the sun must shine
And everyone be glad
For our sakes.

The 2,4,6,8,2 pattern is usually easier to write. Just as with the haiku and the tanka, so some cinquains can be linked to form a longer piece, as in:

The Old Steam Train Arrives at the Station

2 We saw
4 the steel monster
6 Steaming and scattering
8 Huge piles of white and dark grey smoke
2 Skywards,
2 And then,
4 With a squeal of brakes,
6 And mighty clanking groans
8 She slowed down, shuddered, squeaked and sighed;
2 Then stopped.

This idea of using patterns based on syllable count has great merit as most people are able to count syllables. Also, the discipline of working within a set pattern is a good one. It forces the writer to be specific, to use words in a very careful way; if there is a two-syllable word like "ocean", and only a one-syllable word wanted, the writer learns to substitute "sea" or some other one-syllable word. All this is invaluable practice, for poetry must be specific, must use the *mot juste*, cannot afford to be verbose, sloppy, vague, or foggy. Clarity and the desired emotional tone are brought about in this way, through constant practice in writing within a specific structure. Admittedly, this is a very demanding structure, but that is the whole point. If we start neophyte writers in the intricacies and entanglements of rhyme, we demand the impossible. We are likely to end up with such verbal slop as:

I have a funny little dog
He likes to sit upon a log
He looks just like a frog.

How much more valuable to have the beginner write Haiku, Tanka, Cinquain.

Borrowing is an ancient and honourable technique. Take this:

The Evening Sky

The evening sky spreads out its poor array
Of tattered flags,

Saffron and rose
Over the weary huddle of housetops
Smoking their evening pipes in silence.

John Gould Fletcher

Talk about it and then suggest that the writers change the *flags* to the *sails* on a big sailing ship, and take it from there. You come up with:

The evening sky spread out its rich array
Of billowing sails,
Bright white, blue, red,
Wafting across the dying day,
Sailing serenely onward.

Hundreds of examples can be studied. Use this as a base and as a means of building the confidence of the writer.

Four-line Verse

Another form of highly structured free verse (if that is not a total contradiction in terms, like Jumbo Shrimps!) can be written by giving a subject, such as *dog*. The writer must then write four lines.

- Line One is a noun (connected with dog, of course)
- Line Two is two adjectives (describing the dog)
- Line Three is three verbs (again connected with the dog, its movement, sound, etc.)
- Line Four can either repeat Line One, or can be a thought about the whole piece, a wrap-up, e.g.,

Puppy
Frisky, happy
Jumping, laughing, playing
How I do love you!

or

Doberman,
Silent, Fierce,
Watches, Warns, Guards.
Careful there!

or

Puppy
Frisky, happy
Jumping, laughing, playing:
Puppy!

The possibilities and permutations are endless. The shape need not be four lines. It could be more, or less. Nouns, verbs, adjectives, and of course, adverbs as well, of any required number will give a specificity and structure to what they write. The demands are simple, yet present. Vagueness is the enemy! The motto must be "le mot juste"!

Acrostics

Acrostics can be amusing. They are structured enough, and yet there is freedom too.

C	becomes:	Cheerful	or	Comical
L		Lovable		Laughter bringer
O		Optimist		Only he knows
W		Wonderful		Why each
N		Nice.		Night he weeps.

Here is an acrostic on *Columbus*, written by Jamie (age 10):

Charts
Of the oceans
Left lots out
Until he sailed across the
Main and
By chance discovered the
United
States.
(He didn't really, but it is near enough.)

Admittedly, not a perfect piece, but a beginning from which we might fashion something better, by extending it, perhaps.

Then you can do the same thing; write a word vertically and ask the writers to write *not one word, but a group of words,* like this: (using names is often a good idea)

G — Good friend to me
R — Real, ready to help me
E — Easy to get along with
G — Generous, a great sharer
O — Outwardly shy, really warm and nice
R — Ready for a laugh always
Y — You're lucky if you have a friend like him

This is the rough stuff. It might be worked into something neater, or it could be left. Acrostics can be used with people's names, historical figures' names, place names, things — the list is endless. From there you can go on devising ever more complex and difficult ways of doing it.

A point to recall: all poets try out weird and often very complex patterns. Look at various poems by various poets, from the point of view of technique. Ask yourself the questions: "How did the writer do this? Why? Was it successful?" As a writer of poems you have the right to ask such questions. If you only read, and never put pen to paper yourself, there is absolutely no point in asking such questions. There is no doubt that trying to write your own poetry makes you truly appreciate the poems of others.

If you want to get really tough with yourself, try something like this:

Line One: 5 syllables, and rhyme A
Line Two: 5 syllables, and rhyme A
Line Three: 2 syllables and rhyme B
Line Four: 5 syllables and rhyme A
Line Five: 5 syllables and rhyme A
Line Six: 2 syllables and rhyme B

As a warm-up, try lines rhyming A and B:

Line One: 5 Under the blue sky
Line Two: 5 Jamie, Jan, and I
Line Three: 2 Wander

Limericks

The appeal of the limerick is its prescribed metred structure. Humor arises from blending content with puns, surprising words, distorted meaning, and juxtapositions. Limericks foster inventive language play and help us think in different ways. The more inventive the line, the more interesting the limerick. The rhyme scheme is simple: AABBA.

The rhythmic pattern is simple:

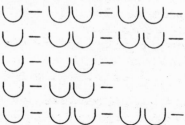

The topics upon which limericks are written are without limit. It is usually wise to censor limericks presented to you, before reading them aloud to mixed company. A few simple limericks follow. Most are by Anon:

> The limerick gets laughs anatomical,
> Into space that is quite economical,
> But the good ones I've seen,
> So seldom are clean,
> And the clean ones so seldom are comical.

> There was a young man of Calcutta,
> Who coated his tonsils with butter,
> Which converted his snores
> From thunderous roars
> To a soft, oleagenous/mutter

The greatest of known limerick writers was Edward Lear. His limericks often had the final line as a repeat, or a near repeat of the opening line:

> There was a young man called O'Brien
> etc. . . .
> That amazing young fellow O'Brien.

Children can have fun playing with the limerick. Start them out writing a limerick on their own name: There was a young fellow called Bill; there was a young lady called Patty; etc. In this way, we often avoid problems. One other point about the limerick: while the rhythm is as shown earlier, it is just as often:

$$\cup - \cup\cup - \cup\cup - \cup$$
$$\cup - \cup\cup - \cup\cup - \cup$$
$$\cup - \cup\cup - \cup$$
$$\cup - \cup\cup - \cup$$
$$\cup - \cup\cup - \cup\cup - \cup$$

Longer Pieces of Writing

There are several stages in putting a poem together once you have gone beyond the "five-finger exercises" we have been discussing thus far.

First, there is the *inspiration* — something strikes you, some sounds perhaps, or a view, or an action; something makes you think that you could write something about it. Then comes *putting it down on paper*. Here is where all kinds of ideas, approaches, words, groups of words, possible phrases are jotted down over a period of time. Some of these will be used later. Others will go into the discard.

The next step is to try to put these words into some kind of shape. This step could be called *clarification*. Clarification sometimes takes many days of working fitfully. At other times, it bursts upon you like the light Paul saw on the road to Damascus. Clarification includes your decision as to *how* you want to write the piece: in free verse, haiku, rhymes, or some other form. Now you mess about with all different possibilities for your piece. You write lines, scratch them out, change words, worry about bits, leave out adjectives until the right one hits you, etc. This level of working might take weeks, days, hours, minutes. The piece gradually seems to be taking on some sort of shape. Put it away for a time. Let it ride. Let the juices ferment. Let the subconscious mind work on it. Later, take it out, look at it again. See its weaknesses and strengths. Slash, change, enlarge, suppress, carve, smooth, as the spirit moves. This might be called the editing phase. This phase might go on for the rest of your life. Tennyson never stopped editing his pieces.

Here is a fairly typical progression. I went through this when writing a poem about the end of summer. Incidentally, and unusually, the first line actually suggested the piece.

W.H.M. Writes a Poem

The inspiration, or the idea of writing the poem, came one late summer evening, while I was sitting in the garden. Someone said, at one point, "Summer's nearly over now." It might have been "Summer's almost over now." The rhythm of the words hit home.

Here are some ideas which were jotted down:
Colours of fall
red . . . orange . . . russet . . . pumpkins . . . browns . . . oak leaves . . . maples, apples reddening . . . blushing? heavy weight of apple boughs . . . bending
Sounds of summer
summer evening. . . crickets . . . bashing? sawing? rasping? chattering? clattering . . . thin, thin sounds

Sights
on the blackness of night . . . warmth dying, compare dark night
with bright flashes of fireflies . . . thick draws the dark

General thoughts
squirrels preparing for winter . . . absentmindedness, always los-
ing nuts . . . compare professors . . . speed with which they nib-
ble windfalls . . . quivery movement . . . birds flying round . . .
preparing for winter migration . . . how do they do it? navigation
exercises, map reading . . . brilliant blue of fall skies . . . crystal,
crystal clear . . . cobalt . . . azure . . . cerulean . . . crisp . . . cloud-
less . . . fireflies . . . whiteness . . . like neon lights . . . strobes
. . . tiny strobes . . . silent flashes hanging in the hedges . . . like
rhythm there . . . chestnuts in green containers . . . so beautiful
. . . because so useless? like medieval ball on chain used by knights
. . . name (found much later to be Morningstar) . . . inside chestnuts the white velvet setting . . . like Cartier's or Tiffany's, color
of ripe nut like chestnut horse . . . haunch of glossy horse . . . bay
. . . stallion . . . auburn, cinnamon, mahogany . . . sounds at night
. . . smells . . . damp, garden smell . . . river-bottom smell . . .
colors in the dark . . . are they there? yes . . . feel the end of a cycle
of the year, and parallels life cycle too . . . gradual decline . . . rather
sad . . . and yet . . . sweet sorrow . . .

These ideas were all jotted down and thrashed around. The
inspiration and the *putting-it-down-on-paper* steps were done. The
next step was to try to knock some of the ideas into some sort of
poetic shape . . . *clarification.* As always happens, many ideas were
rejected. The first poem, after many, many drafts, came out this
way:

Poem for the End of Summer

Summer's nearly over now:
Apples blush, heavy, on bending branches;
Heatbugs rasp and saw
Through goldenrod endless afternoons.

Later crickets clatter,
Stitching warm darkness with thin strings of sound.

In the bushes a hundred fireflies
Flitter and fade, pointing the night
With silent white flashes.

A professor squirrel natters and chatters,
Rapid-mouthing fallen fruit,
Hustling his rustled nuts to special hiding
Against winter's coming;
Then forgets, in sunwarm days,
As another apple drops.

Businesslike birds practise navigation
Through the autumn air,
Whirring, gyrating, against the cobalt clarity;
So many precision pilots
Passing the secret word.

Long shadows in the afternoon;
Peaches yellow in mellow sunshine;
Squash brilliant and bumpy on market stalls;
And the occasional early pumpkin.

Evenings are cooler, nights longer;
Summer's almost over now.

W.H.M.

First I had tried a series of Haiku:

Squirrels

Businessmen squirrels
Invest my garden with nuts
Hedging winter bets.

Fireflies

At night, in my hedge
Hundreds of pale stars shining
Pinpoints of moonlight.

Crickets

Crickets stutter thin
Lines of sound in thick, warm, night;
Netting the darkness.

Birds

Flung against the vault,
Climbing the empty blue,
Handful of black birds.

Summer's End

Slowly summer fades.
Leaves redden, crimson, brown, bronze,
And shadows lengthen.

Here is my poem in rhymed couplets:

Summer's almost over now,
Red the apple on the bough;
Rust the leaf upon the oak,
Blue the gardener's fires smoke.
Purple grapes suggest perfume,
August marigolds still bloom;
Checking flight plans, white geese fly
Patterned vees on crystal sky;
Gold the summer's ending sun;
Black and grey the squirrels run
Chattering through the windfall grass.
Fast the warm weeks winnow past.
Bright the days, but cool the nights,
Flickering with a thousand lights
From a hundred fireflies;
Slowly now the summer dies.

It is not finished yet, in any of the three forms.

W.H.M

Following the series on the end of summer, have the children
try writing a series on:
• winter's here at last
• the early snows
• spring signs
• window on the night
• blizzard
• the old man (woman)
  Remind them to go through the steps:
• Inspiration . . . this is not really fair or natural. In real life the
inspiration would *come* to you. Here, as we are working for practice and experience in manipulating words, the *inspiration* step is
laid upon you.
• Putting it down on paper
• Clarification
• Editing phase

By this time, the children may be ready to play around with rhyme. The first attempts might be made with rhymed couplets. Give them a line. They are to complete the second line.

> The king sat on his golden throne;
> No queen was there, he was . . . (alone)

> The castle, on its hill of flowers,
> Had thick stone walls and . . . (towers)

and so on.

From the couplet of AA rhyme, you can then move along to other rhyme schemes, such as AABB, ABAB, ABCB, etc.

Writing blank verse is a good discipline. Remember, it has five beats to a line and they are iambics . . .

> The curfew tolls the knell of parting day.

Let the children complete lines, following lines that you give them:

> As I was going down our village street,

or

> My dog is fierce, his teeth are very big,

or

> When red leaves fall, and colder winds do blow,
> etc.

Ballads are fun to write. The pattern is usually the same. Read several ballads, and have the children try to write one, with this format:

Line One: four iambics	It was the happiest time of year,
Line Two: three iambics	When Robin and his men,
Line Three: four imabics	Went forth to shoot the king's red deer,
Line Four: three iambics	For they were hungry then . . .

The rhyme scheme is usually ABAB.

Another way to get started on writing might be to take a poem, read it, and see where the spin-offs begin.

Collective Writing

Many young children can write alone with ease and fine results. Other writers of any age many need to do a large proportion of their writing as collaboration, and some students may periodically return to collective writing for support or because group thinking is required. Collective writing workshops form an important adjunct to solo writing. Talking about a composition or trying it out on a friend helps a writer think out what he or she has to say.

Collective writing occurs when youngsters work together to produce a single piece of writing. The children decide together what they want to write and how they want to go about it. Then they work out what they want to say line by line, as one of the group writes it down, as well as making contributions. This scribing by a child is good practice in the transcriptive part of writing. In the process, someone proposes a line and others accept it or amend it. Members may have to stop and work out underlying problems of selection and organization before they can resume dictating. When the composition is finished, the scribe reads back the composition and everyone listens for places needing revision. Members can check punctuation by having the piece read aloud. Once the class can create a collective selection, the children can work in small groups with one partner, two, three, four, or five, as soon as the individuals can handle that degree of co-operation.

Activity directions should state the main steps, and as the children proceed you can find out if they need help. Some groups may need the teacher to sit in until they get going well; but the process will work well as a self-directed activity only if they become responsible for it themselves. The teacher should not contribute to the composition but rather suggest alternatives only on procedures. The class generates ideas that the theme or topic suggests; then the teacher writes in point form on the blackboard those phrases chosen by the class. These serve as the basis for developing poetic images and thought by the children; and a piece of poetry writing is created as a model for composition. Individual students can then write their own poems motivated by the group's efforts.

Example 1:
Subject: Poplar trees at night in autumn
1. Spider webs across the moon.
2. The boughs of the leafless trees interlace like the threads of a web.
3. They set traps to catch the moon.
4. I want to break the web and let the moon escape.

Trees at Night

The trees weave magic webs across the moon
With interlacing boughs,
Like giant spiders setting traps
To catch a tasty morsel.
Moon, shall I break the threads
And let you go?

Example 2:
Subject: Autumn
1. Red maple leaves are like flames or spears.
2. Both are pointed, sharp, fragile looking, but strong.
3. They make me think of the end of year, and of life.
4. I think of winter coming,
5. And my death.

> Fearful, I see
> Crimson daggers slash
> Scarlet spears strike
> Bloody flames destroy the days.
> Smokeless fires burn out the ends of summer,
> As red-coat leaves march in
> Winter's harbingers.

The children gain practice in turning ideas into images that suggest poetry, and often such brainstorming as this gives children shapes and suggestions for writing about their own interests on their own time.

I've found the cluster of forms known as collaborations to be extremely fruitful, especially as training. Due to the continual trade-offs in the compositional method, the burden of intentionality is lifted. Writing together we tend to concentrate on finding a common language to speak rather than on making a point. The absence of purpose tends to fill with association and response. Fragmentation of story and sense encourages a focus on syntax as play — a big attitudinal step toward mastery. I have often made collaborative poems with my own children, using any number of simple methods.

Jack Collom

Publishing the Poems of Children

The Product: "Methods" that add to the visual appeal:

- People *do* judge books by their covers; make the cover attractive, and for a professional look, repeat the cover design on the title page.
- Give the book an overall "look" by tying it together *visually:* e.g., use a *border* on each page, *typeset* certain pieces (such as titles or names), use a *design motif* throughout (such as a fancy first letter for each piece or a graphic pattern repeated periodically — known in the printing business as a "dingbat").
- Use *press type* (also known as "transfer type" or "rub-off letters") for titles, names, etc. Press type can be frustrating. Some tips: after using the press type, xerox your page, and use the copies for page make-up. Because old, dried-up press type cracks, always use a fresh sheet of the press type; protect your original pages by spraying them with fixative.
- Get typed pages reduced at your local photocopy store. Reductions are inexpensive; they look crisp, sometimes almost typeset; they allow you to get more material on a page. You can also use reductions for variety on the page. But don't go overboard and make the page tiny and cramped.
- Use *calligraphy* or some form of *"fancy"* lettering for effect, but use it judiciously. Usually, children can do this art work.
- If you need copies of a book for promotion, staple most of the print run to save money, but bind a few (most photocopy stores can bind, or you can bind them by hand).
- Because most of us are doing books in black and white only, capitalize on the *contrast* between these colors (especially if you're "printing" on a photocopy machine). Cut-offs, silhouettes, stencils, or collages work well — simply give students black and white paper. (A black page with white lettering or cut-outs is especially dramatic.)
- Collections of writing are usually enhanced by artwork and students love to illustrate their books. Some ideas:
  a) Pick out objects or places mentioned in the poems or stories and make a list to give students ideas for drawings;
  b) Hand out different sizes of paper so you get different-sized drawings (small pieces of paper help you collect miniature drawings like those that grace the pages of *The New Yorker*);

c) For younger children who may not be able to manage a small sheet of paper, you can use a photocopy reduction of their drawing;

d) Use black magic markers to get good contrast in the drawings.

- Headlines and other type of newspapers and magazines can be cut up and used effectively.
- Stencils can be used for lettering, which can be done by the students.
- Use art work creatively throughout the book — e.g., a poem can be typed *onto* a drawing.
- For picture stories or comic books, give the students paper with the boxes already drawn, and use a variety of box-formats (e.g., one page divided equally into fourths; one page divided in half, with the bottom half then divided in thirds, etc.).
- Black and white *photographs* can be used in xeroxed books — as art work (e.g., silhouettes) or to document the writing experience (classroom shots) or (as in professional books) to give the reader a picture of the writers.
- A *glue stick* is good for pasting down illustrations. Glue from a glue stick holds fast, but doesn't dry instantly; so you can make last-minute adjustments and straighten illustrations on the page.
- When getting work typed is a problem, and/or to capture the "feel" of the writing as children actually *write*, have children print or write their own poems or stories. These pages can be reduced and a border added.
- Get children's *names* on everything they do, and give them credit on art work, layout design, etc. If you do a play, do a playbill with credits for scenery, costumes, etc.
- Use other resources in the school: e.g., work on the anthology with art classes.
- Be on the lookout for inexpensive ways to add pizzazz to your publication: e.g., a saddle-stitch stapler allows you to make professional-looking books. If you decide to saddle-stitch a book, make a "dummy" of the book first; it will help you organize the layout. You can also use different formats: e.g., folding standard-size paper lengthwise and stapling or gluing the pages, makes an attractive tall, skinny book.

Far too much of the work done by children ends up in desk drawers or is consigned to pretty bulletin board displays — it ends up being forgotten. As much use as possible should be made of the children's work. It should be shared, read, enacted, discussed, reprinted, illustrated, and re-used in a multitude of ways. Reasons for displays should be tied into the ongoing work of the classroom. In this way, language is continually being spread throughout the class, helping to increase ability in both reading and writing.

The Process: Collecting the work and deciding what to publish:

- Keep the children's writing organized from the beginning — individual folders work well.
- Decide on some process for selecting children's work: each child may choose the piece he or she likes best although the teacher or writer may not agree with the selection); a committee of children may select from submissions contributed by the class or school; the teacher or writer may select the work; etc.
- Decide your editorial philosophy for this particular publication (a philosophy that can change with changing circumstances). For example: are you committed to publishing a piece by *every* child? This may be realistic with a small class but becomes infeasible with many classes or a whole school and only a limited publication budget. The general feeling among writers (who usually work with about 100 children) is that, if children are told in advance, they understand that an anthology will contain only selected writings and that not everyone will be represented. However, the writers then make certain that *each* child gets to participate in some way in a "culminating event" that showcases his or her writing (see: "The Alternatives" below). A word of caution: be certain that the *same* children (those who seem to be good at everything) aren't the only ones being published.
- All children can assist in the publication if the typed material is available early enough. You can hand out xeroxes of their typed pieces, and they can revise, copy edit, and proofread them. If at all possible, material for an anthology should be typed on a word processor so that changes are easy to make, and children can be encouraged to edit their own writing freely.
- Just as you need a selection philosophy, so too you need an *editing* philosophy — when and how much to change children's work. Most professional writers value the advice of a good editor, and copy editors leave very few pieces of writing untouched. Between the extremes of treating every child's work as sacred and molding every poem to conform to some ideal, there's good common sense. Most writers agreed on these points:

- they change spelling and grammar when it's incorrect but watch carefully for the offbeat (as in Kenneth Koch's "a swan of bees").
- they feel that invented spelling is acceptable for early drafts, but they find that children want their published work to be correct.
- they sometimes edit for "quality" — often by condensing the child's work. This is best done in conjunction with the child, or when there's time for the child to go over the suggested changes.

The Alternatives: Events and publications that can add to, or replace the traditional student anthology:

- *Broadsides* are single sheets of paper, usually containing one poem or story; they are often decorated with borders or interesting graphics or illustrations. Each child can do a broadside, and each broadside can be duplicated to be collected in a book. Broadsides can be displayed on bulletin boards or handed out in the halls (there's a political history to broadsides). Broadsides can also contain a collection of short poems, a collaborative poem by the class, or a series of one-line poems.
- Create *Poetry Postcards:* you can do this by designating four cards on standard paper (front and back) and having both sides photocopied back-to-back on card stock. A postcard writing day (with postage provided) can get children from other classes excited and involved. You can have children from different classes use the postcards to write messages to each other.
- Children love to create *Tiny Books* (use left-over card stock or cut pieces of regular paper). You can also create those "flip books" that are read by flipping through the pages quickly.
- Poetry Calendars are easy to make (just use a standard calendar format and add the writing and art work). They're also functional: they can be sold to raise class funds or handed out to parents with a school activities schedule.
- Instead of being a multiple-copy book, the class anthology can be a *one-of-a-kind book*. Each child can create his or her individual book, and copy out one piece for the "class book" or "library book." This can also work with a scroll format — use a long sheet of paper that can be rolled and unrolled, and have children add poems, stories, and pictures.

- *Readings* are a good alternative to publication. A reading can be an informal event in a single classroom or a larger event that features the work of many classes. (One writer set up a "poetry cabaret" in the school gym, complete with refreshments.) Children can form a *travelling troupe*, with older children going to younger classes to read their work, or vice versa.
- The school's *video* equipment can be used to tape readings of work (copies of the tape can be made for children who want a visual record of their class, or children who own a VCR can borrow the original tape from the school library and watch it at home).
- Children's writing can be shaped into a *play* or a *dramatic reading*, and different responsibilities can be handed out to all children: e.g., some are the writers, some the actors, some behind-the-scenes people, etc.
- When you print an anthology, do extra copies of various pages, to be used in a display.
- You can create an anthology that is primarily for parents and other teachers. This can be a short book (perhaps 10 pages) that briefly describes on each page the kinds of experiences the children shared during their writing workshop, with selected samples of children's work to show the writing produced. This kind of book allows teachers and writers to share ideas and give parents a sense of the context in which the children are writing.
- Children can produce their own *chapbooks* using any of the techniques described here. You can add to the professional look of these by adding interesting elements: e.g., an author's "bio" (get the children to write theirs) or blurbs on the back cover that quote famous writers (dead or alive) who recommended the book to potential readers.
- Sometimes one child does something so special (either a collection of poems or a story) that it warrants a special publication — seize the time if you can and help him or her preserve the work.

Harry Greenberg and Nancy Larson Shapiro
Teachers and Writers *Vol. IX, No. 2*

Assessment

How do we assess our poetry program? If anything is worth teaching, then it must be assessed or evaluated, so that we can tell how well we are doing. *We* includes both the teacher and the children. The first stage would seem to be the general gut reaction of the teacher: Do they seem to enjoy the poetry lessons? Do they seem to want more? Do they participate, and make interesting suggestions that show they are thinking? Do they talk about poetry? Do they bring poems from magazines, etc.? When it is a funny one, do they understand the humor?

These are all totally subjective ratings, but probably the best. After all, if the poetry lesson is the signal for everyone to groan and ask permission to go to the washroom — there is something wrong.

There are several structured ways of assessing the work in poetry.

One very obvious way is to teach three or four poems, comparing, pointing out various techniques, and then giving the children a *sight piece*, a poem along the same lines, with a few broad questions. If 80-90 per cent of the class do well in answering the questions, then you have taught it well. If most of them cannot answer, then poetry is not "alive and well" in your classroom.

After you have read several haiku, for example, and have had the students write along with you, give them a topic and ask them to write haiku for you. You will soon see who has grasped the notion of the haiku (or cinquain, or couplet, or whatever form you choose).

> But writing, to the young, should never be a task but a
> pleasure, the gratification of desire, and it can only be such
> when the writer is interested in his subject. [So said E.A.
> Greening Lamborn as long ago as 1916.]

Most humans, if the atmosphere in the room is right, can tell if something is good, or at least a good attempt. Again, if most of the class makes a poor showing, the fault lies with the teacher. The skills have not been taught — and there are skills and concepts to be used in the teaching and appreciation of poetry.

We must always avoid the twin pits: the intellectual one where we treat the whole thing as a simile safari, a hyperbole hunt, a punctuation search, a spelling quest; or the emotional bath, where we all simply wallow in vague delight: "I like it because I like it, because I like it." Or, contrariwise, "I hate it, I hate it, I hate it."

Picking a favorite from among three poems on the same topic, or by the same poet, and simply stating, "I like this poem, because . . ." is a simple test, and may tell you much.

Writing is risky business, as every student knows, and sharing honest writing is riskier yet. That's why successful writer-teachers work first to create trusting communities of writers in their classrooms; it makes writing possible for their students, and it makes adopting a fellow writer's stance safe for them as well.

Marie Wilson Nelson

Avoid such questions and statements as: What is the rhythmic pattern of so and so? Or: Note the rhyme schemes of the following. Or, worst of all: Memorize this, and write it out, complete with every comma and semicolon. (Many poems change their punctuation with every new edition.)

Jack Collom's *Moving Windows: Evaluating the Poetry Children Write* is an excellent book on the teaching of poetry writing to children. The author summarized his findings on assessment in these excellent nine points:

1. Candidness and innocence: The simple, unfettered realism children can have. The ability to see a thing as it is, not as it may fit one's world view. Children certainly have biases, which tend to be transparent. Children are also more capable of obvious contradiction, which helps in poetry, as Whitman let us know. These qualities lead not only to pure, simple "takes" on what's seen but also to revelations of the quirks of the human mind and to original use of language.

2. Energy: Children can often leap about rapidly in a richness of ideas and get this into their poems. Their verbal energy, once it's rolling, tends to be uninhibited. They also frequently invest their surroundings with a sense of life, speaking of even inanimate objects as if they had their own wills and spirits.

3. Surprise: Partly because their thoughts are not routinized, kids are likely to respond to the newness of each detail, which allows the natural surprises of the world to turn up in their writings. Their attention dances about, frustrating to teacher or parent, but a possible source of creative power. They also like to surprise, perhaps as a way of being themselves in the face of all they're learning. They create incongruities for the fun of it.

4. Sound: Rhythm and all the music of talk and poetry, including rhyme, assonance, and alliteration. I also include poems showing repetition, extended lists, and onomatopoeia. A physical

cluster of qualities is involved here; there's little barrier between kids and music. Children's great fault, in regard to soundplay, lies in its uncritical use, but they often demonstrate a delicate feel for music in words, especially when the writing is unstructured. Though children need direction, they usually lack the wide command of detail to work well in highly restrictive form, such as a set rhyme scheme. Their sense of rhythm emerges best when the writing is unstructured. Though children need direction, they usually lack the wide command of detail to work well in a highly restrictive form, such as a set rhyme scheme. Their sense of rhythm emerges best when based on their own speech patterns.

5. "Moves": By this I mean surprise as a recurrent quality of the language — sophisticated surprise that seems to emphasize the shifts in meaning more than the shock itself.

6. Show-don't-tell: Keeping the attention on the sensory, not the abstract.

7. Surrealism and metaphor: Images from the mind. Surrealism uses connections from dreams and the unconscious (or connections resembling those); metaphor connects, via one's thought, one object to another, usually in the external world.

8. Concision, shapeliness, and understatement: Shortening, shaping, and shutting up.

9. Empathy: According to its roots, empathy means "feel in" (whereas sympathy means "feel with"). The quality of reaching outside the self and becoming affected by the circumstances there.

There is no age limit on writers of poetry. We begin as children, we grow into young adults who still look to poetry as a medium for thoughts and feelings:

I am a ticket to the fair,
You found me lying
In the gutter of my thoughts,
Torn and tattered,
Worn by much handling and
    folding.

You took me up into your
Great clean hands anyway
And loved my faded colors,
Because you could see
What they once were,
And you revived my spirits.

For this I will give you many rides.

Jim McSherry, Grade 11

Johnnie's Poem

Look! I've written a poem!
Johnnie says
and hands it to me
              and it's about
              his grandfather dying
              last summer, and me
              in the hospital
and I want to cry,
don't you see, because it doesn't matter
if it's not very good:
              what matters is he knows
and it was me, his father, who told him
              you write poems about what
              you feel deepest and hardest.

Alden Nowlan

6
Choosing Poems for Children

For Poets

Stay beautiful
but don't stay down underground to long
don't turn into a mole
or a worm
or a root
or a stone

Come on out into the sunlight
Breathe in trees
Knock out mountains
Commune with snakes
& be the very hero of birds

Don't forget to poke your head up
& blink
think
Walk all around
Swim upstream

Don't forget to fly

Al Young

There are literally hundreds of poetry books for children today, all types of anthologies arranged chronologically, organized by themes, collected works of a single poet, the illustrated printing of a single poem as a complete book, and even talking books of poems read by the poets or by professional actors. Some collections may be very specialized, arranged around certain subjects, such as pets or weather, or around the origins of the poems, such as those from the Inuit or from North American Indians. Some may use a form of poetry, such as ballad or limerick, as organization.

Wise teachers must choose the poems that will have the most significant impact on their children. Some poems are useful for sharing with the whole class; the teacher can read them aloud several times, display them on overhead projectors or chart paper, engage the children in reading them aloud, and share both the shape and the form, the melody and the meaning of the poem. Other poems are useful for small groups to read and discuss or use as the basis for further explorations. Still other poems can be met one on one, as the child selects, reads, and responds to a particular poet or a thematic grouping of poems.

The teacher with a wide selection of poetry anthologies can provide the most service to the children and to poetry. With the help of the public library, the classroom library, and the child's own choice of books at home, the teacher can provide each child with the types of poetry most suitable at his or her developmental stage.

Some poetry is inappropriate for children. While there can be many levels of sophistication in a poem and different children can respond according to their own understanding, there are some topics that are not useful, such as some aspects of love, sexuality, theological or philosophical musing, and some types of religious writings. It is important to remember that the language of some poems may give the children so much difficulty that the meanings are obscured. Allusions, allegory, vocabulary, symbolism, syntax, are integral to poems, but the children must be able to understand enough to make meaning happen, to make the poem real. The conventions, grammars, and conceits of poetry must not surpass the interest and meaning levels of the children.

Poems must be normal modes of appreciation within range of the children's capabilities to be part of their educational network. They must not be seen as "exotic, esoteric, or irrelevant, or poetry will be seen as a source of frustration" (*Barbara Baskin*). These will be present in all poetry but at varying levels, but the images, ideas, and structures of a poem for children must have worth within the experiential background of the children. They should be able to interpret symbols, make sense of the images, examine the issues, and be emotionally involved in their new awareness. This does not mean that we as teachers should pander to children, choosing poems with predictable end rhymes only, or obvious, accented, simplistic verses. By our choosing poems that are grouped around some concept, the children can have their attention drawn to key aspects of poetry, and we can offer subtle guidance in helping children respond to the qualities that are poetic. The pleasures of poetry are very particular, and young readers that read accessible, intellectually demanding, and emotionally satisfying poems will sharpen their awareness of both language and perception.

> *Every poem in this collection will not speak for you, but perhaps one, or two, will. And that will be enough. A particular poem is not for everybody. It is for that person who reads or listens to it, finding in its words something that appeals to him. Not everybody will hear the same tune. If there is to be a beginning for most children, we ask teachers to bring the poem to them. We must do it in such a way that they want more. They want to continue to journey into words and feelings.*
>
> Myra Cohn Livingston

Reading an anthology of poetry can be a difficult task. As we turn page after page of unrelated poems written by various authors over the centuries, we ought to make sense of the bits and pieces, put them into a holistic frame, and this is not always easy to do. While they attempt to provide variety, anthologies may give poems by many authors in isolation. You read a short poem, turn the page and another one pops up. Conflicting styles, different contents, contrasting points of views, from one writer to another, can add frustration on the part of the reader. Perhaps we need coherence in an anthology, some type of underlying structure that helps us make sense of the poems on the page. There must be a context for the poems, a network of support that helps children make the most meaning possible. What context can we give children for appreciating the poems in an anthology?

One connecting tissue lies in choosing a sequence of poems by one poet where the point of view or persona emerges. Knowledge of the poet helps us thread together the poetic experience: one poem helps us understand the next. Themes that involve the child, such as school and friendship, while being less cohesive, can give a setting for the reading of the poems. Authors and editors can collect poems with strong rhythms, poems that touch on the bawdy or naughty, poems with funny rhymes as beginning points for presenting a cohesive picture. An illustrated picture book version of the poem can help children sense the poem as they turn the page and discover new meanings with each line.

Young children like poetry with songs and nursery rhymes. They can be illustrated, played, or danced. The pattern of sound, the color, the sharing with adults, apparently connects the nursery rhyme with the child. Rhyme stories such as those of Dr. Seuss or Margaret Wise Brown, stories with poetry embedded, such as the poems and songs in *The Hobbit, Winnie the Pooh*, and in *A Baby Sister for Francis* by Russell Hoban have a narrative strength that gives the poetry its strong appeal. Poetry chosen with a unity somehow gives the child an underlying understanding that ties the poems together, and helps the reader see himself or herself as a reader of poetry. The anthology, for all its value, must be carefully chosen, because most children read poems in an anthology containing several poets' work.

It is important that we choose the poems we use for children with a consideration of the content and the necessary understanding. It is a good idea to mix poems from the past with contemporary poems. Often the emotional impact of the poem will make the children want to read it again or to choose poems like that one. If poems are being read aloud, by the teacher, then vocabulary problems are not so great, and the emotional appeal of the poem will give meaning to those words. In using themes, you must be careful not to let the desire to find poems on that theme outweigh the value of the poetry. It is best to choose wide-ranging themes that are non-concrete in nature, so that many poems can be hooked into that framework and explored by children. For example "change" is better than "autumn". Children themselves can locate poems on a particular theme as they read through the various anthologies in the classroom, and thus build the framework co-operatively with the teacher. One issue within that theme can be magnified into a further thematic exploration.

Some publishers feel that a poetry book should not have illustrations. Some go all out and use lavish color in a large picture book of poetry. Mother Goose has been illustrated by almost every major illustrator. The answer has to be in what the child needs and in what the teacher feels would work most effectively. For that reason, poems come in a variety of formats. It is interesting to use different types of books for different types of avenues that are being explored with a class of children. Some anthologies work better one on one; others are put together for large-group purposes.

As children become more familiar with poetry, they begin to discriminate. If their ears become tuned to the subtleties of rhythmic patterns, they will begin to understand and detect rhythm and rhyme that is forced and mediocre. The language of poetry — the exact descriptive words, the sensory connotations, the evocative, delicate, precise language — is what makes good poetry. The secret of effective poetry is that it creates experiences that provoke strong emotional responses.

Finding the Poems

A wide choice of resources is vital in a poetry program. A competent resource teacher/librarian and a wide range of materials are your most valuable assets.

It is also important to maintain a classroom library containing books, magazines, pictures, audio-tapes, records, and child-produced material. This poetry library should be changed frequently: its material will come from the school library, from the public library, and from other sources, such as the children's own collections. Even if you do have a school library, your class should also visit the local public library if it is convenient. The school librarian is an important team member for the classroom and must be included in unit-planning if suitable resources are to be available for learning centres and whole-class sharing.

> The primary source for finding such poetry remains the anthology. A collection of poetry can be a quick and easy reference tool, simple to dip into for those few moments at the end of a class period when one wants to. Knowledge of the poet helps us to read a piece out loud just for the ideas or for the mood; or the anthology can be a source for sustained study. But simply having an anthology available does not solve the selection problem. Many poems which appear in anthologies do not work well when it comes to stimulating student interest in poetry. Therefore, a teacher must be quite familiar with the contents of many collections and select only those poems which will be appropriate for particular students. For the same reason, a particular anthology should not be kept too long as a prime resource. New collections appear frequently, and the teacher should attempt to become familiar with these, selecting those which seem to have the most appropriate selection to add to a desk or room collection.
>
> Charles R. Duke

For some children, poems are readily available — at home, in school, in libraries, at children's bookstores, and from mail-order houses. For others, poems are scarce commodities, and individual needs may seldom be met without the teacher's help.

For some children, meeting poems and songs as babies was an everyday occurrence, and sharing poems with loving adults was always a happy experience. For others, school provided the only poems they met, and those often took the shape of traditional lessons in appreciation or memory work, with little or no allowance for individual needs and wants.

Most adults need help in bringing the poems to children at the appropriate moment. We rely on knowledgeable teachers, poets, librarians, critics, friends, children's choices, and recommended lists to build our own selections. There are many books about poems on the market. As educators who work with teachers, parents, and children we are always building our own collections. These include poetry anthologies that work well in one-on-one situations, and with groups of chidren. Distinguishing between poems children want to read and listen to, and poems they can be encouraged to read and listen to, is a delicate balance.

Pre-school Children

It is important to introduce young children to poems, songs, jingles, and rhymes as early as possible in their lives. Psychologists tell us that the greatest part of our intellectual development takes place before the age of five, and another half of that again before the age of eight. The child's pre-school years are therefore the most critical ones developmentally. It follows that this period of a child's life requires the richest of educational experiences.

Poetry is not irregular lines down the printed page, but, in the words of Northrop Frye, "something very close to dance and song, something to walk down the street keeping time to". Poetry, with its shapes, patterns, and forms, its rhythms and rhymes, and its imagery, has been rightly called the music of language and literature. Young children have a strong affinity for this music: poetry elicits the most acute and active listening. It engenders conversation, and it stimulates all kinds of often spontaneous participation through movement and game and play. Young children should be immersed in poetry and music.

The Primary Years

How children feel about poems may alter in the primary years because they begin the process of learning to read. The fact that their ability to understand that their need for complex, meaningful stories doesn't match their reading skills may lead to frustration or eventually the abandoning of books altogether. Because the task of learning to read can be a difficult one for many children, it is important that adults continue to read aloud to them from as rich a selection of poetry as possible. Children must be encouraged to see in poems a world of excitement and satisfaction. As they listen to them, look at and listen to wonderful picture versions, join in with songs, chants, and poems, they will be building the necessary vocabulary, language systems, and experiences that will serve them well as they become independent readers. The initial enthusiasm that beginning readers feel about reading must be supported by and balanced by poems rich in language and image.

Poetry and song build a child's awareness of rhythm and rhyme and bring pattern and shape to print. Adults can sing or read the lines aloud, or share the print with children as they read together. Today, poetry anthologies and song books abound. Children can choose from all types to fill their particular interests. Some of the books are beautifully illustrated, while others depend on the strength of the imagination. Authors and song writers select past favorites, often adapting or rewriting them, and use well-known patterns on which to build new ideas and create wonderful new sounds and images to delight children through the ear. The language structure and vocabulary that are embedded in poem and song give word power for further meaning-making with print.

Adults who understand the need for poetry will continue to share poems with children, extending their young worlds, modelling a love of poetry, developing language and imagination, and building an atmosphere of trust and appreciation.

The Middle Years

The years between nine and twelve reveal the individualization of both the interests and the abilities of children. The lives of the children are filled with clubs, lessons, sports, and television, and poems can take a back seat if not supported by interested adults. Although many readers have reached a level of independence, their listening abilities still outreach their independent reading abilities, and therefore it is still important for them to be read to. The pressure of the peer group may determine their reading choices: those children with limited poetry success may need a great deal of support from adults to continue growing with poems. Poetry provides both sources for sharing and for silent reading. Children can learn about many aspects of life vicariously through poems while having enriching literary experiences. Since poems are forms of art, the perceptions and views built up through literature will give children a strong affective and cognitive basis for life as well as a secure grounding in the world of poetry.

An explosion of poetry for children in the middle years began with the success of Shel Silverstein. The humor, pathos, and wonder that can be created in a few words seem to represent perfectly the needs of these youngsters. The successful poets know both the interests and the nature of children in the middle years; they evoke significant and emotional responses that may surprise adults. Freed from the rhythms and rhymes of the jingles and verses of young children, the writers explore all types of formats of poetry. Children are able to join in the word play because there is intellectual and emotional satisfaction as well.

The Young Adolescent Years

In the beginning years of adolescence, the lives of children are changing drastically. These developments are reflected in both the content of the poems they read and in their attitudes toward poetry in general. Family patterns are changing. The young people are becoming critical of parents, of adults in authority, and of siblings. They depend more and more on peer groups. Children begin to have models drawn by entertainment stars, by sport heroes, by friends, and from books. Future careers are talked about, and they begin to look forward to their own independence, testing their own positions at every stage. Many develop a sense of history and of their own place in society; they are becoming concerned with justice and the unfair treatment of minority groups. They are able to understand better the complexities of issues. Of course, their physical development is a central factor influencing their lives, their relationships, and their identities. Poetry may provide insight into these changes, giving young people roles for identification, situations for reflection, and opportunities for examining issues. Poetry gives the young readers sensitive glimpses into all aspects of life and presents intimate pictures for personal experience. It is also a time for adults to continue to model reading aloud for young people, bringing them poems they might not select, and interpreting the words with power and effect. Adults who provide opportunities and materials for them must continue to observe their needs and wants closely.

During these years, some young people find poetry of particular interest with its emotional appeal, its unusual forms, its brevity, and its succinctness. With so many new collections written for this audience, it is important that poems be made available for both private reading and shared experiences, so that many adolescents will have opportunities to meet poetry during these formative years. The language of many contemporary songs has poetic quality and can be used as a springboard for exploring poems.

Bringing Poetry to Children

1. Collect your own anthology of useful poems. Categorize them under different topics:
   poetry that touches the senses; poems that involve sight, smell, touch, sounds; poems that have to be read in small voices, or shouted, or chanted. Let the actual experience of sharing the poem be a sensory one.
2. Choose poems that are comparable in their content, structure, and feeling. Let children experience three or four poems about flight, about love, about death; or let them become aware of how a poet uses poetry, by choosing poems with similar rhythms, melodies, metaphors, and images.
3. Select favorite poets and collect 10 or 20 poems by that artist, demonstrating the themes he or she chooses, the words he or she likes, the structures and patterns and techniques he or she uses.
4. Choose poems that celebrate special occasions, holidays, festivals, newscasts, news events, sports days, bake sales, students who are moving away, birthdays.
5. Find poems about the past, about the community or the country, about the hard life of the immigrants, or newcomers to this country. Choose poems about the land that they left behind, the hardships on the journey. Help children realize that poets record everyday life as well as special events.

6. Choose poems about the future of space travel, poems that are harbingers of what is to come, or else parody or satirize the future. Let children see that poets think about what the future holds as source material for their visions.

7. Choose poems which deal with the present lives the children are living. Let them see that poets reflect, illuminate, and report on the experiences that they the children are undergoing. Poems can be about school, family, fights, friendships, death of pets, new possessions, and not getting Christmas gifts that they want. Let them see it's the poet's view and voice that matters, not only the content.

8. Choose poems that have a particular style, such as call and response, dialogue, monologue, narration containing dialogue, lists, chants, invocations, and hymns, so that the children can hear the voice of the poem and thus join in with the words.

9. Choose poems with a similar voice, comparable situations or conflict as material for discussion. They can tape-record their poems, put them on overhead transparencies, or make interesting mobiles that hang from the ceiling.

10. The class can make a poetry magazine for other classes or for parents. It can use various formats that are used in bookmaking. It can include poems, pictures, stories of poets, found poetry, their own poetry, ideas for poetry. They can include poems written by others in the school or by parents. They can attempt to send these poems to local newspapers or various interested journals.

11. They can set up a bulletin board of particular themes or genres of poetry. The board can contain favorite poems or interesting poetic phrases. The children can bring in poems from other publications, magazines, periodicals, and share these with others.

12. They can make display tables of poetry anthologies or, perhaps more interestingly, artifacts and objects that may encourage poetry reading and writing. A theme table on the desert, with shells, sand and cacti, may inspire children to collect, read, and write poems on this theme.

13. The children can create a mural that demonstrates a kind of poetry, a theme, or a particular style. For example, with poems about weather, we can create a weather mural that uses graphs from the newspaper, weather maps, etc. Collage work is most effective in tying together visual arts and poems.

14. Build your own anthology. Begin by choosing your favorites from several anthologies and putting them in a journal, on file cards (or photostats).
15. Memorize a poem alone or along with the children. You will gain great strength from owning poetry in this way.
16. Examine a volume of work by one individual poet. Decide which poems you enjoy the most, which represent the poet, which have been anthologized in other books.
17. Examine some new anthologies and discern the range of poetry that is presented. What picture of poetry was the anthologist trying to paint? What is the balance of traditional and contemporary poetry?

AFTERWORD

We still become excited by a new anthology after all these years, or when children find fun in the old, slightly worn verses from before even our time. Our thoughts on the poetry in our lives — personal and professional — have let us reflect on the good years of teaching, when we met the children with the poems, face to face.

The magic of poetry for us lies in its memories, every word replete with the voices of the children who passed through our lives. It was never work, really, finding the poems, sharing them, exploring them, learning them, discovering them again in another anthology, like a friend from childhood. They were gifts for us, as well as for the children, full of the energy and hope that infused all those faces in front of us for all those years. We are still looking for the new poem, anticipating its pleasure, and rediscovering our past delights in sharing poems with children.

We end with poems for you . . . and us . . . and them.

Me and Poetry

I used to think
Poems had to rhyme
All the time.
I used to think
Poems had to be about fairies
And smarty kids who always did the right thing.
I use to think
That if it had short lines,
With capitals at the beginning
It was poetry.
I used to think
That normal people didn't like it,
Or want it,
Or understand it.
Then I met my teacher,
Who showed me that it was
Fun, pleasure,
Laughter, tears,
Like a movie in your head,
With music, music, music.

Now I like it.
I even got a book of poems
For Christmas.

W.H.M.

Classroom Poems

I live in fear
that I
will teach the poem
and they
will lose the poet
and the song
and the self
within the poem.

I live in fear
that I
who love the poem
and the children
will lose the poem
and the children
when I teach the poem.

But I will teach the poem
Live with the fear
Love the children
Sing the song
Find the self
And know the poet
is beside me
Just as afraid
But full of hope.

D.B.

Annotated Bibliography

Selecting Anthologies

We are both devoted fans of poems and use them in our work with teachers, parents, and children, with our families, and for our own pleasure. We want to recommend poems to be shared with children of all ages — at home, at school, at camp, and at the library. We want to help adults find suitable poems for a special child to meet at a particular time, poems that would engage the youngster, pull him or her inside the print, and cause reading to be a meaning-making activity from the very beginning. We want every child to meet poems freed from tension and failure, ready to challenge, appreciate, wonder, and laugh. We want poems to be the normal treasures of childhood, not to be revered nor tasks to be completed.

Most of all, we want to share our own delight in experiencing poems and exploring them with children and adults. So many favorites, so many treasures. How would we make them accessible to the readers of this book?

Poetry books are often available in both hardback and paperback editions. We generally present the most recent publishing information in the Bibliography. A paperback book may be handled by different distributors in different areas or at different times. Your library or bookstore can help you locate the books that best fit your needs.

We have written this book for you as an adult entrusted with the responsibility of bringing children and poems together, and of encouraging a warm relationship between the two.

The annotations in this bibliography are brief descriptions of what the books hold in store. Other books by or about the same poet are included under the annotation. Because of the nature of poetry, it is useful to have several anthologies available to make selection and choice effective and suitable. Not every poem in a book will be useful; depending upon the child or the group of children, the teacher will have to group poems together. Observe carefully the responses of the listener(s), and then select poems that create a positive reaction. Build on success. Taste is acquired from significant experience. The books in this section will help you to begin to awaken and develop an interest in, and a passion for this particular concentrated art form.

The anthologies listed in this bibliography are representative of the selection of anthologies that is available to children today, and are arranged alphabetically in six categories. The teacher or adult wishing to use an anthology with a child or with a group of children should be aware of the appeal of the poems in the book. They should investigate the poet or poets represented, the type of poems they write, the content of the poems, the style and form, the arrangement (by theme, etc.), the reason for the collection, the layout of the poems on the page, and the accompanying illustrations.

Adoff, Arnold. *Birds Poems*. New York: J.B. Lippincott, 1982.
Arnold Adoff's poems are about birds, looking for seeds and worms, worrying over squirrels, and hunting cats, and flying weather.

————. *Sports Pages*. New York: J.B. Lippincott, 1986.

————. *OUTside INside Poems*. New York: Lothrop, Lee & Shepard Books, 1981.

————. *Friend Dog*. New York, New York: J.B. Lippincott, 1980.

————. *I am the running girl*. New York, Hagerstown, San Francisco, London: Harper & Row, Publishers, 1979.

————. *Eats*. New York: Lothrop, Lee & Shepard Books, 1979.

Agard, John. *Say It Again, Granny!* London: The Bodley Head, 1986.
Twenty poems created from Caribbean proverbs.

————. *I Din Do Nuttin and other poems*. London, Sydney, Toronto: The Bodley Head, 1983.

Behn, Harry. *Crickets and Bullfrogs and Whispers of Thunder*. San Diego, New York, London: Harcourt Brace Jovanovich, 1977.
The anthologist Lee Bennett Hopkins has selected fifty of Harry Behn's poems, grouping them in three sections: the seasons; fantasy; and familiar objects.

————. (transl.). *Cricket Songs* (Japanese Haiku). New York: Harcourt, Brace and World, Inc., 1964.

Belloc, Hilaire. *The Bad Child's Book of Beasts*. London: Duckworth, 1974 (1896).
A satirical reflection on the Victorian morality poems.

————. *Cautionary Tales for Children*. Duckworth, 1973 (1907).

Ciardi, John. *You read to me, I'll read to you*. Harper & Row, Publishers, 1962.
This book is full of poems that can be read to and by children.

Dawber, Diane. *Oatmeal Mittens*. Ottawa: Borealis Press, 1987.
The poems evoke memories of childhood rivalries, conflict, joys, and sadness.

de la Mare, Walter. *The Voice*. London, Boston: Faber and Faber, 1986.
Catherine Brighton takes 13 poems by Walter de la Mare, and arranges them in a sequence that runs from dawn to night and offers glimpses into the lives of three children living in a shadowy house by a lake.

Edwards, Richard. *The WORD Party*. New York: A Young Puffin, Viking Penguin Inc., 1986.

Playing with words, rhythms, and imaginative ideas, these poems will be much enjoyed by young children.

Farjeon, Eleanor. *Invitation to a Mouse and other poems*. London: Knight Books, Hodder and Stoughton, 1983.

The contents of this collection of Eleanor Farjeon's poetry provide a welcome introduction to her work.

Fisher, Aileen. *Out in the Dark and Daylight*. New York: Harper & Row, Publishers, 1980.

In 140 new poems by Aileen Fisher, young people will discover ant villages under rocks, rabbits in moonlight, and puddles for feet to splash in.

Frost, Robert. *You COME Too*. New York: Holt, Rinehart and Winston, 1959.

Frost gathered a group of his poems to be read to, and by young people.

Giovanni, Nikki. *Spin a Soft Black Song*. New York: Hill and Wang, 1985.

Spin a Soft Black Song includes a wide variety of poems that share the common thread of being about black children.

Glenn, Mel. *Class Dismissed II*. New York: Clarion Books, 1986.

Mel Glenn presents 70 new poems based upon the emotional lives of the students he has taught.

————. *Class Dismissed*. New York: Clarion Books, 1984.

Gowar, Mick. *So Far So Good*. London: Collins, 1986.

Mick Gowar expresses the feelings of teenagers — intense emotions, fun, frustrations, and anxieties.

Grimes, Nikki. *Something On My Mind*. New York: Dial Books for Young Readers, 1978.

A collection of prose-poems that expands on thoughts and feelings of black children.

Halloran, Phyllis. *i'd like to hear a flower gr O W*. Portland, Oregon: Reading Inc., 1985.

Gentle, lyrical poems of reflection and observation.

Heidbreder, Robert. *Don't Eat Spiders*. Toronto: Oxford University Press, 1985.

Robert Heidbreder has developed an ear for the sound patterns and rhythms that delight children.

Holman, Felice. *At the Top of My Voice and other poems*. New York: Charles Scribner's Sons, 1970.

The poems in this anthology have such inviting voices that children are encouraged to join in.

Hughes, Langston. *The Dream Keeper*. New York: Alfred A. Knopf, 1986 (1932).
A selection of 60 poems by the black poet Langston Hughes. The book is divided into five sections including short lyrics of great beauty, stanzas in serious vein, rollicking songs, and some very fine blues.

Hughes, Ted. *Season Songs*. London, Boston: Faber and Faber, 1985.
Ted Hughes has said that his *Season Songs* began as children's poems, but they grew up. *Season Songs* is generally regarded as one of the Laureate's finest collections.

———. *Ffangs the Vampire Bat and the Kiss of Truth*. London, Boston: Faber and Faber, 1986.

———. *What Is the Truth? A Farmyard Fable for the Young*. London, Boston: Faber and Faber, 1984.

———. *CAVE BIRDS: An Alchemical Cave Drama*. London, Boston: Faber and Faber, 1975.

———. *Moon-Bells and Other Poems*. London: Chatto & Windus, 1978.

———. *CROW*. New York, Evanston, San Francisco, London: Harper & Row, Publishers, 1971.

———. *Meet My Folks!* London, Boston: Faber and Faber, 1961.

huigan, sean o. *the ghost horse of the mounties*. Windsor, Ontario: Black Moss Press, 1983.
In this award-winning book, the poet creates a dream world of horses, a story of the mounted police, and a fantasy filled with power and beauty.

———. *well, you can imagine*. Black Moss Press, 1983.

———. *The Dinner Party*, Black Moss Press, 1984.

———. *scary poems for rotten kids*. Black Moss Press, 1982.

Kennedy, X.J. *ONE WINTER NIGHT IN AUGUST and Other Nonsense Jingles*. New York: Antheneum, 1975.
Though the verses can be enjoyed privately, they can be shared and are perfect for reading aloud.

Krauss, Ruth. *Minestrone*. New York: Greenwillow Books, 1981.
Ruth Krauss presents a selection of her poetry, mini-plays, Kraussian definitions, short prose texts, and a selection of her clever, witty Thumbprints.

Kuskin, Karla. *Dogs & Dragons; Trees & Dreams*. New York: Harper & Row, Publishers, 1980.

Through introductions and notes written especially for this collection of poems, the poet explores how she writes her poems.

Little, Jean. *Hey World, Here I Am!* Toronto: Kids Can Press, 1986.
Kate Bloomfield was first heard from as a minor character in Jean Little's *Look Through My Window*. Now, in her own book, Kate proves herself to be a sensitive, articulate, likable and a poet of promise.

Livingston, Myra Cohn. *Sea Songs*. New York: A Holiday House Book, 1986.
Myra Cohn Livingston creates poetic images of the sea that reflect its many moods. From the moon's "midnight witchery" to sandpiper prints in "the clean morning sand" to "underground dungeons", she probes the sea's ever-changing aura.

————. *A Song I Sang to You*. San Diego, New York, London: Harcourt Brace Jovanovich, Publishers, 1984.

————. *4-Way Stop and other poems*. New York: Atheneum, 1976.

McCord, David. *One at a Time*. Boston, Toronto: Little, Brown and Company, 1986.
This book contains the collected poems of David McCord. He writes of seasons and holidays, of passing summers and crackling fires, of cats and butterflies and shells on a beach, all the small things in life that take on new significance through the poet's eye.

————. *Every Time I Climb a Tree*. Boston, Toronto: Little, Brown and Company, 1980.

McGough, Roger. *Nailing the Shadow*. London: Viking Kestrel, Penguin Books Ltd., 1987.
Roger McGough's collection of poems is full of invention and delight in words; poems which take a new look at accepted views, poems which challenge opinions and show how words are always within reach.

————. *Sky in the Pie*. London: Viking Kestrel Books, 1983.

Merriam, Eve. *Fresh Paint*. New York: Macmillan Publishing Company, 1986.
In this collection, award-winning poet Eve Merriam paints 45 vivid pictures of the wonders of the world that open our eyes.

————. *A Sky Full of Poems*. New York: A Yearling Book, Dell Publishing Co. Inc. 1986.

————. *Blackberry Ink*. New York: William Morrow & Company, 1985.

————. *JAMBOREE Rhymes for All Times*. New York: A Yearling Book, Dell Publishing Co., Inc., 1984.

————. *A Word or Two with You, New Rhymes for Young Readers*. New York: Atheneum, 1981.

Milne, A.A. *When We Were Very Young*. New York: A Yearling Book, Dell Publishing Co. Inc., 1985.

From out of the world of Christopher Robin and Winnie the Pooh comes A.A. Milne's delightful verse of childhood, full of nonsense and rhythm.

————. *Now We Are Six*. Toronto: McClelland and Stewart, 1986.

Moore, Lilian. *Think of Shadows*. New York: Atheneum, 1980.

Shade, shadow, moving mist — all are explored in poems that describe moments that would otherwise be lost.

————. *I Feel the Same Way*. New York: An Aladdin Book, Atheneum, 1967.

Musgrave, Susan. *GULLBAND Thought Measles Was A Happy Ending*. Vancouver: J.J. Douglas Ltd., 1974.

This book is a blend of simplicity and fantasy that brings together 43 poems from Susan Musgrave.

Nash, Ogden. *Zoo*. New York: Stewart, Tabori & Chang, 1987.

Ogden Nash's *ZOO* is a new collection of some of the master's best-loved verses about animals.

————. *Custard and Company*. Harmondsworth: Puffin Books, 1983.

nichol, bp. *Once: A Lullaby*. New York: Greenwillow Books, 1983.

''Once I was a little horse'' begins this lullaby, and the rhythmic words and tapestrylike pictures tell what happens to that little horse and 17 other small creatures.

————. *Giants, Moosequakes & Other Disasters*. Windsor, Ontario: Black Moss Press, 1985.

Nicholls, Judith. *Midnight Forest and other poems*. London: Faber and Faber, 1987.

The poet expresses mysteries of fantasy — fairy tale spells, the darkness of the woods, etc.

————. *Magic Mirror*. London, Boston: Faber and Faber, 1985.

Owen, Gareth. *Song of the City*. London: Collins, 1985.

These poems will take you through the city and show you ordinary things from extraordinary angles.

Patten, Brian. *Gargling with Jelly*. Harmondsworth: Puffin Books, 1986.

A mixture of hilarious, absurd, lyrical, and serious poems from one of Britain's new poets.

Prelutsky, Jack. *My Parents Think I'm Sleeping*. New York: Greenwillow Books, 1985.

The author's poems demonstrate what it is like to go to bed and not to sleep.

———. *The New Kid on the Block*. New York: Greenwillow Books, 1984.

———. *The Headless Horseman Rides Tonight. More Poems to Trouble Your Sleep*. New York: Greenwillow Books, 1980.

———. *Nightmares*. New York: Greenwillow Books, 1976.

Reaney, James. *POEMS*. Toronto, Ontario, Canada: new press, 1972.

Many of Reaney's poems deal with the humblest aspects of rural and small town life, in the counties of Ontario, in the forty-three fields of a Perth County farm.

Reeves, James. *The Wandering Moon and Other Poems*. Harmondsworth: Puffin Books, 1987.

James Reeves is a poet who makes you feel the power of words, and who loves the odd and mysterious.

———. *Complete Poems for Children*. London: Heinemann, 1973.

Rieu, E.V. *The Flattered Flying Fish*. New York: E.P. Dutton & Company, Inc., 1962.

The poems range from an evocation of spring to the strange phenomenon of a little boy washing himself without being told to.

Rosen, Michael. *HAIRY TALES and NURSERY CRIMES*. London: Fontana Young Lions, 1985.

Amazing things happen in the middle of the porridge, in the wicked witch's house on the streets of Hamelin. Rosen's free verse parodies are full of word play and strong feelings.

———. *Smelly Jelly Smelly Fish*. London: Walker Books, 1986.

———. *When Did You Last Wash Your Feet?* London: André Deutsch, 1986.

———. *Quick, Let's Get Out Of Here*. London: André Deutsch, 1983.

———. *You Can't Catch Me!* London: André Deutsch, 1981.

———. *You Tell Me*. Harmondsworth, Puffin Books, 1979.

———. *Mind Your Own Business*. London: Collins Lions, 1974.

Sandburg, Carl. *Wind Song*. New York: A Voyageur Book, Harcourt, Brace & World, Inc., 1953.

Here are the words and sounds, the imaginative fire that makes Carl Sandburg's poetry outstanding.

Silverstein, Shel. *A Light in the Attic*. Harper & Row, Publishers, 1981.

Shel Silverstein's collection of poems and drawings is funny, often moving, and very popular.

————. *Where the Sidewalk Ends*. Harper & Row Publishers, 1974.

Simmie, Lois. *An Armadillo Is Not a Pillow*. Saskatoon, Saskatchewan: Western Producer Prairie Books, 1986.

This new collection of 53 poems, accompanied by Anne Simmie's line drawings, captures the imagination, spontaneity, and concerns of the child's world.

————. *Auntie's Knitting a Baby*. Saskatoon, Saskatchewan: Western Producer Prairie Books, 1984.

Sneyd, Lola. *The Concrete Giraffe*. Toronto, Canada: Simon & Pierre, 1982.

In her book *The Concrete Giraffe*, Toronto poet Lola Sneyd touches on many of the special Toronto places that children enjoy.

————. *The Asphalt Octopus: A Child's World in Poetry*. Toronto, Canada: Simon & Pierre, 1982.

Souster, Raymond. (Selected by Richard Woollatt). *Flight of the Roller-Coaster*. Ottawa, Canada: Oberon Press, 1985.

Raymond Souster is one of the best-known Canadian poets of his generation. Souster's lyrics have the kind of simplicity and clarity that make them especially inviting to a child.

Stevenson, Robert Louis. *A Child's Garden of Verses*. London: Victor Gollancz Ltd,. 1985.

A collection of the favorite poems of a favorite poet, illustrated by Michael Foreman.

Swede, George. *High Wire Spider*. Toronto, Canada: Three Trees Press, 1986.

High Wire Spider is a collection of brief, witty, and thoughtful poetry for children.

————. *Tick Bird*. Toronto, Ontario: Three Trees Press, 1983.

————. *Time Is Flies*. Toronto, Ontario: Three Trees Press, 1984.

Wallenstein, Barry. *Roller Coaster Kid and Other Poems*. New York: Thomas Y. Crowell, 1982.

The characters in the poems "can take off to any place in any way". The author also shares how his poems were conceived, developed, and completed.

Worth, Valeria. *small poems again*. New York: Farrar, Straus and Giroux, 1986.

Small Poems Again is a collection of brief lyrics on such simple but remarkable phenomena as the water lily, the telephone pole, the giraffe, the octopus, and the kaleidoscope.

Wright, Kit. *Hot Dog and Other Poems.* Harmondsworth: Puffin Books, 1981.
A humorous collection of witty and sharply detailed poems.
Viorst, Judith. *If I Were In Charge Of The World and other worries.* New York: Atheneum, 1983.
The poet turns her some of her worries into laughter.
Zolotow, Charlotte. *Everything Glistens and Everything Sings.* New York: Harcourt, Brace Jovanovich, 1987.
In this collection of 72 poems, Charlotte Zolotow displays her ability to see things with a child's eye.

Story-Poem Collections

Causley, Charles. *Figgie Hobbin.* Harmondsworth: Puffin Books, 1985.
One of the most popular and well-loved collections of poems for children, *Figgie Hobbin* is Cornish in flavor, sometimes savory and sometimes sweet.
Coleridge, Samuel Taylor. *The Rime of the Ancient Mariner.* London: Chatto & Windus, 1971. Illustrated by C. Walter Hodges.
A vivid and exciting picture-book version of Samuel Taylor Coleridge's famous poem.
Edwards, Dorothy. *Mists and Magic.* London: Fontana Young Lions, 1983.
Dorothy Edwards brings together stories old and new in this book of folk tales, legends and poems.
Keeping, Charles. *Tinker Tailor.* Brockhampton Press, 1972.
Charles Keeping has taken the old saying, ''Tinker, tailor, soldier, sailor, richman, poorman, beggarman, thief'', and chosen a traditonal tale in the form of a folk song to represent each character.
Kipling, Rudyard. *Gunga Din.* New York: Harcourt Brace Jovanovich Publishers, 1987. Illustrated by Robert Andrew Parker.
This illustrated verson of *Gunga Din* is a tale of courage and loyalty. Written by Rudyard Kipling in 1890, this poem stands today as a testament and reminder of a harsh era in India's history.
Lisowski, Gabriel. *On the Little Hearth.* New York: Holt, Rinehart and Winston, 1978.

"On the Little Hearth", popularly known as "Oif'n Pripitchik", is one of the best loved and most familiar of Jewish songs. *On the Little Hearth* addresses itself to several layers of Jewish life.

Norris, Leslie. *Merlin & The Snake's Egg*. New York: The Viking Press, 1978. Illustrated by Ted Lewin.

Leslie Norris casts a spell that demonstrates his power to infuse words with the magic of his vision.

Noyes, Alfred. *The Highwayman*. New York: Lothrop, Lee & Shepard Books, 1983. Illustrated by Charles Mikolaycak.

Alfred Noyes's tragic ballad about the highwayman and Bess, "the landlord's daughter, the landlord's black-eyed daughter", has long been a favorite with readers of every age.

————. *The Highwayman*. London: Oxford University Press, 1981. Illustrated by Charles Keeping.

Patten, Brian (Chosen by). *Gangsters, Ghosts and Dragonflies*. London: Piccolo Books, 1981.

Brian Patten has chosen a selection of poems from the very best comtemporary poets. Each poem tells a story from "The Last Gangster" and "The Ghost of our Least Favorite Uncle" to the "Dragonfly".

————. *The Sly Cormorant and the Fishes*. London: Viking Kestrel Books, 1977.

Rylant, Cynthia. *Waiting to Waltz: A Childhood*. Scarsdale, New York: Bradbury Press, 1984.

A collection of mood poems that reminisce about a childhood in a small town.

Schenk de Regniers, Beatrice. *Jack The Giant-Killer*. New York: Atheneum, 1987.

In verse, Beatrice Schenk de Regniers re-tells the familiar story of Jack the Giant-Killer in his first adventure. The author and illustrator offer other interesting lore about giants.

Seeger, Peter. *Abiyoyo*. New York: Macmillan Publishing Company, 1986.

Pete Seeger's storysong, made up for his own children, finds its match in Michael Hays' masterful paintings.

Serraillier, Ian. *I'll Tell You A Tale*. Harmondsworth: Puffin Books, 1976.

Included are ballads and poems of love, murder, and faithless men; of false knights, brave gentlemen, and maidens.

Tennyson, Alfred Lord. *The Charge of the Light Brigade*. New York: Golden Press, 1966. Illustrated by Alice and Martin Provensen.

Alfred Lord Tennyson immortalized the most dramatic and useless battle of the Crimean War (1854-1856).

———. *The Lady of Shalott.* New York: Franklin Watts, Inc., 1968. Illustrated by Bernadette Watts.

Vavra, Robert. *tiger flower.* London: Collins, 1968.

When Robert Vavra first saw Fleur Cowles' painting, he was so captivated by the imaginative quality of her birds, animals, and flowers that he thought these were paintings in search of a story, so the story of "Tiger Flower" was created.

Picture Book Poetry

Ahlberg, Janet and Allan (Illustrators). *Each Peach Pear Plum.* London: Fontana Picture Lions, 1978.

A beautifully illustrated version of the gentle old nursery rhyme.

Ashford, Ann. *If I Found A Wistful Unicorn.* Atlanta, Georgia: Peachtree Publishers Ltd., 1978. Illustrated by Bill Drath.

Questions and answers form the basis of this poetic look at relationships.

Baylor, Byrd. *I'm In Charge of Celebrations.* New York: Charles Scribner's Sons, 1986. Illustrated by Peter Parnall.

Byrd Baylor's text captures and shares some of the special experiences in the Southwest's desert country that have inaugurated her private celebrations.

Boulanger, Claudette, and Fran Newman. *Sunflakes & Snowshine.* Richmond Hill, Ontario: North Winds Press, 1979.

Delightful poems arranged as a calendar for the year.

Cendrars,Blaise. *Shadow.* New York: Charles Scribner's Sons, 1982. Illustrated by Marcia Brown.

The village storytellers and shamans of an Africa that is passing into memory called forth for the poet Blaise Cendrars an eerie image, shifting between the beliefs of the present and the spirits of the past.

Coleridge, Sara. *January Brings the Snow.* New York: Dial Books for Young Readers, 1986. Illustrated by Jenni Oliver.

Here is one special moment from every month, each with the hints of children having just passed through.

Ipcar, Dahlov (Adapted and illustrated by). *The Cat Came Back.* New York: Alfred A. Knopf, 1981.

A delightful picture-book version of the old folk-song.

Kovalski, Maryann. *The Wheels on the Bus.* Toronto, Ontario: Kids Can Press, 1987.
While a grandmother and grandchildren wait for the bus, they sing the title song with such energy they miss their bus.

Kherdian, David (Collected by). *If Dragon Flies Made Honey.* New York: Greenwillow Books, 1977. Illustrated by Jose Arvego and Ariane Dewey.
Editor David Kherdian has collected 25 short and lively poems representing the lighter side of leading modern poets.

Lane, John. *What Are Uncles For?* Toronto, Ontario: Harbour Publishing Co. Ltd., 1984.
Through the eyes of his four-year-old nephew, John Lane sees the familiar world reflected as a fantastic place.

Langstaff, John (Compiled by). *Soldier, Soldier, Won't You Marry Me?* Garden City, New York: Doubleday & Company, Inc., 1972. Illustrated by Anita Lobel.
Young children love the repetition in this gentle old folk song about clothes and dressing up.

Livingston, Myra Cohn. *Celebrations.* New York: Holiday House, 1985. Illustrated by Leonard Everett Fisher.
From New Year's Eve, when "old is dying, new is born," to Christmas Eve, when "He is coming from far, by the light of a star," the author and illustrator present a panorama of the traditions, memories, and symbols of important days through the year.

————. *A Circle of Seasons.* New York: Holiday House, 1982.

Lobel, Arnold. *On Market Street.* New York: Greenwillow Books, 1981. Illustrated by Anita Lobel.
Inspired by 17th-century French trade engravings, Anita Lobel has created paintings of the shopkeepers on Market Street — each composed of his or her wares.

Peterson, Jeanne Whitehouse. *While the Moon Shines Bright.* New York: Harper & Row, Publishers, 1981. Illustrated by Margot Apple.
In this illustrated picture book, a little boy's bedtime routine becomes a soothing bedtime chant.

Poe, Edgar Allen. *Annabel Lee.* Montreal, Quebec: Tundra Books, 1987. Illustrated by Gilles Tibo.
In a series of illustrations as lovely as the poem, artist Gilles Tibo has set the scene in the 1930s on the Gaspé Peninsula of his own province.

Willard, Nancy. *A Visit to William Blake's Inn.* New York, London: Harcourt Brace Jovanovich,1981. Illustrated by Alice and Martin Provensen.

Inspired by Blake's work, Nancy Willard has written a book of magical poems about life at an imaginary inn, run by none other than William Blake himself.

Wynne-Jones, Tim. *Mischief City.* Toronto, Vancouver: Groundwork Books, 1986. Illustrated by Victor Gad.

In *Mischief City,* Winchell's daytime life is mirrored by a wild nighttime life that he shares with his imaginary friend Maxine. The story, told in poems, takes place on a stage set, and plays with what is real and what is pretend.

Yolen, Jane. *Owl Moon.* New York: Philomel Books, 1987. Illustrated by John Schoenherr.

Jane Yolen has created a gentle, poetic story that depicts the special companionship of a young child and her father as well as humankind's close relationship to the natural world.

————. *Ring of Earth: A Child's Book of Seasons.* San Diego, California: Harcourt Brace Jovanovich, Publishers, 1986.

Rhymes Old and New — Old

Alderson, Brian (Chosen by). *The Helen Oxenbury Nursery Rhyme Book.* Toronto: Stoddart, 1986.

This book of nursery rhymes presents a collection of some of the best-loved children's traditional verse, drawn from *Cakes and Custard,* an anthology devised by Brian Alderson.

Banyard, Julie, and Colin West. *A Moment in Rhyme.* New York: Dial Books for Young Readers, 1987.

A collection of original nursery rhymes perfect for the very young. Some of Colin West's poems appeal for their dry humor; some celebrate the joys of everyday living; and others express deep-felt dreams and longings.

Baring-Gould, William S. and Ceil. *The ANNOTATED Mother Goose.* New York; Bramhall House, 1962.

This gathering, containing more than 1000 separate rhymes from the earliest surviving publications to the present day, is a very complete collection. The rhymes are usually given in their earliest published form, which was often later suppressed, and the authors have included most of the known variations of the original.

Blake, Quentin. *Quentin Blake's Nursery Rhyme Book*. London: Jonathan Cape, 1983.
The artist's nursery rhyme characters jump off the page with energy.

Bodecker, N.M. *Let's Marry Said the Cherry and Other Nonsense Poems*. New York: An Aladdin Book, Atheneum, 1974.
N.M Bodecker's dry humor, his sense of the absurd, his love of word play, his illogical logic, his awareness of the sadness that lies close to laughter, are all reflected in these verses.

————. *Hurry, Hurry, Mary Dear!* New York: Atheneum, 1978.

Briggs, Raymond. *Fee Fi Fo Fum: A Picture Book of Nursery Rhymes*. Harmondsworth: Puffin Books in association with Hamish Hamilton, 1964.
Raymond Briggs' gloriously colorful paintings capture the warmth and happiness of the nursery rhymes.

Brown, Marc. *Play Rhymes*. New York: E.P. Dutton, 1987.
A lively picture book of 12 well-known cheery play rhymes.

Delamar, Gloria T. *Children's Counting-Out Rhymes, Fingerplays, Jump-Rope, and Bounce-Ball Chants and Other Rhythms*. Jefferson, North Carolina, London: McFarland, 1983.
An interesting collection of rhymes and games (some adapted, others collected) that includes the many types of children's lore.

Evans, Delphine. *Fingers Feet and Fun!* London: Hutchinson, 1984.
A mixture of traditional and original material, action rhymes and songs, counting rhymes, fun rhymes, and stories.

Fowke, Edith. *Sally Go Round the Sun*. Toronto, Montreal: McClelland and Stewart Limited, 1969.
A collection of sandlot, street-corner, playroom poetry that will delight youngsters and tickle an adult's nostalgia, including 300 singing games, skipping and ball-bouncing rhymes, taunts, teases, and silly songs, culled from the innocent vernacular of Canadian children by Edith Fowke, one of Canada's foremost authorities on the country's folklore.

Glazer, Tom. *Eye Winker, Tom Tinker, Chin Chopper: Fifty Musical Fingerplays*. Garden City, New York: Doubleday & Company, Inc., 1972.
Tom Glazer, the balladeer, has gathered songs, music for piano and guitar, and fingerplays into an illustrated book.

Ireson, Barbara (Ed.) *The Faber Book of Nursery Verse*. London: Faber and Faber, 1983.

A complete collection of poems and verse for young children.

King, Karen (Compiled by). *Oranges & Lemons*. Toronto: Oxford University Press, 1985.
An illustrated collection of modern and traditional singing and dancing games that demonstrate how they are done.

Langstaff, John (Chosen by). *Hot Cross Buns and Other Old Street Cries*. New York: Atheneum; 1978.
John Langstaff, a distinguished singer and musicologist, has gathered together this collection of old English street cries and their simple musical notes for children to use and enjoy.

Lobel, Arnold (Selected by). *Gregory Griggs and Other Nursery Rhyme People*. New York: Greenwillow Books, 1978.
Lobel brings to life his favorite nursery rhyme characters with his wonderful drawings.

————. *The Random House Book of Mother Goose*. New York: Random House, 1986.

Lucas, Barbara (Selected by). *CATS by Mother Goose*. New York: Lothrop, Lee & Shepard Books, 1986.
Barbara Lucas and Carol Newson rediscover the cats found in the rhymes of Mother Goose.

Matterson, Elizabeth (Compiled by). *This Little Puffin*. . . . Harmondsworth: Puffin Books, 1969.
This treasury of finger plays and singing and action games will persuade young children to join in musical activities, either in groups or individually.

Opie, Peter and Iona (Assembled by). *The Oxford Nursery Rhyme Book*. London: Oxford University Press, 1955.
This book is a full repository of the nursery rhymes and ditties which are the heritage of our oral tradition. It contains all the well-known rhymes, and the rare ones too, including a number of rhymes and versions of rhymes not previously printed.

Petersham, Maud and Miska. *The Rooster Grows: A Book of American Rhymes and Jingles*. New York: Aladdin Books, 1973 (1945).
Here is a collection that includes the favorite playtime rhymes that are a part of America's and childhood's heritage.

Prelutsky, Jack (Selected by). *Read-Aloud Rhymes for the very young*. New York: Alfred A. Knopf, 1986.
A collection of more than 200 verses that will open young minds and eyes to the magic and meaning of words.

Roeske, Cornelia C. (Music by). *Finger Games for nursery and kindergarten*. New York: Merrimack Publishing Corp.

A collection of finger plays that children have been playing, learning from, and enjoying for centuries.

Rosen, Michael, and Susanna Steele, (Collected by). *Inky Pinky Ponky*. London: Granada, 1982.
A fascinating collection of children's playground rhymes illustrated with contemporary settings.

Rowe, Christopher, and Barbara Ireson. *Over and Over Again*. Markham, Ontario: Beaverbooks, 1978.
Emphasis has been placed on simple rhythm and verse patterns and the treatment of themes important to young children, and all the songs have a melody line and guitar chords.

Stones, Rosemary, and Andrew Mann (Chosen by). *Mother Goose Comes to Cable Street: Nursery Rhymes for Today*. London: Viking Kestrel Books, 1977.
The artist has given new life to these comtemporary children's rhymes by placing them in contemporary settings that will tell a whole story.

Tashjian, Virginia A. (Selected by). *Juba This and Juba That*. Boston, Toronto: Little, Brown and Company, 1969.
A book of rhymes and songs to sing and play, stories to tell, and riddles to guess.

Tripp, Wallace. *Marguerite, Go Wash Your Feet*. Boston: Houghton Mifflin Company, 1985.
Wallace Tripp adds fun and zest to original nursery rhymes with his cartoonlike story-filled drawings.

————. *Granfa' Grig Had A Pig: and Other Rhymes Without Reason from Mother Goose*. Boston, Toronto: Little, Brown and Company, 1976.

Warne, Frederick (Ed.), *Beatrix Potter's Nursery Rhyme Book*. Harmondsworth: Penguin, 1984.
This is a collection of most of the rhymes which Beatrix Potter intended for her books. Some of the rhymes are traditional, quoted here from Halliwell if Beatrix Potter's reference was too scanty; some are Beatrix Potter's special adaptations; and others are Potter originals.

Williams, Sarah. (Compiled by). *Round and Round the Garden*. Toronto: Oxford University Press, 1983. Illustrated by Ian Beck.

Sanson, Clive (Chosen by). *Speech Rhymes*. London: A. & C. Black Ltd., 1974.
For this new edition the rhymes have been re-edited, new rhymes have been added, and the selection has been completely re-set.

Sanson, Ruth (Chosen by). *Rhythm Rhymes*. London: A. & C. Black, 1964.

Lively activity rhymes for young children, with plenty of opportunities for self-expression in a wide variety of moods.

Smith, William Jay. *Laughing Time*. New York: A Yearling Book, 1980.

Fun and games by a poet who brings ear-humor to his readers.

Watson, Clyde. *Catch Me & Kiss Me & Say It Again*. New York, Cleveland, London: Collins, 1978.

A collection of rhymes to celebrate the happy, loving times of childhood. Each of these new poems also suggests an occasion or an activity.

———. *Father Fox's Pennyrhymes*. Richmond Hill, Ontario: Scholastic Book Services, 1971.

Yolen, Jane. *The Three Bears Rhyme Book*. San Diego, California: Harcourt Brace Jovanovich, 1987.

This collection of new, playful rhymes and delightful pictures celebrates the everyday life of Goldilocks and the Three Bears. A delightfully illustrated collection of traditional play rhymes.

Rhymes Old and New — New

Ahlberg, Allan. *Please Mrs. Butler*. Harmondsworth: Puffin Books, 1983.

This collection of poems about school is full of typical classroom events that will be recognized by everyone.

Causley, Charles. *Early in the Morning*. London: Viking Kestrel, 1986.

This book is a fascinating mix of ancient and modern verse which combine to form a heritage linking generations of parents and children.

———. *Jack the Treacle Eater*. London: MacMillan Children's Books.

Dahl, Roald. *Revolting Rhymes*. New York: Alfred A. Knopf, Publisher, 1982.

The poet treads on all the taboos that children do seem to enjoy but parents don't.

Dodson, Dr. Fitzhugh. *I wish I had a computer that makes waffles . . .* La Jolla, California: Oak Tree Publications, Inc., Publishers, 1978.

The aim of this book of contemporary verse is to introduce to children reading, counting, distinction of colors, shapes, and abstract concepts.

Dunn, Sonja. *Butterscotch Dreams*. Markham, Ontario: Pembroke Publishers Limited, 1987.

In *Butterscotch Dreams* more than 60 original chants explore the magic of friendship, holidays, food, exotic places, and even space travel. Each is a rhythmical sound poem that can be enjoyed on its own or used to introduce or extend areas of learning.

Hoberman, Mary Ann. *Yellow Butter, Purple Jelly, Red Jam, Black Bread*. New York: Viking Press, 1981.

Children will be delighted with the humor and directness in this bouncy and rhythmic collection of verses.

Ireson, Barbara (Collected by). *Rhyme Time*. Markham, Ontario: Beaverbooks, 1977.

Rhymes to sing, skip to or count to, riddles, limericks and tongue-twisters can all be found in this collection. Over 200 poems portray the young child's world.

Lee, Dennis. *The Difficulty of Living on Other Planets*. Toronto: Macmillan of Canada, 1987.

Dennis Lee's collection of light verse shows the poet as comedian and philosopher — spinning from lyricism through satire to black humor, and can be useful with children.

————. *Jelly Belly*. Toronto: Macmillan of Canada, 1983.

————. *Garbage Delight*. Toronto: Macmillan of Canada, 1979.

————. *Alligator Pie*. Toronto: Macmillan of Canada, 1974.

Lobel, Arnold. *Whiskers & Rhymes*. New York: Greenwillow Books, 1985.

All the nursery rhymes in this collection are new. Children will take them to heart as soon as they hear them.

————. *The Book of Pigericks: Pig Limericks*. New York: Harper & Row, 1933.

Mitchell, Cynthia. *Hop-Along Happily and Other Rhymes for the Playground*. London: Heinemann, 1979.

A collection of ball-bouncing rhymes, choosing rhymes, and rhymes to hop and jump to. Natural and uncontrived as nursery rhymes, these are verses children will enjoy reading and chanting.

————. *Halloweena Hecatee and Other Rhymes to Skip to*. New York: Thomas Y. Crowell, 1979.

Prelutsky, Jack. *Ride A Purple Pelican*. New York: Greenwillow Books, 1986.

Jack Prelutsky and Garth Williams have created a nursery world, peopled with unforgettable characters.

Sanson, Clive (Chosen by). *Speech Rhymes*. London: A. & C. Black Ltd., 1974.

For this new edition the rhymes have been re-edited, new rhymes have been added, and the selection has been completely re-set.

Sanson, Ruth (Chosen by). *Rhythm Rhymes*. London: A. & C. Black, 1964.

Lively activity rhymes for young children, with plenty of opportunities for self-expression in a wide variety of moods.

Smith, William Jay. *Laughing Time*. New York: A Yearling Book, 1980.

Fun and games by a poet who brings ear-humor to his readers.

Watson, Clyde. *Catch Me & Kiss Me & Say It Again*. New York, Cleveland, London: Collins, 1978.

A collection of rhymes to celebrate the happy, loving times of childhood. Each of these new poems also suggests an occasion or an activity.

———. *Father Fox's Pennyrhymes*. Richmond Hill, Ontario: Scholastic Book Services, 1971.

Yolen, Jane. *The Three Bears Rhyme Book*. San Diego, California: Harcourt Brace Jovanovich, 1987.

This collection of new, playful rhymes and delightful pictures celebrates the everyday life of Goldilocks and the Three Bears.

Rhymes Old and New — Songs

Carlin, Richard. *Animal Songs for Children*. New York, London, Sydney: Amsco Publications, 1985.

A wide range of more than forty animal songs enjoyed by children the world over.

Challis, Evelyn. *Jumping, Laughing & Resting*. New York, London, Sydney: Amsco Publications, 1974.

A collection of songs gathered together for children from 3 to 10. There are songs for very little ones, tender lullabies, and singing games.

Keeping, Charles. *Cockney Ding Dong*. London: Viking Kestrel Books, 1975.

Charles Keeping has brought together and illustrated many songs from the Edwardian music hall, from the First World War trenches, from the American dance hall, or from the streets.

Marzollo, Jean. (Compiled by). *The Rebus Treasury*. New York: Dial Books for Young Readers, 1986.

The Rebus Treasury is for beginning readers to enjoy on their own, and for younger children to "read" aloud with their parents.

Mitchell, Donald (Selected by). *The Faber Book of Nursery Songs*. London, Boston: Faber and Faber, 1985.

This collection of 90 songs for small children includes accompaniments that are simple without being routine, and suggestions for involving a number of children.

Nelson, Esther L. *The Great Rounds Song-book*. New York: Sterling Publishing Co., Inc., 1985.

Here are 116 rounds — every one of them complete with melody line, lyrics, and part numbers.

————. *The Funny Song-book*. New York: Sterling Publishing Co., Inc., 1984.

Raffi. *The RAFFI Singable Songbook*. Toronto: Chappell, 1977.

A collection of 51 songs from Raffi's first three records for young children.

————. *The Second Raffi Songbook*. Toronto: Homeland Publishing (Troubador), 1986.

————. *Baby Beluga*. Toronto: McLelland and Stewart Limited, 1983.

Sharon, Lois, and Bram. *Sharon, Lois & Bram's Mother Goose*. Vancouver, Toronto: Douglas & McIntyre, 1985.

Sharon, Lois & Bram's Mother Goose brings you a collection of songs, nursery rhymes, dandling poems, tickling verses, and games for children from six months to seven years.

————. *Elephant Jam*. Toronto: McGraw-Hill Ryerson Limited, 1980.

Westcott, Nadine Bernard. *Peanut Butter and Jelly*. New York: E.P. Dutton, 1987.

A popular play rhyme gets a new life in this book illustrated by Nadine Bernard Westcott.

Yolen, Jane (Ed.) *The Lullaby Songbook*. San Diego, California: Harcourt Brace Jovanovich, Publishers, 1986.

Soothing lullabies are found in this collection of beloved favorites from around the world.

Themed Anthologies

Adams, Adrienne (Selected by). *Poetry of Earth*. New York: Charles Scribner's Sons, 1942.

Adrienne Adams has chosen 33 poems that speak to her of the earth and its creatures in the simple and authentic language of poets.

Bauer, Caroline Feller (Ed.). *Rainy Day*. New York: J.B. Lippincott, 1986.

A collection of stories and poems — all about rain to fit every kind of rainy day.

Beisner, Monika. *Secret Spells & Curious Charms*. London: Jonathan Cape, 1985.

Subtle, evocative poems in the form of spells, incantations, charms, and chants.

Belting, Natalia. *Our Fathers Had Powerful Songs*. New York: E.P. Dutton & Co., Inc., 1974. Illustrated by Laszlo Kubiny.

The lyrics in the poems were inspired by the rich songlore of many Native Peoples.

Bennett, Jill (Selected by). *A Packet of Poems*. London: Oxford University Press, 1982.

A new collection of poems all about food.

Calmenson, Stephanie (Selected by). *Never Take A Pig To Lunch and other funny poems about animals*. New York: Doubleday & Company, Inc., 1982.

Stephanie Calmenson has selected these funny poems, and the poems are illustrated with Hilary Knight's witty pictures.

Causley, Charles (Compiled by). *The Sun, Dancing: Christian Verse*. London: Viking Kestrel Books, 1982.

In selecting poems written from a Christian standpoint, or embodying a Christian point of view, the editor has produced a wide-ranging collection of verse in a variety of forms.

———. *The Puffin Book of Salt Sea Verse*. Harmondsworth: Puffin Books, 1978.

———. *The Puffin Book of Magic Verse*. Harmondsworth: Puffin Books, 1974.

Cohen, Mark (Collected by). *The Puffin Book of Tongue Twisters*. Harmondsworth: Puffin Books, 1986.

A collection of the trickiest, slippiest, most infuriating tongue-twisters in the world.

Cole, William. *A Boy Named Mary Jane and other silly verse*. New York: Avon Camelot, 1977.

The silly, funny poems in this illustrated collection include "Piggy", "Sneaky Bill", "After the Elephant Sneezed", "Lies, All Lies", and many more.

Cole, William (Selected by). *Poem Stew.* New York: J.B. Lippincott, 1981.

A feast of poems about food by such popular writers as William Cole, Odgen Nash, John Ciardi, and Shel Silverstein, seasoned with Karen Ann Weinhaus's comical illustrations.

————. *Oh, How Silly!* New York: The Viking Press, 1970.

————. *Beastly Boys and Ghastly Girls.* New York: A Yearling Book, 1964.

Corkett, Anne. *The Salamander's Laughter and other poems.* Toronto, Ontario: Natural Heritage/Natural History Inc., 1985.

The Salamander's Laughter presents the combined artistry of two creative individuals, poet Anne Corkett and illustrator Sylvia Hahn.

Covernton, Jane (Compiled by). *Petrifying Poems.* Melbourne, Australia: Omnibus Books, 1986.

A collection featuring some frightening favorites, as well as 35 new poems by Australia's poets.

Davis, David (Compiled by). *A Single Star.* Harmondsworth: Puffin Books, 1982.

An anthology of Christmas poetry.

Eliot, T.S. *Old Possum's Book of Practical Cats.* London: Faber and Faber, 1939.

These lovable and intricate cat poems were written by T.S. Eliot for his godchildren and friends.

Farber, Norma. *How Does It Feel To Be Old?* New York: A Unicorn Book, E.P. Dutton, 1979.

Norma Farber writes about loneliness and love, about the past and the present, about hope and memory linked in the relationship of a lonely old woman and a child.

Fisher, Robert (Ed.). *Ghosts Galore: Haunting Verse.* London: Faber and Faber, 1983.

Here are sinister ghosts and comic ghosts, sad ghosts and rollicking ghosts, unsuccessful ghosts and hopeful ones.

————. *Amazing Monsters: Verses to Thrill and Chill.* London: Faber and Faber, 1982.

Fleischmann, Paul. *I Am Phoenix.* New York: Harper & Row, Publishers, 1985.

I Am Phoenix is a verbal, visual, musical celebration of the sound, the sense, and the essence of birds. The poems and drawings evoke birds singing, soaring, complaining, confessing, revealing, rejoicing.

———. *Joyful Noise: Poems for Two Voices.* New York: Harper & Row, Publishers, 1988.

Foster, John. *Spaceways: An Anthology of Space Poetry.* London: Oxford University Press, 1986.

An excellent selection of all types of poetry relating to outer space and space exploration.

Fox, Siv Cedering. *The Blue Horse and Other Night Poems.* New York: A Clarion Book, The Seabury Press, 1979.

In this collection of 14 original poems, Siv Cedering Fox sets free her imagination to create vivid, childlike scenes of sleeping, dreaming, and waking.

De Gasztold, Carmen Bernos. *The Creatures' Choir.* New York: The Viking Press, 1965.

Each animal, bird, fish, reptile, or insect voice makes a statement of its situation, its circumstances in prayers.

Hill, Helen, Agnes Perkins, and Alethea Helbig (Selected by). *Dusk to Dawn: Poems of Night.* New York: Thomas Y. Crowell, 1981.

Here are American and British poems rarely found in children's anthologies — poems describing images of the beauty of the world at night.

———. *Straight On Till Morning.* New York: Thomas Y. Crowell Company, 1977.

Hooper, Patricia. *A Bundle of Beasts.* Boston: Houghton Mifflin Co., 1987.

Over the years, people have given names to groups of animals, and, in *A Bundle of Beasts*, the poet improvises on these names.

Hopkins, Lee Bennett (Selected by). *A Song In Stone: City Poems.* New York: Thomas Y. Crowell, 1983.

A Song In Stone is a lyrical celebration of the city.

———. *Creatures.* New York: Harcourt Brace Jovanovich, Publishers, 1985.

———. *Dinosaurs.* New York: Harcourt Brace Jovanovich, Publishers, 1986.

———. *My Mane Catches the Wind.* New York: Harcourt Brace Jovanovich, Publishers, 1979.

Janeczko, Paul B. (Selected by). *Strings: A Gathering of Family Poems.* New York: Bradbury Press, 1984.

Families inspire stories, love letters, toasts, memories, hopes and prayers, RSVPs, IOUs, admonitions, visions, and dreams. Paul B. Janeczko's *Strings* draws together 128 such tributes from 84 poets.

Kherdian, David (Ed.). *I Sing the Song of Myself*. New York: Green-willow Books, 1978.

In this unusual collection, the reader is aware of the poet's pre-occupation with everyday relationships, with love, death, and work.

Larrick, Nancy (Selected by). *Tambourines! Tambourines To Glory!: Prayers and Poems*. Philadelphia: The Westminster Press, 1982.

Nancy Larrick has gathered prayer poems from the world over.

———. *Room for Me and a Mountain Lion: Poetry of Open Space*. New York, Bantam Books, 1975.

Lewis, Naomi (Selected by). *A Footprint On The Air: an anthology of nature verse*. London: Hutchinson, 1983.

In the four sections of this book (on birds, on animals, on plants and flowers, on creatures that hop or swim or creep), each poet has caught some essence of the bird or flower or creature in the poem.

Livingston, Myra Cohn (Selected and edited by). *I Like You, If You Like Me: Poems of Friendship*. New York: Margaret K. McElderry Books, 1987.

This anthology offers a selection of 90 poems by contemporary and traditional poets. The book is divided into nine sections that reflect the diversity of feelings and thoughts about friends and the importance of friendship.

———. *Poems for Jewish Holidays*. New York: A Holiday House Book, 1986.

———. *Valentine Poems*. New York: A Holiday House Book, 1987.

———. *Why Am I Grown So Cold? Poems of the Unknowable*. New York: Atheneum, 1982.

———. *Callooh! Callay! Holiday Poems for Young Readers*. New York: Atheneum, 1978.

———. *A Tune Beyond Us*. New York: Harcourt, Brace and World, Inc., 1968.

———. *O Frabjous Day! Poetry for Holidays and Special Occasions*. New York: Atheneum, 1977.

Margolis, Richard J.*Secrets of a Small Brother*. New York: Macmillan Publishing Company, 1984.

The hidden thoughts and private complaints of a small brother find a voice in this collection of poems told from the younger boy's point of view.

Milligan, Spike, *Goblins*. London: Hutchinson of London, 1978.

Humorous verses by a poet skilled in word play.

——. *Unspun Socks From A Chicken's Laundry*. Harmondsworth. Puffin, 1981.

——. *Badjelly the Witch*. London: Joseph and Hobbs, 1973.

——. *Milliganimals and The Bald-Twit Lion*. Harmondsworth: Puffin, 1968.

——. *Silly Verse For Kids*. Harmondsworth: Puffin, 1988 (1959).

Morrison, Lillian. *The Sidewalk Racer and Other Poems of Sports and Motion*. New York: Lothrop, Lee & Shepard Co., 1977.
Most of the poems express "how it feels" for athletes-in-action, both men and women, — the exhilaration of perfectly executed moves, the disciplined ease, the pains and pleasures of the game, as well as sports seen through the spectator's eyes in sensitive word pictures that bring memorable athletic moments to life.

Morrison, Lillian (Compiled by). *Sprints and Distances: Sports in Poetry and the Poetry in Sport*. New York: Thomas Y. Crowell Company, 1965.
Lillian Morrison has gathered a collection in which poets in many times and countries have caught the grace and precision of motion, the excitement of competition, and the deep satisfaction that sport can bring.

O'Neill, Mary. *Hailstones and Halibut Bones*. New York: Doubleday & Company, Inc., 1961.
With a compelling sense of rhythm and images that are clear and fresh, Mary O'Neill explores the spectrum in 12 poems about different colors, from the show-off shout of red to the blueness of wind over water, to the quiet white of a pair of whispers talking.

Oppenhaim, Joanne. *Have you seen Birds?* Richmond Hill, Ontario: North Winds Press, 1986 (1968). Illustrated by Barbara Reid.
Spring, summer, autumn, and winter birds, woodland, meadow, marsh, and sea birds — all are brought to life in lively, lyrical prose and rich plasticene-relief illustration.

Parrott, E.O. (Chosen by). *Limerick Delight*. Harmondsworth: Puffin Books, 1985.
Here are over 300 quirky and curious verses, old favorites and new.

Plotz, Helen (Chosen by). *Eye's Delight: Poems of Art and Architecture*. New York: Greenwillow Books, 1983.
Over 100 poems document the inspiration these arts have provided poets through the ages. They are divided into four sec-

tions: poems about pictures, about sculpture, and the last two on architecture, public and private.

———. *This Powerful Rhyme: A Book of Sonnets.* New York: Greenwillow Books, 1979.

———. *Life Hungers To Abound: Poems of the Family.* New York: Greenwillow Books, 1978.

———. *As I Walked Out One Evening: A Book of Ballads.* New York: Greenwillow Books, 1976.

Regniers, Beatrice Schenk de. *This Big Cat and Other Cats I've Known.* New York: Crown Publishers, Inc., 1985.

Beatrice Schenk de Regniers celebrates cats — their wiles and guiles, their quirks and winning ways — in a series of poems for cat lovers, young and old.

Ryder, Joanne. *Inside Turtle's Shell and Other Poems of the Field.* New York: Macmillan Publishing Company, 1985.

Joanne Ryder has written 41 poems of nature that are delicate, lively, and profound.

Streich, Corrine (Selected by). *Grandparents' Houses: Poems about grandparents.* New York: Greenwillow Books, 1984. Illustrated by Lillian Hoban.

Grandparents are given their due in this illustrated anthology. The 15 poems included are culled from many cultures, among them Zuni, Japanese, Chinese, Hebrew, American, and German.

Turner, Ann. *Street Talk.* Boston: Houghton Mifflin Company, 1986.

Here are 29 poems that catch the drama of the city. There are poems about street games and street people, break dancing and graffiti, cruelty and kindness, youth and old age.

Wallace, Daisy (Ed.). *Ghost Poems.* New York: Holiday House, 1979.

All kinds of ghosts float eerily through these 17 poems, some of them original, by Lilian Moore, Jack Prelutsky, X.J. Kennedy, and others.

———. *Giant Poems.* New York: Holiday House, 1978.

———. *Monster Poems.* New York: Holiday House, 1976.

Wells, Carolyn (Collected by). *A Nonsense Anthology.* New York: Dover Publications, Inc., 1958.

245 of the most nonsensical nonsense verses ever written, are here assembled by the anthologist, Carolyn Wells.

West, Colin (Chosen by). *The Land of Utter Nonsense.* New York: Sparrow Books, 1983.

Here are some of the craziest characters ever imagined, and some of the funniest stories.

Wilson, Raymond (Chosen by). *Nine O'Clock Bell: Poems about School*. Harmondsworth: Puffin Books, 1987.

Nine O'Clock Bell is a collection of poems with one thing in common — school. Getting ready for it, going to it, liking it, hating it, and even playing truant from it.

Woodward, Zenka and Ian (Chosen by). *Witches' Brew: Spooky Verse for Hallowe'en*. Markham, Ontario: Beaverbooks, 1984.

The reader will meet ghouls, sorcerers, and goblins; walk through haunted houses, graveyards and other dark, lonely places; learn a charm against hiccups, a spell to bring sleep, and a curse for your enemies.

Woolger, David (Chosen by). *The Magic Tree: Poems of fantasy and mystery*. London: Oxford University Press, 1981.

Here is a collection of poems about witches, mermaids, ghosts, sea serpents, wizards, fairies, visitors, journeys and struggles, weird music, transformations, and other strange happenings.

General Collections and Anthologies

Abercrombie, Barbara (Ed.). *The other side of a poem*. New York: Harper & Row, Publishers, 1977.

This book came out of many poetry readings and discussions, and the poems and parts of poems are all by modern American writers.

Blishen, Edward (Compiled by). *Oxford Book of Poetry for Children*. New York: Franklin Watts, Inc., 1963.

Edward Blishen set out to compile an anthology that would introduce poetry to younger children and help them make the leap from nursery rhymes to "serious" verse. It is a collection that leads children toward an appreciation of the richness and variety of English poetry.

Bold, Alan , Gareth Owen, and Julie O'Callaghan. *Bright Lights Blaze Out*. London: Oxford University Press, 1986.

Three contemporary poets combine in one volume to present the best of their new unpublished poems for children.

Bogan, Louise and William Jay Smith (Compiled by). *The Golden Journey: Poems for Young People*. Chicago: Henry Regnery Company, 1965.

The authors offer only poems that they have themselves enjoyed and read and remembered with pleasure; old and new poems;

poems written in English, but written sometimes in far countries, such as Australia; poems about many and diverse subjects.

Butler, Dorothy (Chosen by). *I will build you a house*. London: Hodder and Stoughton, 1984.
The poems in the collection have themselves lived for years and years as honored guests in a house full of children.

———. *For me, me, me: Poems for the very young*. London: Hodder and Stoughton, 1983.

Charlesworth, Roberta A. (Ed.). *The Second Century Anthologies of Verse — Book 1*. Toronto: Oxford University Press, 1969.
A carefully chosen collection of children's poetry from over the years.

Cole, Joanna (Selected by). *A New Treasury of Children's Poetry*. New York: Doubleday & Company, Inc., 1984.
In this personal collection, Joanna Cole introduces children to the fun and enjoyment of poetry.

Corrin, Sara and Stephen (Eds.) *Once Upon a Rhyme: 101 Poems for Young Children*. Harmondsworth: Puffin Books, 1982.
Sara and Stephen Corrin, well-known for their collections of stories for children, have collected poems young children will really enjoy.

Elkin, Judith (Ed.). *The New Golden Land Anthology*. Harmondsworth: Puffin Books, 1984.
Not only traditional stories, tall stories, and tongue-twisters, but new stories, nonsense poems and nasty tales, rhymes and riddles, songs and stories of the supernatural are included in this anthology.

Foster, John (Compiled by). *A Very First Poetry Book*. London: Oxford University Press, 1984.
The first in a series of poems for children throughout elementary school, representing poetry mainly from the United Kingdom.

———. *A First Poetry Book*. London: Oxford University Press, 1979.

———. *A Second Poetry Book*. London: Oxford University Press, 1980.

———. *A Third Poetry Book*. London: Oxford University Press, 1982.

———. *A Fourth Poetry Book*. London: Oxford University Press, 1982.

———. *A Fifth Poetry Book*. London: Oxford University Press, 1985.

Graham, Eleanor (Compiled by). *A Puffin Book of Verse*. Harmondsworth: Puffin Books, 1953.

An anthology intended simply to give pleasure. Every boy or girl who browses among its pages will find something to enjoy.

———. *A Puffin Quartet of Poets*. Harmondsworth: Puffin Books, 1984.

Hall, Donald (Ed.) *The Oxford Book of Children's Verse in America*. New York: Oxford University Press, 1985.

Bringing together poems written for children and also poems written for adults which children have enjoyed, the book includes anonymous works, ballads, and recitation pieces, and ranges from the Calvinist verses of the 17th century right up to the nonsense of the present.

Harvey, Anne (Chosen by). *Poets in Hand: A Puffin Quintet*. Harmondsworth: Puffin Books, 1985.

An inspiring anthology from a quintet of poets, writers of children's verse: Charles Causley, John Fuller, Elizabeth Jennings, Vernon Scannell, John Walsh.

Hendra, Judith (Ed.) *The Illustrated Treasury of Humor for Children*. New York: Grosset and Dunlap Publishers, 1980.

A collection of children's stories and poems by masters old and new.

Hopkins, Lee Bennett (Selected by). *And God Bless Me: Prayers, Lullabies, and Dream-Poems*. New York: Alfred A. Knopf, 1982.

Warm and comforting verses for children are collected in this assortment of prayers, lullabies, and dream-poems.

———. *Thread One To A Star*. New York: Four Winds Press, 1976.

———. *The Sky Is Full Of Song*. New York: Harper & Row, Publishers, 1983.

———. *Potato Chips and a slice of moon*. Richmond Hill, Ontario: Scholastic Book Services, 1976.

Heaney, Seamus and Ted Hughes (Selected by). *The Rattle Bag*. London: Faber and Faber, 1982.

The verse chosen is meant to develop foundations of poetry and to amplify notions of what poetry is.

Ireson, Barbara (Compiled by). *The Young Puffin Book of Verse*. Harmondsworth: Penguin Books, 1970.

This is a collection of poems, verses, nursery rhymes, and jingles for children up to the age of eight.

Janeczko, Paul. *Going Over to Your Place: Poems For Each Other*. New York: Bradbury Press, 1987.

In Paul Janeczko's latest anthology, the reader meets 132 poems that reveal the extraordinary hidden in the familiar, everyday love and loss.

————. *Don't forget to fly*. New York: Bradbury Press, 1981.

————. (Ed.). *Postcard Poems*. New York: Bradbury Press, 1973.

Kemp, Gene (Ed.). *Ducks and Dragons*. Harmondsworth: Puffin Books, 1983.

A mixture of poems is found in this collection — some familiar, some not.

Kennedy, X.J. and Dorothy M. *Knock At A Star: A Child's Introduction to Poetry*. Boston: Little, Brown and Company, 1982.

In this anthology, X.J. and Dorothy Kennedy have collected a flock of poems that are lively, funny, and memorable.

Koch, Kenneth and Kate Farrell (Selected by). *Talking To The Sun*. New York: The Metropolitan Museum of Art, 1985.

The splendid and diverse treasures of The Metropolitan Museum of Art are combined with an inspired selection of poems in this unique anthology.

Larrick, Nancy (Selected by). *Bring Me All Of Your Dreams*. New York: M. Evans and Company, Inc., 1980.

Nancy Larrick has brought together a collection of poems about dreams and dreamers, including fun and fantasy, humor and pathos, beauty and tragedy.

Lewis, Naomi (Compiled by). *Messages*. London: Faber and Faber, 1985.

Messages, compiled by the distinguished critic and writer Naomi Lewis, is designed for readers of 11 to 15 or so, and revisit some of the great poets of yesterday and explores the writings of today.

Leuders, Edward and Primus St. John (Compiled by). *Zero makes me hungry*. New York: Lothrop, Lee & Shepard Company, 1976.

Drawn almost entirely from the 20th century, the collection includes poets from a wide range of ethnic and cultural traditions as well as many female poets.

McGough, Roger (Ed.). *The Kingfisher Book of Comic Verse*. London: Kingfisher Books, 1986.

Roger McGough has chosen over 200 poems to make up this collection, ranging widely from old favorites by Lewis Carroll, Edward Lear, and Hilaire Belloc, to the work of some of the best poets writing today.

————. *Strictly Private: An Anthology of Poetry*. Harmondsworth: Puffin Books, 1984.

Moore, Lilian (Chosen by). *Go With The Poem* . New York: McGraw-Hill Book Company, 1979.

This is a collection of some 90 poems for today's middle-graders.

———. *Something new begins*. New York: Atheneum, 1982.

Moss, Elaine (Chosen by). *From Morn to Midnight*. London: Heinemann, 1977.

A collection of 20 poems, chosen to give young children a first taste of poetry, and illustrated by Satomi Ichikawa.

Nicoll, Helen (Chosen By). *Poems for 7-Year-Olds and Under*. London: Puffin Books 1983.

Peck, Richard (Ed.). *Pictures That Storm Inside My Head: poems for the inner you*. New York: Avon, 1976.

Pictures That Storm Inside My Head voices an affirmation of honest emotions that can be best examined through poetry.

Prelutsky, Jack (Selected by). *The Random House Book of Poetry for Children*. New York: Random House, 1983. Illustrated by Arnold Lobel.

An excellent anthology of poems, from the past and present.

Rosen, Michael (Selected by). *Poetry*. New York: Little Simon, 1985.

Each poem, from the romantic to the whimsical, will spark young readers' imaginations and warm their hearts.

Rumble, Adrian (Collected by). *Have You Heard the Sun Singing?* London: Evans Brothers Limited, 1981.

Large numbers of poems by modern writers are included as well as some of the best traditional verses.

Smith, William Jay (Compiled by). *A Green Place*. New York: Delacorte Press, 1982.

There are poems on many subjects and in many forms, all the way from simple rhymes to complex stanzaic patterns.

Waters, Fiona (Chosen by). *Golden Apples*. London: Heinemann, 1985.

This new poetry anthology for 8-12 year olds has simple poems and challenging ones, the familiar and the completely new, poems that range from the lyrical to the comic.

Webb, Kaye (Selected by). *All in a day*. Ladybird Books, 1985.

The poems which are gathered in this book have been written from a child's eye view.

———. *I Like This Poem*. Harmondsworth: Puffin Books, 1979.

Wilner, Isabel (Compiled by). *The Poetry Troupe*. New York: Charles Scribner's Sons, 1977.

Over 200 poems from a variety of children's poets, ideal for reading aloud by individuals or groups.

Wright, Kit (Chosen by). *Poems for 9-Year-Olds and Under.* London: Viking Kestrel Books, 1984.
  Kit Wright's anthology of the very best poems enjoyed by children age 9 years and under, is full of laughter, nonsense, and sheer fun.
———. *Poems for Over 10-Year-Olds.* Harmondsworth: Puffin Books, 1984.
Untermeyer, Louis (Selected by). *The Golden Treasury of Poetry.* London: Collins, 1982.
  This book contains over 400 carefully chosen poems. Louis Untermeyer, a distinguished poet and anthologist, has poems from every period of English literature.

Cultural Collections and Anthologies

Bierhorst, John (Ed.) *The Sacred Path.* New York: William Morrow and Company, 1983.
  Spells, prayers, and power songs of the American Indians.
———. *In The Trail of The Wind.* New York: Dell Publishing Company, 1971.
———. *Songs of Chippewa.* New York: Farrar, Straus Giroux, 1974.
Bold, Alan (Compiled by). *A Scottish Poetry Book.* London: Oxford University Press, 1983.
  An unusual collection of poems and verse originating in Scotland.
Brand, Dionne. *Earth Magic.* Toronto, Ontario: Kids Can Press, 1979.
  Dionne Brand's poetry is alive with the spirit, song, and magic of her Trinidadian childhood.
Butler, Dorothy (Collected by). *The Magpies Said: Stories and Poems from New Zealand.* Harmondsworth: Puffin Books, 1980.
  A collection of stories and poems by New Zealand writers, but for children all round the world.
Cronyn, George W. (Ed.). *American Indian Poetry.* New York: Ballantine Books, 1972.
  An anthology of songs and chants which reveal the thoughts, feelings, and desires of the Indian, vividly brought to life.
Day, David, and Marilyn Bowering (Eds.). *Many Voices.* Vancouver: J.J. Douglas Ltd., 1977.
  An anthology of contemporary Canadian Indian poetry.

Downie, Mary Alice, Elizabeth Green and M.A. Thompson (Eds.). *The Window of Dreams*. Toronto, Ontario: Methuen Publications, 1986.
The Window of Dreams is an anthology of 30 stories and poems for children. The collection has been distilled from more than 600 submissions received from across Canada.

Downie, Mary Alice, and Barbara Robertson (Compiled by). *The New Wind Has Wings: Poems from Canada*. Toronto, Ontario: Oxford University Press 1978.

Griego, Margot C., Betsy L. Bucks., Sharon S. Gilbert, and Laurel H. Kimball (Selected by). *Tortillitas Para Mama And Other Nursery Rhymes*. New York: Holt, Rinehart and Winston, 1981.
A collection of Latin-American nursery rhymes, preserved through the oral tradition.

Heylen, Jill and Celia Jellett (Selected by). *Someone is Flying Balloons: Australian Poems for Children*. Sydney, NSW: Omnibus Books, 1983.
In this collection of poetry for children, some of Australia's finest contemporary poets and the best of our traditional writers combine to give a fresh view of Australian life as it was, and is today.

Hofmann, Charles, *Drum Dance*. Toronto, Ontario: Gage, 1974.
Legends, ceremonies, dances, and songs of the Inuit.

Jones, Hettie (compiler). *The Trees Stand Shining*. New York: Dial Press, 1971.
Illustrated by Robert Andrew Parker, this volume contains poems and songs of many Indian Peoples, telling how they feel about the world and what they did in their lives.

Lewis, Richard (Ed.). *I Breathe A New Song*. New York: Simon and Schuster, 1971.
Richard Lewis has selected 90 representative poems, magical chants, lullabies, and songs to bring luck while hunting, songs to taunt enemies.

———. (Ed.). *Out of The Earth I Sing*. New York: W.W. Norton and Company, 1968.

Lowenfels, Walter (Ed.). *From the Belly of the Shark*. New York: First Vintage Books Edition, 1973.
The voices of contemporary Indians, Puerto Ricans, Chicanos, Inuit, and others who are Americans in the most deep-rooted sense, are included in this anthology.

Mezey, Robert (Selected by). *Poems from the Hebrew*. New York: Thomas Y. Crowell Company, 1973.

Robert Mezey has dramatized the poetic continuity from the shepherds and warriors of 25 centuries ago to the writers now living in the cities of Israel.

Peirce, Maggi Kerr. *Keep the kettle boiling.* Belfast: The Appletree Press Ltd., 1983.

The rhymes and songs included here come from Maggi Kerr Peirce's own memories of a childhood spent in the city and surrounding countryside in the '30s and '40s.

Pomerantz, Charlotte. *Had a Paka: Poems in Eleven Languages.* New York: Greenwillow Books, 1982.

Poems in Serbo-Croatian, Swahili, Vietnamese, and other languages.

Rollings, Laurie McFarlin. *Mother Goose Rhymes, Versos Infantiles, Vers d'Enfance.* Colorado: Matterplay, Inc., 1986.

Mother Goose in three languages chosen because of their shortness, rhyme, and metre, and familiarity to most children. Included in the poems are the numbers 1-20, days of the week, months of the year, and many of the more frequently used nouns and verbs.

Ross, Sandy Thomas. *Bairnsangs: Nursery Rhymes in Scots.* Ayr: Alloway Publishing, 1982.

Bairnsangs is the result of the collaboration in 1955 of three Ayrshire men: "Sandy" MacMillan, Thomas Limond, and A.L. (Ross) Taylor. It was published under the collective name of Sandy Thomas Ross.

Strickland, Dorothy S. (Ed.). *Listen Children: An Anthology of Black Literature.* Toronto, Ontario: Bantam Skylark, 1982.

Listen Children is an introduction to black literature for young people who are learning about values and feelings.

Wyndham, Robert (Selected and edited by). *Chinese Mother Goose Rhymes.* New York: Philomel Books, 1982.

The poems in this book are all traditional. Some have been translated especially for this collection, others have been selected from other books.

References

Arnstein, Flora J. *Poetry and the Child*. New York: Dover Publications, Inc., 1962.

Baskin, Barbara H., and Karen H. Harris. *Books for the Gifted Child*. New York & London: R.R. Bowker Company, 1980.

Brown, Rosellen, Marvin Hoffman, Martin Kushner, Phillip Lopate, and Sheila Murphy (Eds.). *The Whole Word Catalogue*. Teachers & Writers Collaborative, 1972.

Bennett, Jill, and Aidan Chambers. *Poetry for Children*. Ed. Nancy Chambers. England: The Thimble Press, 1984.

Benton, Michael, and Geoff Fox. *Teaching Literature: Nine to Fourteen*. London: Oxford University Press, 1985.

Bierhorst, John (Ed.). *The Sacred Path: Spells, Prayers & Power Songs of the American Indians*. New York: William Morrow and Company, 1983.

Birney, Earle. *The Cow Jumped Over The Moon: The Writing and Reading of Poetry*. Toronto: Holt, Rinehart and Winston of Canada, Limited, 1972.

Booth, David W., and Stanley Skinner. *ABC's Of Creative Writing*. Toronto: Globe/Modern Curriculum Press, 1981.

Booth, David, Larry Swartz, and Meguido Zola. *Choosing Children's Books*. Pembroke Publishers Limited, 1981.

Boyd, Gertrude A. *Teaching Poetry in the Elementary School*. Columbus, Ohio: Charles E. Merrill Publishing Company, 1973.

Brownjohn, Sandy. *What Rhymes with "Secret"?: Teaching children to write poetry*. London: Hodder and Stoughton, 1982.

Cass, Joan E. *Literature and the Young Child*. 2nd ed. Longman, 1967.

Ciardi, John, and Miller Williams. *How Does A Poem Mean?* 2nd ed. Boston: Houghton Mifflin Company, 1975.

Collom, Jack. *On Evaluating Collaborations*. New York: Teachers & Writers Collaborative. Nov-Dec. 1985, Vol. 17 #2.

_____. *Moving Windows: Evaluating the Poetry Children Write*. New York: Teachers & Writers Collaborative, 1985.

Cronyn, George W. (Ed.). *American Indian Poetry: An Anthology of Songs and Chants*. New York: Ballantine Books, 1972.

Cullinan, Bernice E. (Ed.). *Children's Literature in the Reading Program*. Newark, Delaware: International Reading Association, 1974.

Delamar, Gloria T. *Children's Counting Out Rhymes, Fingerplays,*

Jump-Rope and Bounce-Ball Chants and Other Rhythms: A Comprehensive English-Language Reference. Jefferson, North Carolina: McFarland, 1983.

Duke, Charles R., and Sally A. Jacobsen (Eds.). *Reading and Writing Poetry: Successful Approaches for the Student and Teacher.* New York: Oryx Press, 1983.

Egoff, Sheila. *Only Connect.* Toronto: Oxford University Press, 1980.

Egoff, Sheila. *The Republic of Childhood.* Toronto: Oxford University Press, 1975.

Farber, Norma. "Bilingual Children". *Innocence and Experience.* Harrison & Maguire. New York: Lothrop, Lee & Shepard, 1987.

Fox, Geoff. "Pro Patria: Young Readers and the 'Great War'." *Children's Literature in Education,* Vol. 16, No. 4, 1985. New York: Agathon Press, Inc.

Gallo, Daniel R. (Ed.). "Poetry: Reading, Writing and Analyzing It." *Connecticut English Journal,* Vol. 10, No. 2. A Publication of Connecticut Council of Teachers of English, Spring 1979.

Geldart, William, illus. *Words On Water: An Anthology of Poems.* Harmondsworth: Puffin, 1978.

Geller, Linda Gibson. *Wordplay and Language Learning for Children.* Urbana, Illinois: National Council of Teachers of English, 1985.

Gensler, Kinerth, and Nina Nyhart. *The Poetry Connection: An Anthology of Contemporary Poems with Ideas to Stimulate Children's Writing.* New York: Teachers & Writers Collaborative, 1978.

Golick, Margie, Ph.D. *Playing With Words.* Markham, Ontario: Pembroke Publisher Ltd., 1987.

Gough, John. "Poems in a context: breaking the anthology trap." *Children's Literature in Education,* Vol. 15, No. 4, Winter 1984, pp. 204-210.

Harms, Jeanne McLean, and Lucille J. Lettow. "Poetry: Invitations To Participate." *Childhood Education,* Vol. 63, No. 1, Oct. 1986, pp. 6-10.

Hayhoe, Mike. "Sharing the Headstart: An Explanatory Approach To Teaching Poetry." *English Quarterly,* Vol. 17, No. 3, Fall 1984, pp. 39-44.

Hazzard, Russell. *It scares me but I like it: Creating Poetry With Children.* Markham, Ontario: Fitzhenry & Whiteside, 1979.

Hopkins, Lee Bennett. *Pass the Poetry Please!* New York: Harper & Row, Publishers, 1987.

Huck, Charlotte S., Susan Helpler, and Janet Hickman. *Children's*

Literature in the Elementary School. 4th ed. New York: Holt, Rinehart and Winston, 1987.

Hughes, Ted. *Poetry in the Making: An Anthology of Poems and Programmes from "Listening and Writing".* Faber and Faber, 1967.

Ingham, Jennie. *Books and Reading Development: The Bradford Book Flood Experiment.* London: Heinemann, 1982.

Ireland, R.J. *The Poet's Craft.* Toronto, Ontario: Academic Press Canada, 1984.

Kimzy, Ardis. *To Defend A Form: The Romance of Administration and Teaching in a Poetry-in-the-Schools Program.* New York: Teachers & Writers Collaborative, 1977.

Kirkland, Glen, and Richard Davies. *Inside Poetry.* Academic Press Canada, 1984.

Koch, Kenneth. *Rose, Where Did You Get That Red?: Teaching Great Poetry To Children.* New York: Vintage Books, 1974.

Koch, Kenneth, and Kate Farrell. *Sleeping on the Wing: An Anthology of Modern Poetry with Essays on Reading and Writing.* New York: Vintage Books, 1982.

Larrick, Nancy (Ed.). *Somebody Turned on a Tap in These Kids: Poetry and Young People Today.* New York: Delacorte Press, 1971.

Lewis, C. Day. *Poetry For You.* Oxford: Basil Blackwell, 1940.

Livingston, Myra Cohn. *The Child as Poet: Myth or Reality?* Boston: The Horn Book, Inc., 1984.

Lopate, Phillip. *Being With Children.* New York: Doubleday and Company, 1975.

Lukasevich, Ann. "Making Poetry a Natural Experience for Young Children." *Childhood Education*, Vol. 61, No. 1, Sept/Oct. 1984, pp. 36-42.

Lynd, Robert. *An Anthology of Modern Verse.* London: Methuen, 1912.

Lynn, Joanne L. "Runes to ward off sorrow: rhetoric of the English nursery rhyme." *Children's literature in education*, Vol. 16, No. 1, 1985. New York: Agathon Press, Inc.

Martin, Bill, and Peggy Brogan. *Instant Readers: Teacher's Guide, Level 3.* New York: Holt, Rinehart and Winston, Inc., 1972.

McCracken, Robert A., and Marlene J. McCracken. *Stories, Songs, and Poetry to Teach Reading and Writing: Literacy through Language.* Winnipeg: Peguis Publishers Ltd., 1987.

McNeil, Florence. *When Is A Poem? Creative Ideas for Teaching Poetry: Collected from Canadian Poets.* Toronto, Ontario: The League of Canadian Poets, 1972.

McVity, Walter, ed. *The PETA Guide to Children's Literature.* Rozelle, N.S.W., Australia: Primary English Teaching Association, 1985.

Mearns, Hughes. *Creative Power: The Education of Youth in Creative Arts.* New York: Dover, 1958.

Meek, Margaret. *Learning to Read.* London: The Bodley Head, 1982.

Merriam, Eve. "Sharing Poetry With Children." *Learning,* Vol. 14, No. 2, Sept. 1985, pp. 78-80.

Millett, Nancy C., and Helen J. Throckmorton. *How to Read a Poem.* Ginn and Company, 1966.

Newbolt, Sir Henry. *New Paths on Helicon.* London: Nelson, 1922.

Newman, Judith M. "Online: Using a Database in the Classroom." *Language Arts,* Vol. 63, No. 3, March 1986.

Padgett, Ron, and Bill Zavatsky (Eds.). *The Whole Word Catalogue.* Teachers & Writers Collaborative, 1976.

Painter, Helen. *Poetry And Children.* Newark, Delaware: International Reading Association, 1980.

Palgrave, F.T. *The Golden Treasury.* Oxford: University of Oxford Press, 1928.

Patrick, Geoff. "Questions to ask about poems." *Elementary English,* January 1975.

Perrine, Laurence. *Sound and Sense: An Introduction to Poetry.* 3rd ed. San Diego, California: Harcourt Brace Jovanovich, 1969.

Powell, Brian. *Their Own Special Shape: Further approaches to writing from classrooms around the world.* Toronto, Ontario: Collier-Macmillan Canada, Ltd., 1976.

Ramsden, Madeleine. *Dreams and Challenges: Writing Poetry.* Toronto, Ontario: Macmillan of Canada, 1976.

Rogers, Wanda C. "Teaching for poetic thought." *The Reading Teacher,* Vol. 39, No. 3, Dec. 1985, pp. 296-300.

Rouse, John. "On Children Writing Poetry." *Language Arts,* Vol. 60, No. 6, September 1983, pp. 711-716.

Saltman, Judith. *Modern Canadian Children's Books.* Toronto: Oxford University Press, 1987.

Sears, Peter. "What Do You Say About a Terrible Poem?" *Teachers & Writers,* Vol. 16, No. 5, May/June 1985.

Sebesta, Sam Leaton, and William J. Iverson. *Literature for Thursday's Child.* Toronto, Ontario: Science Research Associates, Inc., 1975.

Shapiro, Jon E. *Using Literature & Poetry Affectively.* Newark, Delaware: International Reading Association, 1979.

Shapiro, Sheila. "An analysis of poetry teaching procedures in

Sixth-grade basal manuals." *Reading Research Quarterly*, Vol. 20, No. 3, Spring 1985, pp. 368-381.

Smith, Richard J. *Using Poetry to Teach Reading and Language Arts: A Handbook For Elementary School Teachers*. New York and London: Teachers College Press, 1985.

Stafford, William. "Exploring the Wild, Surprising World of Poetry." *Learning*, Vol. 13, No. 5, Jan. 1985, pp. 38-40.

Summerfield, Geoffrey (Ed.). *Junior Voices: An Anthology of Poetry and Pictures*. London: Penguin, 1967.

Sutherland, Zena, and May Hill Arbuthnot. *Children and Books*. 7th ed. Chicago, Illinois: Scott, Foresman and Company, 1986.

Swanger, David. *The Poem As Process*. New York: Harcourt Brace Jovanovich, Inc., 1974.

Terry, Ann. *Children's *Poetry Preferences: *A National Survey of Upper Elementary Grades*. (*no. 16 in a series of research reports sponsored by the NCTE Committee on Research). Urbana, Illinois: National Council of Teachers of English, 1974.

Tomlinson, Brian. "Using poetry with mixed ability language classes." *ELT Journal*, Vol. 40, No. 1, Jan. 1986, pp. 33-41.

Travers, D. Molly Murison. "The Poetry Teacher: Behavior and Attitudes." *Research in the Teaching of English*, Vol. 18, No. 4, December 1984.

Tunnicliffe, Stephen. *Poetry Experience: Teaching and writing poetry in secondary schools*. London/New York: Methuen, 1984.

Untermeyer, Louis. *The Albatross Book of Verse*. London: Collins, 1947.

Valentine, Sonia L. "Beginning Poets Dig for Poems." *Language Arts* , Vol. 63, No. 3, March 1986.

Walter, Colin. "The Many Years of Telling: A Tradition of Failed Practice of Teaching Poetry in the Primary School." *English in Education*, University of London Goldsmith's College, 1985.

Walter, Nina Willis. *Let Them Write Poetry*. New York: Holt, Rinehart and Winston, 1962.

Whitin, David J. "Making Poetry Come Alive." *Language Arts*, Vol. 60, No. 4, April 1983.

Index